Workplace Justice
Without Unions

Workplace Justice Without Unions

Hoyt N. Wheeler
Brian S. Klaas
Douglas M. Mahony

2004

W.E. Upjohn Institute for Employment Research
Kalamazoo, Michigan

Library of Congress Cataloging-in-Publication Data

Wheeler, Hoyt N.
  Workplace justice without unions / Hoyt N. Wheeler, Brian S. Klaas, Douglas M.
Mahony.
     p. cm.
  Includes bibliographical references and index.
  ISBN 0-88099-312-X (pbk. : alk. paper) — ISBN 0-88099-313-8 (hardcover : alk.
paper)
     1. Employee rights—United States. 2. Arbitration, Industrial—United States.
3. Employees—Dismissal of—United States. I. Klaas, Brian S. II. Mahony,
Douglas M. III. Title.
HD6971.8W5   2004
331'.01'10973—dc22

                              2004009579

W.E. Upjohn Institute for Employment Research
300 S. Westnedge Avenue
Kalamazoo, Michigan 49007–4686

The facts presented in this study and the observations and viewpoints expressed are
the sole responsibility of the authors. They do not necessarily represent positions of
the W.E. Upjohn Institute for Employment Research.

Cover design by Alcorn Publication Design.
Index prepared by Nairn Chadwick.
Printed in the United States of America.
Printed on recycled paper.

This book is dedicated to the memory of
Marco Biagi; to Liz, Alice, and Rachel; and to
Hannah and Mary Frances Johnson

Contents

Tables

Acknowledgments

The research that forms the basis for this book was derived from a large number of organizations and persons, without whose cooperation it would not have been completed. First, we would like to thank the W.E. Upjohn Institute for Employment Research for providing the major funding for the project. Also, the Riegel and Emory Human Resources Research Institute at the Moore School of Business, University of South Carolina, provided substantial financial support. Hillary McDonald of the Research Division of the Moore School provided invaluable assistance in obtaining and administering the research grants.

Arbitrators Dennis R. Nolan and Sara Adler spent a good deal of time and energy helping us to pretest research instruments. Michelle Oswald and Yvonne Bennett, students in the Master of Human Resources program at the Moore School of Business, did an excellent job in assisting our research. One of the more challenging aspects of the project was gathering data from judges in a number of different countries, and Arturo Bronstein and Enrique Marín of the International Labour Office in Geneva, Switzerland, greatly facilitated this by inviting one of us to a meeting of Labour Court judges. These judges, who will remain nameless to respect the confidentiality of their responses, are also due our thanks for spending significant amounts of time and effort to fill out our rather lengthy research instruments. Maria Isabel Brage and Alice Adams, both graduate students at the University of South Carolina, provided translations of our questionnaires into Spanish and French, respectively, and translation of some of the responses.

The American Arbitration Association, and in particular Robert Meade, the association's senior vice president, provided us with copies of employment arbitration awards, as well as names and addresses of employment arbitrators. In addition, we had the aid of South Carolina citizens who had served on juries, a federal district court judge who supplied us with their names and addresses, human resources officers of companies, company employees who had served on peer review panels, labor arbitrators, and employment arbitrators. Those who responded to our research instruments deserve special appreciation, given that responding to our rather complex scenarios required substantial time and effort on their part. Our pledge to them regarding the confidentiality of their responses prevents us from thanking them by name.

Hoyt N. Wheeler
Brian S. Klaas
Douglas M. Mahony

1
Workplace Justice in the United States: An Introduction

Where there is no rule of law but only the command of persons, where secrecy and arbitrariness reign, where one never knows when or why the axe will fall, there justice weeps. (Wolterstorff 2001)

Human dignity at the workplace requires just treatment by those holding authority. At the crux of this matter is protection from arbitrary action—action that is based upon personality rather than merit, and is not predictable on any reasoned basis. When a human being is treated merely as a means to an end or a thing to be employed by others, rather than as a person deserving justice, justice does indeed weep. This is especially true where a person's job is at stake. In our society, an individual's job is not only a source of economic goods, but also an important part of how we define ourselves—and others define us—and our role in society. Where workers can be terminated from their employment for any reason, or none at all, arbitrariness reigns. Yet, this is historically the basic principle of the law of employment termination in the United States.

The situation is quite different in Western Europe and nearly all other countries. In these countries, there exists a general principle of law that dictates that workers cannot be terminated without cause. This principle is enforced either in labor courts, other specialized courts, or in the general court system.

The American rule of employment-at-will—that a person can be fired at any time for any, or no, reason—has deep roots in the nation's jurisprudence. It was announced in a legal treatise in 1877, and is known as "Wood's rule," named for the author of the treatise, Horace Gay Wood. He stated, "With us [in America, unlike in England] the rule is inflexible that a general or indefinite hiring is *prima facie* at will" (Willborn, Schwab, and Burton 1993, p. 15). It has remained the general rule ever since. Its practical result is that, absent a statute or contract to the contrary, workers have no right to insist upon a just cause for their termination.

If employment were simply an economic transaction where a commodity called labor is bought and sold, we would need not concern ourselves about justice. The conventional wisdom in economics takes just such a view of employment. From this perspective, employment-at-will simply reflects the reality of a market. However, it is reasonably clear that, although there are aspects of employment that are congenial to an economic view, the full reality of employment is much more than that. As David Ewing, a former editor of *Harvard Business Review,* has said: "A company is a kind of society, its management a type of government, and managements that manage justly, as employees see justness, gain potent advantages over managements that do not" (Ewing 1989, p. 3). For a society to be managed justly, the substantive rules of workplace behavior must be just, and there must be mechanisms in place that deliver procedural "due process" (Ewing 1989).

Corporations are social organizations arranged in a hierarchy in which those at the top exercise authority over those at the bottom. This inevitably means that control must be exerted over those who are employed by others. In such circumstances, both human nature and differing interests between the employed and the employer give rise to a situation in which an abuse of power is not only possible, but highly likely (Wheeler 1997). In the workplace, there are order-givers and order-takers, and a common instrument of control by order-givers is the threat of a termination of the relationship. Ultimately, employees who do not behave as they are ordered will be separated from the organization—fired.

Fortunately, since the days when Wood's employment-at-will principle was adopted by American courts in the late nineteenth century, there has been considerable erosion of it. In fact, management attorneys have recently claimed that it is gone entirely, but the reality of the matter is a bit more complicated than that. What has occurred over a period of about 90 years is the construction of a patchwork of limitations on employment-at-will. This has been aptly described as the gradual slicing away of an entire pie of rights that at one time wholly belonged to employers, until the remainder is only a remnant of what once was (Bennett-Alexander and Hartman 2001). Yet, in truth, the employer's portion is still quite substantial. Arguably, it has grown significantly by virtue of recent U.S. Supreme Court decisions that will be discussed later in this book.

THE HISTORICAL DEVELOPMENT OF AMERICAN WORKPLACE JUSTICE

The road to the present system of workplace justice in the United States has been long and convoluted. Perhaps the clearest starting point is the enactment of the Clayton Act, effective in 1914. Hailed as "labor's Magna Carta" at the time, it declared that "the labor of a human being is not a commodity or article of commerce." Although the Supreme Court's interpretation kept the Clayton Act from being a boon to labor, at least the principle was recorded as a part of American labor policy.

With the Great Depression and New Deal came the Wagner Act in 1935, which protected workers from termination based on their union activity. Legislation adopted in the 1960s prohibited termination on the basis of race, color, national origin, religion, sex, or age (Title VII, Civil Rights Act of 1964; Age Discrimination in Employment Act of 1967). The Occupational Health and Safety Act of 1970 prohibited employers from terminating employees for seeking remedies for safety and health hazards. Based on this legislation, employees are protected against discrimination on the basis of union activity, race, color, national origin, sex, age, and their actions to ensure a safe workplace.

In the 1980s, state courts began creating exceptions to the employment-at-will doctrine. Terminations that violated public policy, implied-in-fact contracts (often based on employee handbooks or company rules), and implied-in-law contractual obligations of good faith and fair dealing were held to give rise to legal claims on the part of employees. The manner of a termination, if abusive, could make the employer liable for damages.

The 1980s and early 1990s brought a spate of employment legislation. The Immigration Reform and Control Act of 1986 prohibited employers from discriminating against legal aliens; the Employee Polygraph Protection Act of 1988 limited the use of lie detectors in firing workers; and the Worker Adjustment and Retraining Notification Act of 1988 (WARN Act) required employers to give 60 days' advance notice of a plant closing or mass layoff.

One of the more significant changes in the law over several decades was the adoption of the Americans with Disabilities Act in 1990. It expanded protection to employees against termination for physical and mental disabilities. This was a right that had already been granted to employees of federal contractors in the Vocational Rehabilitation Act of 1973. Another major boon, the Civil Rights Act of 1991, gave employees the right to a jury trial, and to both compensatory and punitive damages, when they were terminated for reasons of race, color, national origin, religion, or sex. Further, the Family and Medical Leave Act (FMLA) of 1993 protected workers from being terminated for taking unpaid leave for family and medical purposes.

At the same time that Congress was expanding the protection of workers against unfair terminations for *particular reasons*, two other things were occurring that gave workers a claim to just treatment as a general right. First, beginning in the 1940s, collective bargaining agreements came to commonly include a provision that workers could be discharged or disciplined only for just cause. This obligation was enforced through labor arbitration, in which a neutral third party (an arbitrator) could make a legally binding determination that the employee had been unjustly discharged. Because the courts adopted a policy of keeping their hands off this process in the Steelworkers Trilogy of cases (*United Steelworkers v. American Mfg. Co.* 1960; *United Steelworkers v. Warrior & Gulf Navigation Co.* 1960; *United Steelworkers v. Enterprise Wheel & Car Corp.* 1960), there was virtually no way that a labor arbitrator's decision could be overturned on appeal. This system has been generally viewed as highly successful, delivering justice to employees without significantly interfering with management's ability to manage effectively. Its chief limitation is that, because of the decline of unionization, it only covers a small proportion of the private sector workforce (about 8.2 percent in 2003).

The second major development has been the voluntary, management-initiated adoption of organizational justice procedures by nonunion employers, the more advanced forms of which have come along relatively recently. Based on data gathered in the late 1970s, Fred Foulkes (1980) found that, at that time, by far the most common employer device for handling employee grievances was the open-door policy, which is a very rudimentary workplace justice procedure. More advanced forms of nonbinding policies have included 1) installing an ombudsman—a corporate employee who independently deals with worker problems; and 2) mediation, where a neutral third party works to facilitate a resolution of the dispute (McDermott and Berkeley 1996).

An especially interesting organizational justice procedure originated in the 1980s—peer review panels. Here, a panel of employees (and sometimes managers) makes a final decision or recommendation regarding an employee's grievance (Grote and Wimberly 1993).

The management-initiated organizational justice system to most recently rise to prominence is employment arbitration. In employment arbitration, a nonunion employer requires employees to agree to submit any complaints (or sometimes any allegations of violation of law on the part of the employer) to a neutral arbitrator whose duty it is to render a final and binding decision on the matter (Clark 1997).

There are several questions that need to be answered in regard to the various management-initiated workplace justice systems. First, do they deliver substantive results that are fair and reasonably similar to those obtained in other systems, such as the courts or labor arbitration? Second, do they provide due process? Third, how do they compare to one another on these dimensions? It is these questions that the study reported in this book aims to address.

PLAN OF THE STUDY

The first task in which we engaged was a survey of the literature on nonunion justice systems. This literature is quite extensive and will be summarized both here and in Chapters 2 and 3.

The empirical portion of our study has several aspects. In order to judge the substantive results obtained under these various procedures, we analyze overall win/loss rates by employees in termination cases in labor arbitration, employment arbitration, and the federal courts. The most intensive research strategy is our attempt to determine the degree to which the same result would be reached in the same cases across different processes. This is tested by posing scenarios to labor arbitrators, employment arbitrators, managers, members of peer review panels, jurors in employment discrimination cases, and labor court judges from other countries. By analyzing the responses to these scenarios, we can compare the relative harshness or leniency of the systems toward employees for different disciplinary offenses, and the criteria used to reach decisions.

Whether each procedure provides due process can only be judged by examining them in some detail. We identify these procedures through a combination of literature search and survey questions posed to the various decision makers, and then compare them. The result is a body of data and analysis that permits us to draw some conclusions on the differences among these systems as to both outcome and procedure, and to compare them on the basis of their merits.

THE LITERATURE ON WORKPLACE JUSTICE

What do we know about workplace justice without unions? The scholarly literature is somewhat helpful in providing ideas and arguments, but is woefully lacking in empirical studies. We will work our way through the existing literature, dealing first with open door policies, ombudsmen, mediation, and peer review panels. We will then turn to the body of knowledge regarding employment arbitration, in order to consider this important and controversial process in some length.

Why Workplace Justice Systems?

As noted previously, David Ewing (1989) has written that the workplace is a kind of society. As such, it requires a justice system. This is consistent with the guiding principles that were instituted in the founding of the American Republic. According to Ewing, "More than any other procedure or device on the business scene, corporate due process brings to the workplace the humanitarian philosophy that lit up the American sky two centuries ago" (1989, p. 118). In the workplace, it means that employees are entitled to the assurance that managers are less likely to make arbitrary decisions about their lives (McCabe 2002).

Yet, these democratic political ideals have seldom been in evidence in the American workplace. This has been attributed, in part, to a philosophy of management described and prescribed by the early and influential management theorist Chester I. Barnard. Barnard (1938) held that managers were the ones best able to distribute, at their discretion, the resources of work organizations. This is thought to justify autocratic, rather than democratic, management. "America has been described as a sea of freedom filled with islands of despotism . . ." (Scott 1988, p. 294). The American corporation has been one of the islands.

The rise of workplace justice procedures in nonunion firms has been attributed to the rising importance lent by workers to the notion of "due process" (McCabe 2002). This may amount to a revolution of expectations on the part of workers, a "second civil rights revolution" (Ewing 1977, p. 39). Additionally, there are many reasons for firms to adopt these procedures, including 1) "developing a relationship of mutual trust and respect with employees"; 2) holding unions "at bay"; 3) "reducing litigation and litigation expenses"; 4) ensuring "greater compliance with the company's personnel policies"; 5) pressuring managers to "deal constructively with their subordinates' complaints and solve them on the spot if possible"; 6) providing feedback on the effects of policies on employees; 7) boosting morale; and 8) attracting and retaining good employees (Ewing 1989, pp. 6–9). Spotting and solving problems at an early stage before they fester is yet another advantage (McCabe 2002).

What is Due Process in the Workplace?

Some of the requirements of workplace due process are that there must be a procedure; it must have—and follow—rules; it must not be arbitrary; and it must be known to employees, predictable so that employees know that previous decisions on worker rights will be followed, "institutionalized," easy to use, perceived as equitable, and applicable to all employees (Ewing 1977, p. 156). It must be "timely, accessible and inexpensive," include the right of the employee to represented by another employee, provide the right to present evidence and rebut charges, have "as much privacy and confidentiality as is practicable," have "a fair and impartial fact-finding process and hearing," provide objective and reasonable decisions with appropriate remedies, and be free from retaliation against the employee (Ewing 1989, pp. 6–7). It has been argued that this should include the right to have outside arbitration or some other mutually agreed-upon process (Werhane 1985).

"Soft" Justice Systems

The justice systems which are the least intrusive upon management prerogatives are those that are considered "soft." These are procedures that do not bind management to any particular outcome. Instead of resulting in a legally binding determination, they provide a means of working out an agreed-upon solution. They sometimes constitute the early stages of more intrusive systems, and are comprised of three different procedures: the open-door policy, mediation, and the use of an ombudsman.

Open-door policy

The most common of the corporate procedures for resolving employee complaints is the open-door policy. In its simplest form, it is a policy statement that says that employees who have a problem are free to discuss it with management. The basic idea is one of managerial openness to employee complaints, even if this involves the employee going over the head of the immediate supervisor.

A study published in 1980 (Foulkes) found open-door policies to be quite "commonplace" (p. 300). The sample of policies reported by Foulkes included some rather complex policies that utilize multiple steps in the management hierarchy. They often include statements that an employee can use the policy without fear of reprisal. Also, they commonly encourage employees to settle their problems at the lowest practicable level of supervision.

The intent of these policies is to encourage employees to talk with managers in a friendly and informal fashion. The door of even such a dignitary as the president of the company is sometimes held open, and the human resources manager may be a step in the process (McCabe 2002). Open-door policies are often broader in their scope than unionized grievance procedures, encouraging employees to raise a wide range of problems and questions (McCabe 2002).

The effectiveness of open-door policies appears to vary from company to company. The interviews with personnel staff and managers reported by Foulkes (1980) show opinions ranging from avid approval to the statement that the policy is merely a "myth" (p. 309). Many times, although the door is supposed to be open, almost no one walks through it (McCabe 2002), or only trivial questions are raised. Employees may believe that they will not get a fair hearing because there is considerable social distance between rank and file employees and high company officials, which may discourage employees from using the procedure to its fullest extent. Perhaps most critically, it is difficult to convince employees that going over their bosses' heads will not lead to reprisals (McCabe 2002). In the case of employment termination, many upper level managers feel a necessity to support the actions of lower level managers, or employees may believe this to be the case. This makes the use of the procedure an unattractive channel for a complaint regarding a discharge.

Unfortunately, we have not been able to locate any rigorous empirical studies of open-door policies. For the purposes of studying termination of employment, however, they are probably not a particularly fruitful subject of inquiry.

Mediation

Mediation utilizes the services of a neutral third party to help the parties to a dispute resolve it. The mediator is not a decision maker; rather, mediators serve as facilitators. The use of mediation is a "soft" form of dispute resolution because it imposes on the parties no binding result. Its methods are those of "win–win" bargaining, and as such, it provides opportunities for the employer and the employee to work out a mutually agreeable solution to an employment problem in a relatively nonadversarial setting (McDermott and Berkeley 1996).

Mediation has been said to provide a forum that is more likely to facilitate settlement than the more adversarial procedures involving adjudication. It is confidential, may produce a settlement at an early stage, provides an opportunity to redirect emotions, is adaptable and flexible, and can provide feelings of personal empowerment in cases such as those involving sexual harassment (Harkavy 1999).

The increase in formal grievance procedures for nonunion employees during the 1980s and 1990s has included an increase in the use of mediation. It has been argued that the overall phenomenon of increased mediation procedures has arisen partly because of "the increased willingness of disgruntled employees to file lawsuits and administrative agency complaints," and the resulting increase in the desire of employers to resolve these complaints by some means other than litigation (Feuille 1999, p. 205). Also, the availability of punitive damages and the right to jury trial given to workers claiming discrimination by the 1991 Civil Rights Act have encouraged employers to seek alternative means of dispute resolution. The related phenomenon of the take-up of employment arbitration by employers in the wake of the U.S. Supreme Court decisions in *Gilmer v. Interstate/Johnson Lane* (1991) and *Circuit City Stores, Inc. v. Adams* (2001a), discussed in Chapter 2, has involved the increased use of mediation (Feuille 1999).

Surveys of employers conducted in the mid 1990s showed large proportions of employers, particularly among the larger corporations, using some form of alternative dispute resolution (ADR), with mediation often being the preferred form (Feuille 1999). A study of five large firms that had adopted employment arbitration by 1997 showed that three of them had various forms of pre-arbitration dispute resolution procedures, including mediation. In 1999, the Equal Employment Opportunity Commission (EEOC) started encouraging employers to use ADR in handling discrimination claims, and initial analyses of this experience yielded positive results (Feuille 1999).

While mediation is widely admired as a dispute resolving process, it may be difficult to apply in the highly stressed atmosphere of a termination case. This is especially true if, as is usually the case, it is utilized subsequent to the discharge. Nevertheless, practitioners are generally of the opinion that it can frequently be helpful and seldom harmful. Therefore, it can be an important element in a workplace justice system.

Ombudsman

The corporate ombudsman "is a neutral member of the corporation who provides confidential and informal assistance to employees in resolving work-related concerns" (Kandel and Frumer 1994, p. 587). In the mid 1990s, it was estimated that about 500 corporations, most of them with 500 or more employees, had an ombudsman system in place (McDermott and Berkeley 1996).

Two crucial elements of an ombudsman program are that the ombudsman keep communications with employees confidential, and that the ombudsman be independent of management (McDermott and

Berkeley 1996). If ombudsman programs meet these conditions, they have considerable potential for removing communication barriers and helping to resolve disputes. A problem for ombudsmen is that they are in a position that is fraught with danger for their own careers. On one hand, they need to be independent of management, while on the other, it is expecting a great deal of upper level managers to assume that they will ignore the negative effects on the company's supervisors and finances that an energetic and assertive ombudsman can sometimes produce. Therefore, it is difficult for an ombudsman to maintain independence, and to be perceived by workers as being independent (Cooper, Nolan, and Bales 2000).

"Hard" Justice Systems

There are several justice systems that, unlike the "soft" ones, may impose a legally binding decision on the employer. These are peer review, employment arbitration, and labor arbitration. Peer review is actually something of a hybrid between soft and hard systems, since it may or may not result in a final and legally binding decision, while the others always do. We will discuss it here, leaving for later consideration the purely hard systems.

Peer review, which originated in the mid 1980s, was originally intended to be primarily a union-avoidance strategy. General Electric's Appliance Park plant in Columbia, Maryland, is where it started (Grote and Wimberly 1993). Recent research (Colvin 2003) provides evidence that union avoidance remains a significant motivation for the establishment of peer review committees. These systems "shift some personnel decisions from the company to the aggrieved employee's peers" (Cooper, Nolan, and Bales 2000, p. 664).

The procedures used by peer review systems vary considerably (Cooper, Nolan, and Bales 2000). However, they follow a general pattern of having worker complaints go to a hearing-like stage where a panel that is comprised of employees makes a decision regarding the worker complaint. The panel usually includes some managers, but the majority of the panel is made up of nonmanagerial employees. The original General Electric panels consisted of three members who were fellow workers and two who were managers (Grote and Wimberly

1993), which is the same makeup used in the Marriott system (Wilensky and Jones 1994).

The Marriott system is fairly typical. In it, 10 to 15 percent of employees in each of 50 business units are trained to be peer review panelists. Their names are placed in a box and drawn by the grieving employee. The employee can draw up to six names of peers, from which the employee chooses three. The employee then draws from a box the names of up to four managers, from whom the employee chooses two. The five persons chosen then make up the panel, which is required to hear and decide the case within 10 days of their selection (Wilensky and Jones 1994).

Other features of the Marriott system that are also considered typical require that the panel only interpret and apply company policies—it does not have the authority to change or abolish company policies. Generally, a human resources professional facilitates the operation of the panel.

The Marriott panels make final and binding decisions. This last element is one in which some companies' procedures vary, as some make the panel's decision only a recommendation for management action. However, making the panel's decision nonbinding may subject it to attack under the provisions of the National Labor Relations Act (NLRA). The NLRA makes it an unfair labor practice for an employer to dominate or interfere with a "labor organization." In the case of *Keeler Brass Automotive Group* (1995), the National Labor Relations Board (NLRB) held that an employee committee of this type that did not make a final and binding decision was engaged in "dealing with" the employer over wages, hours, and terms and conditions of employment, and was therefore a "labor organization" under the law. Setting up and managing such an organization is a violation of Sec. 8 (a)(2) of the NLRA. In *Sparks Nugget, Inc.* (1977), the NLRB had decided that a panel that made a final and binding decision was legal. Interestingly, some companies have made a decision to make peer review panel decisions only recommendatory, requiring the approval of management when they uphold a termination, even though they recognize that this likely violates the NLRA. The reason for a company to ignore the law likely lies in the fact that there are no penalties for violating it, and the worst that can happen is that the NLRB can order the company to change its practice in the future.

How well do peer review panels work? It is claimed that employees like them, primarily because they deliver an objective and fair decision (Wilensky and Jones 1994). Managers tend to like peer review because it helps employees understand the management point of view, with employees being less likely to blame managers for disciplinary actions (Wilensky and Jones 1994; Cooper, Nolan, and Bales 2000). One firm found that peer review dramatically reduced employee filings with the EEOC (Wilensky and Jones 1994). In addition, there is some anecdotal evidence supporting the belief of managers that peers will be more harsh with employees than managers would be (Cooper, Nolan, and Bales 2000). A result attributed to peer review that is to the advantage of both workers and managers is that managers tend to be more careful in making decisions if they know that those decisions will be reviewed by a peer review panel (Wilensky and Jones 1994).

On its face, peer review appears to be an extraordinary delegation of power by management to rank and file employees. From the point of view of traditional analysis of management/employee relations, it is certainly an anomaly. How, then, does one explain this from the standpoint of managers' self-interest? Is it simply that they believe in empowering workers and are willing to give up authority in pursuit of this ideal? Is it that they believe that this will lead to efficiencies and profitability? Is it mainly a union avoidance technique? Or, do they believe that employees will be more severe than managers, so that they are cynically delegating an unpleasant task at no cost, given that punishments will be upheld more often by peer review committees than they would by upper management?

The answer may be some combination of several of the above considerations. The explanation cannot be based simply on ideological grounds. If management believes that satisfied workers perform better, they might favor a procedure that would increase satisfaction, hoping that this would lead to greater productivity. The prevention of litigation would lead to lower costs, thereby contributing to efficiency. The avoidance of unions is certainly among the motivations, and peer review may provide a substitute for one of the main advantages of unionism—an effective grievance system. A human resources manager was overheard to remark that her company's peer review procedure had worked well in its first test because management had won the case. This made it fairly clear what management's criterion was for a successful program—the peer review committee denying the grievance. Also, the establishment of peer review committees has been found to be related to the adoption of more general high-performance management systems (i.e., teams and the like) (Colvin 2003). This may indicate that peer review is often just one aspect of an overall policy of employee involvement.

The most important effects from both the employer and employee perspectives may be more subtle and long-range. It may well be that supervisors take greater care with disciplinary actions when they know that a relatively objective review of these actions will be made. Clearly, this is the hope for positive effects of the "hard" processes generally— that the prospect of having a decision overturned will make for better, more objectively justifiable decisions. It is precisely this that is a prime requirement for the provision of human dignity at the workplace.

From a management perspective, it may be extremely helpful in the long run to have a group of rank and file employees (trained peer review panel members) who have a sympathetic understanding of the difficulties that managers face in discipline cases. The role of a manager is often a difficult one, and it can only be eased by making subordinates aware of this fact.

There are many questions that remain unanswered about peer reviews. Are they fair? How do their decisions compare with those reached in other "hard" processes? Are they indeed more severe than managers would be? Does the presence of managers and the participation of human resources professionals permit the co-opting of employees into accepting management decisions? Are peer review panel members truly independent of management? We attempt to deal with at least a few of these in this study.

PLAN OF THE BOOK

In the next two chapters, we will discuss the literature and evidence on the most heavily studied of the "hard" management-initiated dispute resolution procedures—employment arbitration. In the chapters that follow, we will set out the methods and samples employed in our study, the data gathered, our various analyses of the data, and some general conclusions.

2
Employment Arbitration

Employment arbitration is by far the most controversial of the ADR systems for resolving disputes over termination of employment. This is illustrated by the fact that in November 2002, the Consumer Attorneys of California took the rather extreme step of announcing a boycott of the American Arbitration Association (AAA), in a bitter dispute between claimants' lawyers and the AAA that has arisen out of AAA's opposition to recent California legislation that regulates this process. The intensity of the controversy is derived from an increasing popularity of employment arbitration among employers and strong resistance to it by claimants' attorneys, federal agencies, scholars, and professional groups.

Employment arbitration is a process for resolving disputes among nonunion employees and their employers. It provides an alternative to litigation and, indirectly, to labor arbitration that is available to unionized workers. In an employment arbitration procedure, the employer and the employee agree that claims of the employee against the employer will be taken to an arbitration tribunal rather than to court. Sometimes this is limited to claims for which the law already gives a remedy, such as discrimination on the basis of race, sex, national origin, religion, color, age, or disability, but the agreement may apply more broadly to any type of claim by the employee against the employer, or by the employer against the employee. It is designed by the employer. While there have been attempts to provide for arbitration of employment discharge cases by state law, most notably the Model Employment Termination Act adopted by the Commissioners on Uniform State Laws, only Montana has adopted such a law (Bingham 1996).

The details of employment arbitration procedures vary widely. They can range from a process that is clearly stacked against the employee to one that is relatively even-handed and provides the employee with a fair process. The crucial ingredients are a binding decision by a neutral outsider selected by the parties, and the avoidance of lawsuits. It has been said that employment arbitration is not a substitute for litigation, but rather litigation in a different forum.

The most controversial aspect of employment arbitration is that it is typically mandated by the employer as a condition of employment prior to the dispute in question. Post-dispute voluntary arbitration is universally praised as useful, and can be truly said to be at the option of the employee. Pre-dispute employment arbitration contracts, on the other hand, confront employees with a choice of agreeing to arbitration or losing either their present job or the chance to be hired at a new job. In addition, these are contracts of adhesion wherein there is no bargaining and the procedure is offered to the employee on a take-it-or-leave-it basis. This transaction has the further characteristic of usually being between two parties of greatly unequal bargaining power.

In this chapter, we will discuss the growth of employment arbitration, the reasons for its growth, changes in the law pertaining to it, and the literature on the pros and cons of employment arbitration.

THE GROWTH OF EMPLOYMENT ARBITRATION

Although there is no current comprehensive study of the incidence of employment arbitration agreements, there have been a number of scholarly and government efforts to document the increase in these agreements during the 1990s. These provide us with a picture of a phenomenon that is gaining in popularity, although perhaps not so rapidly as is sometimes assumed in the literature.

One recent study of the telecommunications industry (Colvin 2001) found that about 16 percent of the 302 establishments surveyed had employment arbitration procedures in place. Somewhat surprisingly, the same survey showed a similar (15.9 percent) rate of adoption of peer review practices (Colvin 2003). A national survey of a sample of 1,000 firms that included firms varying in size, location, and industry found that 19 percent of the 123 respondent firms had an employment arbitration procedure (Galle and Koen 2000–2001). According to the 2000 annual report of the AAA, there were over 500 employers employing five million workers covered by AAA's arbitration programs (LeRoy and Feuille 2002).

In the late 1980s, a study by Columbia University showed that 42 to 54 percent of nonunion employers had a written procedure, and about 20 percent of these had third-party arbitration (Lewin 1990). A

1994 survey by the U.S. General Accounting Office (USGAO) found that, of their stratified random sample of 2,000 businesses that filed Equal Employment Opportunity reports in 1992 and had more than 100 employees, 9.9 percent had employment arbitration procedures in place. Of those that had ADR procedures in 1992, 19 percent used arbitration (USGAO 1995, 1997). USGAO concluded in a 1997 report that the use of ADR generally had increased since their 1994 report (USGAO 1997). A 1997 study that received responses from 606 corporate lawyers from the 1,000 largest companies showed that arbitration (not necessarily in its mandatory form) had been used in 62 percent of their employment disputes (Lipsky and Seeber 1999). A survey of the 1,000 largest American corporations found that 79 percent of them used arbitration to resolve a variety of disputes (Zimmerman 1997). This, however, included many types of disputes, not just those regarding employment. One mid-nineties survey (McDermott 1995) reported that most of the 92 companies responding to the survey would consider adopting employment arbitration.

One very broad and comprehensive survey of American workplace practices (Freeman and Rogers 1999) provides some interesting data. It found that 32 percent of workers were covered by a grievance procedure that ended in third-party arbitration. Given that only 13.5 percent of American workers are union members who are covered by a collective bargaining agreement's provision for labor arbitration, this would translate into approximately 18.5 percent who are covered by employment arbitration.

From the above data, we conclude that there has been some growth in the use of employment arbitration during the 1990s. However, there is no hard evidence regarding the extent to which this is currently occurring across American industry.

REASONS FOR GROWTH OF EMPLOYMENT ARBITRATION

Employment arbitration has enjoyed whatever popularity that it has gained for two main reasons: First, employers have felt a need for it, and second, the Federal Government has encouraged it. Congress has encouraged ADR in several statutes, but most importantly, the U.S.

Supreme Court has made it clear that pre-dispute mandatory employment arbitration agreements are enforceable under federal law. We will briefly address the first of these reasons—the employers' perceived need—in this section, and then move on to a more extensive review of the law.

Complaints filed with the Equal Employment Opportunity Commission soared in the early 1990s. Between fiscal years 1991 and 1994, the number of discrimination complaints to the EEOC grew by 43 percent, from 63,898 to 91,189 (USGAO 1997). Between 1990 and 1998, the number of employment discrimination cases filed in Federal District-Court Civil Cases rose from 6,936 to 21,540. In the same period, civil rights cases in U.S. Courts of Appeal increased from 4,729 to 8,466, and 56 percent of these cases were employment cases (Litras 2000). This was paralleled by an increase in the number of discrimination cases decided in federal district courts from 2,418 in 1991 to 3,419 in 1994, and the cases decided annually rose to 5,400 by 2000 (Federal District-Court Civil Cases 2002). The Federal Commission on the Future of Labor-Management Relations (Dunlop Commission) concluded that there had been a veritable "explosion" in lawsuits for enforcement of employee rights (U.S. Departments of Commerce and Labor 1994). However, this conclusion was challenged by one scholar (Stone 1999) who argued that there were no more cases on federal dockets in the mid 1990s than 25 years before, and that the average caseload per judge had gone down. In spite of the fact that studies had lent support to the view that the "so-called litigation explosion is a myth which has little to support it," it is one that "nonetheless plays a powerful role in fueling moves to alternative dispute resolution mechanisms" (Stone 1999, p. 959).

Employment discrimination cases had already been on the rise prior to the 1990s (Coleman and Pangis 2000–2001). In the 1970s and 1980s, the number of employment discrimination cases filed had increased an astonishing 2,166 percent (Donohue and Siegelman 1991).

In its 1997 report, the USGAO concluded that the increase in discrimination cases resulted from the downsizing that was taking place during this period, the passage of the Americans with Disabilities Act in 1990, and the Civil Rights Act of 1991, which provided for the right to jury trial and compensatory and punitive damages. Under this new

Civil Rights Act, compensatory damages can now be awarded for future pecuniary losses, emotional pain, suffering, and the like, but the limit on compensatory and punitive damages is $300,000 for the largest employers.

In addition to the increasing litigation involving violation of federal and state antidiscrimination laws, state courts continued to expand a set of exceptions to the historic employment-at-will rule in the 1980s and 1990s. In some states—particularly California—wrongful termination suits grew in both volume and money damages enough to give rise to concern and calls for arbitration of these cases (Gould 1987–1988). Employment-at-will is a matter of common law in all states except Montana, which has a statute requiring cause for termination. The employment-at-will rule is that employers can terminate employees for any—or no—reason, so long as they do not violate a particular statute, such as Title VII of the Civil Rights Act or the NLRA. This cuts both ways, in that the employee can also terminate the relationship at any time.

The most commonly adopted exception to employment-at-will is the public policy exception, with courts holding that an employee cannot be terminated if the termination would violate public policy. Examples of this are the firing of a worker for refusing to commit perjury or for compliance with a summons to perform jury duty. Other exceptions are the implied-in-fact contract exception, where a handbook or set of company rules can become binding upon the employer under certain circumstances. The courts have also implied-in-law that there is an obligation of good faith and fair dealing implicit in all employment contracts, as it is in other contracts. Finally, liability can arise from firing a worker in an abusive manner (Bennett-Alexander and Hartman 2001).

It is not only the frequency of employee claims and lawsuits that has been increasing; the size of damage awards in jury verdicts has been increasing as well. Between 1994 and 2000, the median jury award in a discrimination case rose 177 percent, from $78,592 to $218,000 (Jury Verdict Research 2002a). During the same period, the chances of winning in front of a jury increased from 50 percent to 67 percent (Jury Verdict Research 2002b). In the arena of litigation in state courts under exceptions to the employment-at-will rule, as well as in statutory cases, there have been a number of very lucrative jury verdicts against employers that have been highly publicized (Eaton and Keefe 1999). In the 1980s, jury verdicts had already become quite substantial. For example, in California between 1980 and 1986, the average award for successful plaintiffs was $640,000 (Dertouzos, Holland, and Ebner 1988). This experience has led to a fear of extreme jury verdicts that, although not entirely justified because of the low probability of their occurrence, has caused employers to search for alternatives to being subjected to the tender mercies of juries (USGAO 1995).

The Dunlop Commission concluded that it was the phenomenon of increasing worker discrimination complaints and litigation that led employers to search for ways other than litigation to resolve these claims (U.S. Departments of Commerce and Labor 1994). One study found that 75 percent of a national sample of 36 employers with employment arbitration had adopted it because of concerns about the cost of litigation (Bickner, Ver Ploeg, and Feigenbaum 1997). This same study found that only 10 percent cited union avoidance as a motivating factor in the adoption of employment arbitration. This lends some support to the view that union avoidance is not the primary motivation (Clark 1997). A number of writers have argued that these procedures have been adopted primarily to avoid the costs and risks of litigation (e.g., Clark 1997; Abraham and Voos 2000).

ENCOURAGEMENT BY THE FEDERAL GOVERNMENT

The federal government's encouragement of the use of employment arbitration has been both legislative and judicial. Congress encouraged the use of ADR by stating a preference for it in the American with Disabilities Act of 1990, the Civil Rights Act of 1991, and the Civil Justice Reform Act of 1990 (which encouraged federal courts to use ADR). In 1992, the EEOC adopted regulations that encouraged the use of ADR in its complaint processes. Likewise, in 1994, the Dunlop Commission recommended increasing the use of ADR in resolving employee claims of violations of discrimination laws (USGAO 1997).

The most powerful stimulus to the adoption of employment arbitration has come from two key decisions of the U.S. Supreme Court which made it clear that pre-dispute mandatory employment arbitration agreements are enforceable: *Circuit City Stores, Inc. v. Adams* (2001a), and *Gilmer v. Interstate/Johnson Lane* (1991).

In *Circuit City Stores, Inc. v. Adams*, by a 5 to 4 vote, the court reversed a decision of the Ninth Circuit Court of Appeals that had held that a mandatory employment arbitration clause in an employment contract was unenforceable. The employee—Adams—had signed an employment application that contained a provision stating that he agreed to take all claims arising from his employment, including statutory ones, to arbitration rather than to court. He later filed a suit against his employer for violating California's Fair Employment and Housing Act.

The Supreme Court ruled that the arbitration agreement was enforceable by finding that the Federal Arbitration Act (FAA) covered such contracts of employment. The court construed the FAA's exclusion of "contracts of employment of seamen, railroad employees, or any other class of workers engaged in interstate commerce" to exempt only transportation workers. The primary rationale of the court in so construing the FAA exclusion was the legal principle of *ejusdem generis*, which holds that "where general words follow specific words in a statutory enumeration, the general words are construed to embrace only objects similar in nature to those objects enumerated by the preceding specific words" (pp. 114–115). Applied to the language of the FAA, this meant that only workers similar to seamen and railroad employees—i.e., transportation employees—were covered by the exclusion from the FAA.

Because federal law is supreme, the FAA as construed by the Supreme Court controls litigation in state courts as well as federal courts, meaning that the authority of the federal government prevents the states from making these agreements unenforceable (*Southland Corp. v. Keating* 1984). The only basis for an arbitration agreement being deemed unenforceable under the FAA is "such grounds as exist at law or in equity for the revocation of any contract." Thus, a contract to arbitrate could be set aside, but only for the same reasons that would make any other contract unenforceable, and this would generally be a matter of state law.

Under the FAA, arbitration awards are not subject to meaningful judicial review. They can be set aside only "where the award was procured by corruption, fraud, or undue means," "where there [existed] evident partiality or corruption [by] the arbitrators," where there was misconduct by the arbitrators, or where "the arbitrators exceeded their powers" (Federal Arbitration Act, 9 U.S.C. §510, 2000; Cooper, Nolan, and Bales 2000). Courts have stated that an arbitration award can also be set aside if the arbitrator acted in "manifest disregard of the law" (*Halligan v. Piper Jaffray, Inc.* 1998). It has been held that manifest disregard of the law exists where the award is: "unfounded in reason and fact; based on reasoning so faulty that no judge, or group of judges, ever could conceivably have made such a ruling; *or* mistakenly based on a crucial assumption that is concededly a non-fact" (*Advent, Inc. v. McCarthy* 1990, p. 8). This decision was based on *dictum* in a U.S. Supreme Court decision, *Wilko v. Swan* (1953).

The stage for *Circuit City Stores v. Adams* was set by the earlier case of *Gilmer v. Interstate/Johnson Lane* (1991). In that case, the court upheld an arbitration agreement contained in Gilmer's application for registration as a securities representative on the New York Stock Exchange. The application provided that he agreed to "arbitrate any dispute, including employment disputes." Interstate/Johnson Lane terminated him several years later when he had reached the age of 62, and Gilmer sued in federal court under the Age Discrimination in Employment Act. The employer defended on the grounds that Gilmer was compelled to arbitrate the matter, and the Supreme Court held that the agreement to arbitrate a statutory claim was enforceable. It said that this did not involve Gilmer giving up substantive statutory rights, but only an agreement on his part to enforce these rights in a different forum. It cited the strong federal policy favoring arbitration that was reflected in the FAA.

Gilmer v. Interstate/Johnson Lane did not involve an agreement between an employer and an employee, but rather one with the stock exchange, therefore, the FAA exemption of employment contracts did not apply. However, the court's reasoning and approach to this case strongly indicated that employment contracts to arbitrate would be enforceable. This decision had the effect of encouraging employers to experiment with mandatory arbitration clauses in their agreements with employees. Indeed, subsequent to the *Gilmer* case, all of the Circuit Courts of Appeal except the Ninth Circuit had reached the conclusion that such clauses were enforceable, even before *Circuit City* was decided.

Subsequent to *Circuit City*, the Ninth Circuit overruled its decision in *Duffield v. Robertson Stephens Co.* (1998), in which it had held that a mandatory employment arbitration covering statutory rights was unenforceable, thus bringing the court into line with the others on this point. However, on the *Circuit City* case itself, which was remanded to the Ninth Circuit, the court held that the agreement in that case was unenforceable because it was "unconscionable" under California law. It based this decision on the fact that the agreement was offered on a take-it-or-leave-it basis, did not require the company to arbitrate its claims against the employee, provided for only limited relief to the employee, and required the employee to pay half of the costs of arbitration (*Circuit City Stores, Inc. v. Adams* 2001b).

As indicated by the Ninth Circuit's ruling in the *Circuit City* remand, there remain a number of questions to be answered with regard to the enforcement of mandatory employment arbitration agreements. Given that these clauses are enforceable as a general proposition, what, if anything, is required of particular agreements in order for them to survive judicial scrutiny under state law or under a developing federal common law?

Partly because the author of the opinion is Harry Edwards, a well-respected authority on employment law, the decision of the District of Columbia Court of Appeals in *Cole v. Burns International Security Services* (1997) is widely cited on the subject of the standards that must be met by employment arbitration agreements. In this case, the court held that it would enforce an agreement to arbitrate, but only because it did not impose on the employee the obligation to pay all or part of the costs of the arbitration. Judge Edwards stated:

> Indeed, we are unaware of any situation in American jurisprudence in which a beneficiary of a federal statute has been required to pay for the services of the judge . . . [yet] arbitration is supposed to be a reasonable substitute for a judicial forum." (p. 1484)

In *Cole*, the court also stated that *Gilmer* required five safeguards for a pre-dispute employment arbitration clause to be enforceable: 1) an arbitrator who is neutral; 2) discovery that is more than minimal; 3) a written award; 4) the availability of all remedies that would be available in court; and 5) the absence of a requirement for the employee to pay either costs that are unreasonable, or any part of the arbitrator's fees.

There have been a number of court decisions on an employee's obligation to share in the costs of arbitration proceedings, and on the effects of that obligation on the enforceability of the employment arbitration agreement. Some have agreed with *Cole* that any sharing of cost renders the agreement unenforceable (*Shankle v. B-G Maintenance Management of Colorado, Inc.* 1999; *Paladino v. Avnet Computer Technologies, Inc.* 1998). Others have viewed the question on a case-by-case basis to see if the particular cost-sharing arrangement is reasonable under the circumstances of the case (e.g., *Midworm v. Ashcroft* 2002; *Baugher v. Dekko Heating Technologies* 2002). An appeals court in Florida held that a provision that the employer and the employee share equally in the costs of the arbitrations rendered the agreement unenforceable (*Flyer Printing Co. v. Hill* 2001). The Ninth Circuit has held that excessive costs being imposed on the employee, along with other "oppressive" provisions, can render the arbitration agreement unconscionable (see below for further discussion of this criterion), and therefore unenforceable (*Ferguson v. Countrywide Credit Industries, Inc.* 2002). The Sixth Circuit has held that cost-splitting agreements are unenforceable, but severed them from the balance of the arbitration agreement, making it otherwise enforceable (*Morrison v. Circuit City Stores, Inc.* 2003). Other courts have refused to sever unconscionable cost provisions, causing them to invalidate the entire agreement to arbitrate (*Plaskett v. Bechtel International, Inc.* 2003). An interesting analysis of this issue has been written by LeRoy and Feuille (2002).

The California Supreme Court in *Armendiaz v. Foundation Health Psychcare Services* (2000) held that, in order to be consistent with the state antidiscrimination statute, and therefore enforceable, an agreement needed to contain the *Cole* safeguards: 1) provide for a neutral arbitrator; 2) not limit statutory remedies; 3) provide for some discovery; 4) require written awards; and 5) not impose limits on the employee's remedies without imposing the same limits on the employer's. *Armendiaz* has been applied to common law claims of termination in violation of public policy (*Little v. Auto Stiegler* 2003).

In *Hooters of America, Inc. v. Phillips* (1999), the Fourth Circuit Court of Appeals held that the employer had violated its agreement to arbitrate by setting up a process that was "utterly lacking in the rudiments of even-handedness," and therefore could not force the employee to submit to the employer's process (p. 933). Hooters' system required the employee, but not the employer, to provide the specifics of the claim at the outset of the proceeding. The employee was also required to provide the employer with a list of witnesses and a summary of the facts known by each. Here, also, there was no such requirement for the employer. The arbitrator was to be chosen from a panel selected by the employer. The employer, but not the employee, could add claims during the course of the proceeding, move for summary dismissal, record the hearing, and vacate or modify the award. The employer could cancel the arbitration process on 30 days' notice, and change the rules without notice at any time. The court characterized this as a "sham system unworthy even of the name arbitration" (p. 940).

To the extent that employment arbitration agreements are adhesive (i.e., form contracts presented on a take-it-or-leave-it basis), they may be unenforceable under state law if the terms are "not within the reasonable expectation of the weaker party and . . . are unduly oppressive or unconscionable" (Cooper, Nolan, and Bales 2000, p. 560); (see also *Graham v. Scissor-Tail, Inc.* 1981). Unconscionability is said by the courts to have two dimensions: substantive and procedural. To be unenforceable, a contract must be unconscionable on both dimensions. Substantive unconsionability "refers to contract terms that unreasonably favor one party over another," while procedural unconsionability "refers to the process of contract formation, and encompasses the inequality of bargaining power and ability, and the use of fine print and convoluted language" (Cooper, Nolan, and Bales 2000, p. 560). It has been held that an adhesive agreement—one that is "drafted or otherwise proffered" by the stronger of two contracting parties—is unenforceable "if two conditions are present: 1) the contract is the result of coercive bargaining between two parties of unequal bargaining strength; *and* 2) the contract unfairly limits the obligations and liabilities of, or otherwise unfairly advantages, the stronger party" (*Brown v. KFC National Management Co.* 1996, p. 167); (see also *Stirlen v. Supercuts* 1997). The U.S. Supreme Court, in *Doctor's Associates, Inc. v. Casarotto* (1996), held that defenses generally applicable in contract cases, such as unconscionability, can be applied without violating the FAA. Some practical guidance for employers drafting agreements that are fair and defensible exists in the literature (Dichter and Ballard 2000–2001). More recently, the Ninth Circuit has held an arbitration agreement to be both procedurally and substantively unconscionable (*Ingle v. Circuit City Stores, Inc.* 2003).

Arbitration agreements have been found to be unenforceable on a few other counts. The Ninth Circuit has held that an arbitration clause buried in a handbook does not constitute a "knowing waiver" of statutory rights, and is therefore enforceable (*Nelson v. Cyprus Bagdad Copper Corp.* 1997). Another circuit has held that an arbitration clause contained in a handbook is enforceable where it is separate from other parts of the handbook and signed separately (*Patterson v. Tenet Healthcare* 1997), and yet another U.S. Circuit Court of Appeals has refused to enforce an arbitration clause that it deemed to be "illusory" because it permitted the employer to change it at any time (*Dumais v. American Golf Corp.* 2002). A federal district court in Ohio has held an agreement to be unenforceable because it favored the employer on procedural matters and required the Ohio resident employee to travel to San Francisco for the arbitration proceeding (*Hagedorn v. Veritas Software Corp.* 2002).

It is clear that a pre-dispute employment arbitration clause is not per se unconscionable or unenforceable. However, whether a particular agreement is unconscionable or, in terms of the analysis in the *Hooters* case, is an agreement to arbitrate at all, probably depends upon whether it meets accepted norms of fairness and due process.

A broad set of standards for fairness was laid down by the Dunlop Commission in its 1994 report. According to the commission, arbitration systems should provide 1) a neutral arbitrator who is knowledgeable about the law and the concerns of the employer and the employee, 2) a method that is both fair and simple by which the employee can secure the necessary information to prosecute the claim, 3) a method of sharing costs that is fair and ensures affordable access of the employee to the process, 4) the right to an independent representative, 5) the same remedies available in litigation, 6) a written opinion explaining the arbitrator's reasoning, and 7) sufficient judicial review to ensure that the arbitrator's decision is consistent with the law.

Probably the most influential set of standards for employment arbitration is the Due Process Protocol created and agreed to in 1995 by the National Academy of Arbitrators, the AAA, the American Bar Association, the American Civil Liberties Union, the Federal Mediation and Conciliation Service, the National Employment Lawyers Association, and the Society of Professionals in Dispute Resolution (Zack 1999). The Due Process Protocol calls for 1) a neutral agency to develop a roster of neutrals who are demographically diverse, 2) neutrals who are trained in the statutes involved, 3) joint selection of the arbitrator from the panel of arbitrators, 4) access by both parties to the names of parties who had recently presented cases to the neutrals, 5) discovery procedures allowing for a reasonable number of depositions, 6) a representative of the employee's choosing, 7) a written decision consistent with the law, 8) a remedy consistent with the statute, and 9) limited judicial review (Zack 1999). Interestingly, the NAA, one of the parties to the Protocol, has taken an adverse position, in principle, to mandatory pre-dispute employment arbitration, although its members may ethically hear such cases. The NAA is joined in its opposition to pre-dispute employment arbitration by the EEOC (1997). In two 1995 cases, the NLRB issued unfair labor practice complaints based on employees' termination for refusing to sign or abide by employment arbitration agreements (*Bentley's Luggage Corp.* 1995; *Great Western Financial Corp.* 1995). However, it is not possible to know the NLRB policy at the present time. In our view, it is likely that the 2004 version of the board will look more favorably upon employment arbitration.

Two of the major agencies that administer employment arbitration cases, the AAA and JAMS/Endispute, have adopted the protocol and announced that they will handle cases only if they are based on agreements that comply with the protocol. In addition, in November 2002, the AAA announced that it had changed its rules to provide that the cost of the administrative filing fee that could be charged to the employee was capped at $125, and that the arbitrator's fee must be paid in full by the employer (National Arbitration Center 2002a).

In our view, pre-dispute employment arbitration agreements will have to meet the requirements of the protocol in order to be enforceable. In addition, an agreement that imposes more than *de minimus* costs on the employee is highly likely to run afoul of the standards set in *Cole v. Burns International Security Services*, and therefore be unenforceable. Requiring the employer to foot the bill for arbitration does seem eminently reasonable, given that it is the employer's process that is substituted for court proceedings at the employer's insistence.

Having spoken to the ability of the employee to assert his or her claim for employment discrimination, there remains the question of what, if any, effect an employment arbitration agreement has on the ability of the EEOC to enforce the statutes under its purview. One of the many arguments against employment arbitration is that it consigns a matter of public law and policy to a private justice system. That is, it is not just the individual right of the claimant that is involved, but rather the public interest in the elimination of discrimination. An answer to this criticism of employment arbitration is the continued ability of the EEOC to enforce the law when it believes this to be necessary.

In *EEOC v. Waffle House, Inc.* (2002), the U.S. Supreme Court held that an employee's agreement to arbitrate did not preclude the EEOC from bringing an action of its own to enforce the law. Furthermore, the EEOC can recover judicial victim-specific relief for the employee, including backpay, reinstatement, and money damages. However, if the employee has failed to mitigate his or her damages (e.g., by attempting to find interim employment) or has accepted a monetary settlement from the employer, this would limit the amount that the EEOC could recover from the employer. This was followed by a Sixth Circuit Court of Appeals decision (*EEOC v. Circuit City Stores, Inc.* 2002), holding that an arbitration agreement did not prevent an employee from filing a charge with the EEOC, or the EEOC from proceeding with a lawsuit seeking victim-specific relief.

This limit on the effects of an arbitration agreement may not be as important as one might think, since the EEOC brings few lawsuits (in 2000 only 291 of the 21,032 discrimination lawsuits were brought by the EEOC). The EEOC, with its limited budget and staff, can take only cases with high publicity potential or where a very large amount of money is at stake.

Employment Arbitration and Collective Bargaining

The interface between collective bargaining agreements and the NLRA, and employment arbitration agreements is still unclear. There are two questions that arise in this context. First, does the agreement of a union to arbitration of employee grievances bind the individual employee in the same manner that an individual's agreement does? That is, is an employee covered by a collective bargaining agreement barred from bringing a lawsuit for violations of employment discrimination laws? Second, what should be the effect of an arbitration clause on an employee's ability to file charges under the NLRA? These are questions that were believed to be settled but have been given new life by *Circuit City Stores v. Adams.*

As to the first question, it has long been the law that neither the existence of a collectively bargained right to arbitration, nor an employee pursuing arbitration under a collective bargaining agreement, bars a lawsuit under federal antidiscrimination statutes (*Alexander v. Gardner-Denver Co.* 1974). An employee can pursue a Title VII claim, even after losing in arbitration.

The decision in *Gardner-Denver* was based in part on the view that the statutory claim and the claim under the collective bargaining agreement were separate. The fact that the same events gave rise to both claims did not prevent the employee from pursuing them both. The court also held that "there can be no prospective waiver of the employee's rights under Title VII," (p. 51) and that, in any event, the *collective* processes of collective bargaining could not waive the *individual* rights of an employee under the law. In addition, the court held that the arbitral forum was ill-suited to dealing with questions of public law because the arbitrator's duty was to enforce the contract, not to enforce public law. Furthermore, the lack of legal training of many arbitrators, and the differing procedures in arbitration, caused the arbitral forum to be inadequate.

Obviously, *Circuit City* plays havoc with the rationale found in *Gardner-Denver.* Although this decision has not yet been overruled, the reasoning of the court in *Gardner-Denver* is no longer subscribed to by the U.S. Supreme Court. Title VII rights, or at least the forum to pursue them, can now be waived. The question is now what does it take for a waiver to exist. In *Wright v. Universal Maritime Service Corp.* (1998), the Supreme Court held that an arbitration clause did not bar an action under the Americans with Disabilities Act because the collective bargaining agreement did not contain a clear and unequivocal waiver of the right of access to court. The court avoided saying whether such a clear and unequivocal waiver by the union would be binding on the part of the employee.

At this writing, it is still unclear whether a union can waive an employee's right, however there are a number of post-*Wright* cases that develop the law on this issue. It has been argued that there may be two ways that a collective bargaining agreement can meet the standard of having a clear and unequivocal waiver. First, the collective agreement's arbitration clause could specifically provide that employees agree that they will submit to arbitration all claims that arise out of their employment. Second, the collective bargaining agreement could state that the obligation to arbitrate applies to "all disputes," or "all disputes concerning the agreement," while at the same time incorporating the discrimination statutes into the agreement (Hodges 2001, p. 515). The courts have tended to be rather strict in their requirements for such waivers (see *Brown v. ABF Freight Sys., Inc.* 1999; *Kennedy v. Superior Painting Co.* 2000; *Quint v. A.E. Staley Manufacturing Co.* 1999). However, the Fourth Circuit has held that a provision in a collective bargaining agreement that arbitration would be the exclusive remedy for "all claims regarding equal employment opportunities" barred a suit under the Americans with Disabilities Act (*Singletary v. Enersys Inc.* 2003).

Two circuits have held that union waivers of statutory claims of individual employees are unenforceable (*Rogers v. New York University* 2000; *Pryner v. Tractor Supply Co.* 1997). The Third Circuit has decided that a collective bargaining agreement arbitration clause does not bar a lawsuit if the employee cannot demand arbitration without the consent of the union (*Martin v. Dana Corp.* 1997). The Eleventh Circuit has set out a three-part test for a collective bargaining agreement barring an employee from litigation. Under this test, a suit is barred only if 1) the employee has individually agreed to arbitrate, 2) the arbitrator is authorized to resolve federal statutory claims, and 3) the employee had the right to insist upon arbitration (*Brisentine v. Stone & Webster Engineering Corp.* 1997). Another circuit has held that the award of an arbitrator against the employee is strong evidence that Title VII has not been violated, and, in the absence of a showing of new evidence or partiality on the part of the arbitrator, the employee fails to make out a *prima facie* case of discrimination (*Collins v. New York City Transit Authority* 2002).

A more troubling question is whether the waiver of individual rights to go to court on discrimination claims under a collective bargaining agreement—if such a waiver would be valid—would be a mandatory subject of collective bargaining under the NLRA. If it is not a mandatory subject of bargaining, then neither party can insist on their position to the point of impasse. Also, it may be possible for the employer to bypass the union and require employees to sign individual agreements to employment arbitration (Hodges 2001). One circuit court of appeals has held that the right of an employee to pursue an individual claim in court in the presence of an arbitration clause in a collective bargaining agreement is not a mandatory subject of bargaining under the Railway Labor Act. It concluded that an employer can, therefore, require an employee covered by a collective bargaining agreement to sign an agreement compelling him or her to arbitrate a discrimination claim (*Air Line Pilots Association v. Northwest Airlines, Inc.* 1999).

The matter of the union waiver of individual rights to pursue their claims in court is one with respect to which a number of questions remain. These will probably stay unsettled until the U.S. Supreme Court rules definitively on them.

Another area of difficulty lies in the policies of the NLRB, with regard to the arbitration of cases that may involve violations of the NLRA. At present, the NLRB will defer to arbitration. It will generally overturn an arbitration award only if the award is "clearly repugnant" to the NLRA (*Spielberg Manufacturing Co.* 1955; *Collyer Insulated Wire* 1971; *United Technologies Corp.* 1984). However lenient the NLRB's standard of review, it still involves a review of an arbitrator's decision on its merits. This would seem to be a more severe review than a court would give an employment arbitrator's decision under the NAA. Yet here, the employee's claim is likely to get at least as capable representation as it would get under employment arbitration. Here, then, is another area of uncertainty in the law that will have to be resolved, probably by the Supreme Court, in order for the law to have the necessary degree of predictability.

LEGISLATION ON EMPLOYMENT ARBITRATION

The State of California is a hotbed of legislative activity on employment arbitration. In its 2002 session, the California legislature passed six statutes having to do with arbitration. The governor vetoed two of these legislative actions, but the four that became law affect employment arbitration in several respects. First, private arbitration providers are required to publish certain information about their cases, including who prevailed, the amount of the award, the arbitrator's fee, and the number of times the employer has been a party to arbitrations or mediations administered by the provider. Second, private arbitration providers are prohibited from having a financial interest in the parties and attorneys, and the parties and attorneys are not permitted to have a financial interest in the provider. Third, private providers are not immune from lawsuits. Fourth, a court's remand of an arbitrator's award cannot go back to the same arbitrator (AAA 2002; National Arbitration Center 2000b). It is a dispute over this legislation that led the Consumer Attorneys of California to boycott the AAA.

For several years, there have been efforts to pass federal legislation prohibiting pre-dispute mandatory employment arbitration. In June 2001, a bill was introduced in the House of Representatives entitled the Preservation of Civil Rights Protection Act. It would amend the FAA to make employment arbitration agreements unenforceable unless they were voluntarily entered into by an employer and an employee after the dispute arose. This bill was developed by the Congressional Progressive Caucus, and cosponsored by 35 Democratic members of the House. It was endorsed by a number of civil rights, labor, and similar organizations, including the Leadership Conference on Human Rights and the National Organization for Women (Bureau of National Affairs 2001a). Similar legislation, entitled the Civil Rights Procedures Protection Act, was first introduced in the U.S. Senate in 1994 by Senator Russell Feingold (D–WI) (Feingold 2002), but stands little chance of passage in a conservative Republican Congress.

A contrary direction is taken in the Model Employment Termination Act that was adopted in 1991 by the National Conference of Commissioners on Uniform State Laws. This act would require "good cause" to be present for the termination of a worker, and would permit employers to require employees to submit future claims to arbitration—i.e., pre-dispute mandatory arbitration (Eastman and Rothstein 1995). At this writing, no state has adopted this model legislation.

THE PROS AND CONS OF EMPLOYMENT ARBITRATION

There is an extensive literature arguing the advantages and disadvantages of pre-dispute mandatory employment arbitration. While interesting and lively, much of it covers the same ground, making the similar arguments to those already covered here in slightly different ways. Accordingly, we will limit ourselves to summarizing the literature by setting out the main arguments and citing a representative set of references for each one.

Arguments in Favor of Employment Arbitration

Public policy

From the standpoint of the courts, employment arbitration offers some relief from the burdensome employment arbitration caseload that has developed over the last few decades. The court process is slow and costly, and better suited to "setting principles and establishing procedures in test cases" than to handling a heavy caseload of employment cases (Bales 1997, p. 9). Arbitration can free the EEOC from handling routine claims and permit it to instead expend its efforts going after wrongdoers who are systematically violating the law (Estreicher 1997). It is said that the courts have been enduring a "tidal wave of employment-related litigation," and need to deal with it by getting rid of some of this burden (Clark 1997, p. 181). It has been persuasively argued that the EEOC and the courts operating under Title VII have failed to deliver what they should—"access to a fair adjudicatory process" to all employees, and the avoidance of employers having to "spend excessive amounts of time and money defending baseless claims" (Sherwyn, Tracey, and Eigen 1999, p. 147). Frivolous claims may be encouraged while meritorious ones "slip through the cracks" and are lost (Sherwyn, Tracey, and Eigen 1999, p. 88).

Congress has emphatically approved employment arbitration. This first occurred in 1925, with the enactment of the FAA. In 1991, Sec. 118 of the Civil Rights Act of that year encouraged arbitration as a means of settling disputes arising under Title VII (Kaswell 1998).

Employers

Employers have an understandable dislike for the jury system, which arbitration avoids. Employers have the view that juries are unpredictable, often decide cases on grounds of emotion and sympathy, and relate to employees more than to employers (Bales 1997; Clark

1997; Sherwyn, Tracey, and Eigen 1999). Arbitrators are expected to be less likely to award excessive damages than juries (Clark 1997).

Employers are attracted to employment arbitration because, compared to litigation in the courts, it is fast and inexpensive (Bales 1997; Clark 1997). It is argued that litigation nearly always involves attorneys' fees of over $50,000, and often exceed $500,000, regardless of the merits of the case (Sherwyn, Tracey, and Eigen 1999), and in most cases, arbitration involves less publicity than a court proceeding (Clark 1997). Recent research (Colvin 2003) provides strong evidence that avoidance of litigation is a powerful motive for employers adopting employment arbitration.

Employees

Low-income employees have greater access to arbitration than to the court system because their low salaries make large awards unlikely, which in turn makes it difficult to attract attorneys, most of whom work on a contingent fee basis. Because arbitration is quick, it is more likely to attract an attorney for the employee. If the employee is unable to find an attorney, he or she may be able to pursue the claim without one, given the informal nature of arbitration. Litigation is highly adversarial and, in addition to the costs involved, may require employees to put their professional lives on hold for several years (Bales 1997).

It has been argued that the new nonunion ADR systems, including employment arbitration, have grown to serve a new managerial and professional class of employees. This is the most rapidly growing segment of the American labor force, currently comprising somewhere between 31 and 40 percent of the labor force (Eaton and Keefe 1999).

It is well documented that there is a hostility on the part of federal judges toward discrimination litigants and their claims. It is argued that

> there is credible evidence to suggest that the crushing discrimnation caseload in Federal courts has caused judges to look askance at even meritorious discrimination claims, and that this attitude may result in unfairness in the eventual result. (Kaswell 1998, p. 93)

Since "justice delayed is justice denied," the fact that it takes years to resolve discrimination cases does injustice to employee claimants (Kaswell 1998).

Employees may prevail more frequently in arbitration than before courts and juries. A study comparing results under the securities industry arbitration system and the U.S. District Court for the Southern District of New York showed employees winning more often in arbitration, and more quickly. We will consider this and other studies below. Prehearing dismissals, which are common in federal courts, are very rare in arbitration (Kaswell 1998).

That strict rules of evidence do not apply in arbitration can work to the advantage of employees. This allows all manner of evidence to be admitted that would not be admissible in court. Also, the relative informality of the procedures makes the process more "user friendly" for employees (Kaswell 1998, p. 96).

Both employers and employees

Both parties benefit because they have a dispute resolution mechanism that is "faster, less costly and less divisive" (Estreicher 1997). Arbitration has been successful for both parties in the securities industry (Kaswell 1998).

Answers to the critics of employment arbitration

Under employment arbitration, an employee does not give up any substantive rights—only the purely procedural right to a judicial forum. This is not a new form of "yellow dog" contract under which employees give up important rights, but rather a simple change of forum. It is argued that many of the critics of arbitration depict the worst case scenario for arbitration and the best possible scenario for litigation, which is misleading. The reality of the court system is that low-wage employees have little access to it. The argument that employment discrimination law will become a system of private law, where no guidance from prior decisions will be generated, is wrong because under any possible circumstances there will still be plenty of discrimination cases for the courts to decide in order to develop the law (Estreicher 1997).

The argument that the loss of the right to jury trial is important fails to take into account that a jury trial is a realistic alternative for very few claimants. Even when cases with lawyers go to trial they are usually disposed of by motions prior to being heard by a jury. Further, the jury trial is a relatively recent innovation in discrimination cases, coming as late as 1991 in the case of Title VII and Americans with Disabilities Act cases. The United States got along well without jury trials for many years, as have the European countries. Also, from the employer's perspective, the prospect of a jury trial introduces so much uncertainty that we may reach the point where employers will refrain from hiring workers for fear of jury trials if they decide to fire them (Estreicher 1997).

In reply to arguments that employment arbitration will inevitably be biased in favor of employers because they can be repeat users and therefore sources of future business for arbitrators, there are several answers. First, adherence to professional standards of ethics may avoid this problem. Second, the plaintiff's bar, which is increasingly well-organized, can police this. Third, the appointing agencies can monitor this problem (Malin 2001). The recent California legislation mentioned above is an attempt to deal with this.

In response to the concern that the removal of the threat of extremely large jury awards will take away a major incentive for employers to obey the law, there are several responses. One is that the fear of losing the "lottery" in jury awards, where some employees receive a lot and most receive nothing, may simply cause employers to construct "bulletproof" workplaces that adopt forms of fairness in order to cover up a reality of discrimination. This can "feed an increasing judicial appetite to grant summary judgment" because of judicial distrust of outlier jury awards (Malin 2001, p. 609). The higher probability of the successful pursuit of relief under arbitration may have a greater deterrent effect on lawbreaking than a remote chance of an employee winning in court (Malin 2001). There is some evidence that most employees who are discharged unlawfully receive only "modest or inadequate awards" that can be less than half of their economic loss, only after three to five years in the courts (Malin 2001, p. 608; Summers 1992). Also, many of the extreme jury verdicts are reduced or set aside on appeal (Summers 1992).

The more limited use of discovery in arbitration can be an advantage to the employee. It shortens the process and makes it less expensive for both the employee and the employer. Leaving the amount of discovery in the hands of the arbitrator (AAA procedures require this) provides the requisite ability to determine the amount of discovery based upon the situation in the individual case (Malin 2001).

Arguments against Employment Arbitration

Public policy

The private nature of arbitration means that it conceals from the public the ways in which statutes are being interpreted and applied. "The public has a right to know and indeed a need to know how the policy is being applied and if it is effective" (Zalusky 2002, p. 4). The lessened exposure to damages will produce "a lessened employer deterrent to employee abuse" in violation of a large number of laws enacted for the protection of workers (Zalusky, 2002 p. 12).

The goal of employment legislation, particularly in the area of civil rights, was to "change the way in which business was being done," not to make it possible for some workers to be benefited while companies "engaged in business as usual" (Silverstein 2001, p. 493). Employers' increasing ability to buy their way out of the obligation to avoid discrimination was not part of the legislative plan. Also, taking away the belief that discrimination will result in legal action allows employers to do the very things that the laws prohibit. When a waiver of the statutory structure occurs, "the loser is the legislative decision to correct market failures through statutory regulation" (Silverstein 2001, p. 495).

Employers

As a practical matter, employment arbitration may furnish the best chance for the ordinary employee to prevail in an employment discrimination claim, meaning that this is the forum in which the employer stands the greatest chance of losing (Green 2000, p. 399; St. Antoine 2001). This is partly because of the great difficulty, not present in arbitration, that employees have in finding legal counsel to represent them in a court action (St. Antoine 2001).

Some managers have concluded that arbitration is no less expensive than litigation, and has the additional disadvantage of the loss of the opportunity to appeal from an unfair result (Green 2000, p. 423). A massive Rand Corporation survey of the Civil Justice Reform Act of

1990, which encouraged the use of ADR in the federal courts, found that there were savings neither in time nor cost. This seemed to stem from the tendency of lawyers to do just as much work in preparing for ADR as for trial (Green 2000).

The differences between litigation and arbitration have been narrowed by the protocol and the adoption of its principles by administering agencies. The requirements of the protocol result in an employee's right to counsel, discovery, a neutral arbitrator who is familiar with the statutory issues, and the same remedies that are available in court (Green 2000).

There has been something of a "political backlash" against mandatory employment arbitration. This has resulted, for example, in the National Association of Securities Dealers, whose process was sustained in the *Gilmer* case, deciding to abandon mandatory arbitration in 1997. There has also been hostility to mandatory employment arbitration in the lower federal courts, which has led them to develop limitations on and standards for employment arbitration systems (Green 2000).

The employers' preference for arbitration because it keeps the dispute private is based on an unrealistic assessment of their ability to avoid public knowledge of what has happened in an arbitration case. A number of high-profile arbitration cases have in fact made their way into the public media (Green 2000).

Limits on discovery in arbitration can be a "double-edged sword" (Green 2000, p. 438). In litigation, employers have had considerable success in bringing out the weaknesses in an employee's case and then obtaining summary judgment from a judge prior to trial. With discovery being limited, the employer may find itself subject to surprise testimony in an arbitration hearing, and may not have been able to fully understand the basis for the employee's claim prior to the hearing (Green 2000).

Large employers, in particular, have a great deal to gain from sticking with the court system. Most of the complaints about the enforcement of civil rights laws revolve around their inadequacy in enforcing worker rights. The obverse of this is that employers have a substantial advantage in the legal system. The practical difficulties of employees in meeting their burden of proof in discrimination cases, the inability of many employees to afford legal counsel, and the increasing frequency of summary judgments against employees by a judiciary that is hostile to discrimination claims all work to the advantage of employers. The EEOC's limited ability to enforce the law, given its large backlog of cases and limited budget, also affects the ability of employees to vindicate their rights in the legal system. About 90 percent of discrimination cases are lost by employees at the summary judgment stage without reaching a jury. Employers simply do better in court than in arbitration (Green 2000).

The fears of large jury awards appear to be exaggerated. As to punitive damages, most large awards are overturned on appeal. The costs of legal counsel in litigation, while high, may pay off in reduced employee recoveries (Green 2000). Anecdotes about horrible costs in frivolous cases "pale in comparison to the results favoring employers in the courts" (Green 2000, p. 461). It is argued that, ". . . given the overwhelming success for employers in the court system and absent some empirical data showing a big bottom-line cost savings from employing arbitration instead of the courts, if it is not broken, why use mandatory arbitration to fix it?" (Green 2000, p. 462).

Small employers have special problems with employment arbitration. For one thing, they are more likely to have employment arbitration agreements than large employers. Also, small employers are much more likely to lose to employees in arbitration than are large employers. However, the advantages in cost and avoiding the hassles of litigation may still make arbitration worthwhile for small employers (Green 2000).

It may be that, by having mandatory employment arbitration, employers will give up being at-will employers. The practical result of having an employment arbitration agreement may be that the breadth of employment discrimination laws, which cover whites as well as minorities, will turn at-will employment into a situation where the employer will end up arbitrating all terminations of employees (Hayford 1995). There is the danger that an arbitrator might imply a just cause requirement from the arbitration agreement, and the arbitrator could decide to apply a fairness standard rather than the standards required by the law. In addition, the arbitration agreement might well persuade an arbitrator that there is a contract present to which the obligation of good faith and fair dealing applies. Another situation in which a contractual relationship other than at-will might be implied would be where the employer has waxed too enthusiastic about its comprehensive dispute resolution system, making statements that indicate a broader obligation on its part than what is stated in its written documents. An employer wishing to avoid this consequence probably needs to state explicitly in the arbitration agreement that it applies only to legal obligations imposed by statute (Bales 1997).

Employees

The National Employment Lawyers Association (NELA), which opposes pre-dispute mandatory employment arbitration, cites the following disadvantages that employment arbitration has for employees:

Arbitration Often Limits or Eliminates Essential Procedural Protections
- Arbitrators do not have to know or follow the law.
- Arbitrators do not grant injunctive or remedial relief.
- Arbitration does not contain the procedural safeguards of court.
- Arbitrators do not have to abide by the federal rules of evidence.
- Arbitrators do not have to abide by the federal rules of discovery.
- Limited compensatory damages and attorneys' fees makes hiring a lawyer difficult.
- Arbitrators do not have to be lawyers.
- Arbitrators rarely issue written opinions.
- Arbitrators do not have to justify their rulings.
- Arbitrators are only regulated in two states.

Arbitration Interferes with the Ability to Fully Enforce Civil Rights Laws
- The EEOC, the U.S. Department of Labor, and NLRB agree that arbitration interferes with their agency's ability to fully enforce civil rights laws.
- Arbitration undermines Congress' intent in passing civil rights laws.

Arbitration Often Favor (sic) Employers
- Studies show that arbitrators favor large corporations.

Arbitration Often Requires Workers to Pay for the Process

- High fees discourage or make it impossible for individuals to pursue their cases.
- Arbitration fees can reach the tens of thousands of dollars, depending on the case.

Arbitrators Often Have Conflicts of Interest

- Some arbitration firms have financial ties to the companies they preside over.

—(National Employment Lawyers Association 2002)

Senator Feingold (D–WI) (1998) has argued that there is an inherent inequality of bargaining power between employees and employers that makes it necessary to outlaw mandatory employment arbitration agreements. As he says, discovery, remedies, and the right to trial by jury may be lost in arbitration. The private nature of arbitration and the lack of meaningful court review renders it a severe impediment to the development of civil rights laws. Senator Feingold's primary objections are to the mandatory nature of employment arbitration and the lack of court review. According to him,

> In terms of fairness, it seems to me that these mandatory agreements cannot be tolerated. It is the most involuntary act, to require someone to sign away his or her right to something that every other American, that everyone, should have as a condition of employment. It just seems to me that, on its face, this is something that is rather abhorrent. (Feingold 1998, p. 10)

Congressman Alfonse D'Amato (D–NY) argues: ". . . if a person is required to sign and say that I waive my rights to go to court as a condition of employment, I don't think it's voluntary" (D'Amato 1998, p. 24).

It is rather clear that "the empirical reality is that mandatory arbitration does not result from a bargained for exchange," but rather is imposed on the employee (Malin 2001, p. 596). When an employee, especially a long-term one, is presented with a choice between signing an arbitration agreement and losing the job, "the employee has absolutely no choice in the matter. There is nothing for the employee to bargain" (Malin 2001, p. 596). While it may seem that a job applicant has more choice, this is illusory: ". . . invariably the agreement to arbitrate is presented in a systematic manner as part of the standard boilerplate—a manner designed to preclude questioning, much less bargaining over it" (Malin 2001, p. 596).

As Malin (2001) argues, there is a problem of "asymmetric information" (p. 596). While the employer is able to make some estimate of the chances of an employee having a claim in the future, an applicant for employment probably would not be taking the job if he or she believed that there was a real chance that the employer may violate the employee's legal rights. Furthermore, a prospective employee would be extremely reluctant to indicate that he or she wanted to preserve the right to litigate against the employer for fear of having the employer change its mind about hiring the job applicant. Except for highly paid executives who may have their contracts negotiated by legal counsel, it is clear that agreements to arbitrate are imposed by employers without any bargaining taking place (Malin 2001).

Congressman Edward Markey (D–MA) (1998) has stated that, "In essence, mandatory arbitration contracts reduce civil rights protections to the status of the company car, a perk which can be denied at will by the employer to the employee" (p. 5). A representative of NELA has maintained that, when Congress passes laws, it should not be up to an employer to pick and choose which laws are going to be obeyed. In effect, pre-dispute mandatory employment arbitration allows employers to "opt out" of laws passed by Congress (Palefsky 1998, p. 17). NELA wants federal laws to be interpreted by judges, not by persons who may have little or no legal background. Further, arbitration is designed primarily to provide finality, with less attention to achieving the correct result under the law than the case would receive from a court. This is inappropriate for the enforcement of civil rights laws. Contrary to the argument that all employees lose is the procedural right to go to a particular forum, the loss by employees of the right to have civil rights laws correctly enforced is the loss of "the ultimate substantive right" (Palefsky 1998, p. 78; Appelbaum 1998). Only pre-dispute—not post-dispute—arbitration involves "a risk of allowing an employer to contract out of the need to comply with the underlying employment statutes" (Malin 2001, p. 600).

The EEOC's legal counsel has pointed out that the weaknesses of mandatory employment arbitration include the fact that arbitration is not always less expensive and more efficient than the courts, and that there are important questions raised about the fairness of arbitration because of problems of arbitrator impartiality and qualifications, the absence of "reasoned decisions and substantive appeals," limits on discovery and remedies, and high forum fees (Vargyas 1998, p. 120).

There is a repeat-user bias in favor of some employers. In labor arbitration, both the company and the union are regular consumers of arbitration services, preventing arbitrators from leaning toward one side or the other to increase their future business. In employment arbitration, only the employer is a potential repeat player (Malin 2001). Employers are far more successful in arbitration than before a jury, and employees who prevail in arbitration do not recover as much money as they would in court (Palefsky 1998). A representative of the National Women's Law Center says: "A strong reason for industry representatives to insist on *mandatory* arbitration of employment disputes is that in reality the deck is stacked, as we believe it is, in the employer's favor" (Appelbaum 1998, p. 105). Because employers design such systems, there is reason to fear that they will design systems that are stacked in their favor. An outrageous example of this is provided by the *Hooters* case discussed previously (Malin 2001). There are numerous examples of employers systematically constructing systems that are weighted heavily in their favor (Malin 2001). Employers who adopt mandatory employment arbitration obviously believe that it works to their advantage. There is some evidence that the stock market reacts in a way that confirms this (Abraham and Voos 2000).

The prestigious National Academy of Arbitrators has adopted a position in opposition to mandatory employment arbitration, as has the Society of Professionals in Dispute Resolution (Palefsky 1998). The EEOC has also condemned mandatory pre-dispute employment arbitration (EEOC 1997).

Employment arbitration is criticized for its private nature; it is inappropriate for arbitrators who are privately appointed to be administering public law embodying public policy. The private nature of arbitration awards hinders the development of the law on civil rights. The limited discovery in arbitration is particularly a problem for employees because the information necessary to the case usually lies in the hands of employers (Malin 2001).

The lack of meaningful judicial review is a serious disadvantage of the mandatory employment arbitration system. By virtue of the courts' traditional respect for the decisions of arbitrators, they may be abdicating their responsibility for interpreting civil rights laws (Malin 2001). It seems clear that the situation is different from that in which a labor arbitrator is enforcing the terms of a contract in the context of industrial common law. Here, we are dealing with statutory rights and duties, and it is the duty of the courts to interpret and enforce these. While appeals to the courts will lessen some of the advantages of arbitration (time and cost), it seems that it is necessary that the courts retain the ability to ensure that arbitrators are applying the law properly (Zalusky 2002).

The processes adopted for the federal district courts in the Alternative Dispute Resolution Act (28 U.S.C. §§651–658, 2000) in 1998 have been suggested as being better than those available under *Circuit City* (Zalusky 2002). Under the Alternative Dispute Resolution Act, the arbitration award is not final, but can be set aside for a trial *de novo* within 30 days after it is filed. The choice of going to arbitration is made post-dispute rather than pre-dispute. The consent to arbitrate is required to be knowing and voluntary.

The waiver of the right to jury trial in arbitration has been the subject of intense criticism. Under the Civil Rights Act of 1991, litigants under Title VII of the Civil Rights Act who claim discrimination on the basis of race, color, sex, religion, or national origin have the right to a jury trial. Jury trial is also a right under the Age Discrimination in Employment Act, and there is a constitutional right to trial by jury in certain cases. This right can be waived, which is what happens when an employee signs an employment arbitration agreement. However, the law generally requires that a waiver of such a right be "knowing, voluntary and intelligent" (Sternlight 2001). It is highly questionable whether this requirement is ordinarily met in mandatory employment arbitration agreements.

It is argued that, at least for the employee, it is doubtful if there are cost savings in arbitration. In arbitration, there is typically a forum fee that, at least for the AAA, starts at $500 and increases for larger claims. Arbitrator fees can run anywhere from $1,100 to $4,000 per day, and a bill of $5,000 to $10,000 for arbitrator fees is what might be expected (Zalusky 2002). However, as noted above, AAA has recently changed its procedures to limit the employee's cost on the filing fee to $125, and prohibits the employee from having to pay any part of the arbitrator's fee.

CONCLUSIONS ON THE LAW AND THE LITERATURE

It appears that the enforceability of pre-dispute mandatory employment arbitration agreements as a general proposition has been settled by the U.S. Supreme Court in the *Circuit City* and *Gilmer* cases. Whatever the merits of this proposition, the Supreme Court has spoken and is unlikely to change its mind any time in the near future. It also seems clear that Congress will take no action on this, at least until the Democrats regain control of both the House and Senate.

What remains unclear about the law are the specific criteria that will be applied to test whether a particular employment arbitration agreement is enforceable. It is probably the case that, whatever rationale the courts use, they will subject these agreements to some scrutiny beyond the grounds explicitly stated in the FAA. They are, we believe, most likely to apply the protocol standards. These require use of a neutral agency, a well-trained neutral, joint selection of the arbitrator from a panel of arbitrators, access to information about the arbitrators, reasonable discovery rights, a right to counsel, a written decision, a remedy that is consistent with the law, and limited judicial review. Many of these criteria are subject to a variety of interpretations. Perhaps the most challenging is the requirement of judicial review. Without it, the courts lose control of the laws that they are charged to enforce. With too much of it, the advantages of speed and low cost will be lost. The law will develop on a case-by-case basis with, hopefully, additional guidance from the U.S. Supreme Court.

The arguments on the pros and cons of pre-dispute employment arbitration are very diverse. There are powerful arguments on both sides. At the root of most of the disagreements among the scholars and practitioners who have engaged in this debate is *qui bene*—who benefits—from arbitration. Answering this question requires that we look at the experience of the parties in litigation and arbitration and attempt to determine under which process the parties fare better. It is to this question that we turn in Chapter 3.

3
The Evidence on
Employment Arbitration

As can be seen from the discussion in the preceding chapters, much of the debate about the merits of employment arbitration has to do with what practical results it is likely to produce for employers as well as employees. This includes considerations of win/loss ratios, amounts recovered, time spent, and cost. With respect to all of these, the pertinent question is how employment arbitration stacks up compared to the alternatives—principally, litigation in court and labor arbitration. In this chapter, we will review and analyze the evidence on these points that has been reported in empirical studies. We will also report the results of our survey of employment arbitrators regarding the workings of the employment arbitration process.

Our discussion will begin with a comparison of win/loss outcomes between employment arbitration, court proceedings, and labor arbitration. Next, we will examine the modest literature on amounts recovered by employees, and then the evidence comparing time and costs. Last, we will report the results of our survey of employment arbitrators, and then draw some conclusions.

COMPARING WINS AND LOSSES

The Literature

Let us first look at the evidence on how employees fare in winning employment arbitration cases. In a widely cited study, Maltby (1998) found that employees prevailed in 63 percent of the cases in a 1993–1995 sample of AAA employment arbitration cases. A 1995 study (Howard 1995) of AAA cases found employees winning 68 percent of the cases. Lisa Bingham has reported employee win/loss percentages in employment arbitration covering several periods. Analyzing cases decided under the AAA Commercial Arbitration Rules in 1992, she found no systematic bias in favor of employers (Bingham 1995). Looking at cases decided in 1993 under both the Commercial Arbitration Rules and the Employment Arbitration Rules, she found that employees won only 2 of the 11 cases involving termination of employment (Bingham 1996).

A study of 270 AAA cases in 1993 and 1994 showed employees winning 63 percent of the time (Bingham 1997). In a later study of AAA cases decided in 1993–1995, the same author found employees obtaining relief in 52 percent of the employment arbitration cases. Employees won 69 percent of the cases where an individual contract of employment was being enforced, compared to only 21 percent where provisions of a personnel manual were involved (Bingham 1998). In this last study, she found that employers who were "repeat players" in employment arbitration did significantly better than those who were not. In another study, however, this effect did not appear (Bingham 1996). Very different numbers were found in an analysis of individual employment arbitration awards between 1990 and 2001 by LeRoy and Feuille (2001). They found that the employer won 61.8 percent of the time, while 17.6 percent were split awards, and the employee won in only 20.6 percent of the cases.

A study of employment arbitration cases decided in the securities industry between 1992 and 1998 showed employees registered with the New York Stock Exchange winning in 38.46 percent of the cases, and those registered with the National Association of Securities Dealers winning 32.57 percent of the time (Kaswell 1998). A study of cases decided between 1990 and 1995 (Bompey and Stempel 1995) found employees winning in New York Stock Exchange cases 41 percent of the time and in National Association of Securities Dealers cases in 24 percent. Other studies have shown employees winning in securities industry cases 43 percent (Bompey and Pappas 1993–1994), 55 percent (USGAO 1994), and 48 percent (Howard 1995) of the time.

From all of this literature we conclude that there is a lack of evidence of any clear pattern of employees winning or losing in cases decided by employment arbitrators. The range found varies from 20 to 68 percent wins, depending on the data set and the period studied. This makes it impossible to draw any conclusions from the existing literature. So, looking at employment arbitration win/loss outcomes in isolation is not particularly instructive, which would seem to call for the gathering of new data.

Comparing the experience of employees in employment arbitration to their experience in the courts complicates matters even further. A major problem is that there are no reliable data on the proportion of the cases that are settled in favor of employees prior to going to court. There is anecdotal evidence that as many as 64 percent of employment discrimination cases handled by lawyers are settled favorably to the employee (Bell 2002). Since many of these cases may never get to court, it must be kept in mind that it may well be that litigation or its threat may be much more powerful than available statistics can show. On the other hand, it seems that only a small proportion of claimants are able to secure a lawyer to handle their claims. There is evidence that only about 5 percent of the cases brought to employment lawyers are accepted by them (Howard 1995; Meeker and Dombrink 1993).

Keeping in mind these limitations, let us view the evidence on the success rates of employees litigating questions of unjust termination. There is some limited evidence with respect to state court outcomes in unjust termination cases. Two studies of wrongful termination cases in California concluded that employees were winning between 68 percent (Dertouzos, Holland, and Ebener 1988) and 70 percent (Jung and Harkness 1988) of the time. Based on a data set maintained at Cornell University, which includes cases terminated between July 1, 1991 and June 30, 1992, state civil court filings were found to be decided in favor of the employee 64 percent of the time (Estreicher 2001).

As might be expected, the greatest amount of scholarly attention has been paid to the outcomes in federal courts. An early study of employment discrimination cases in federal court found that employees received at least a partial remedy in 24 percent of the cases (Burstein and Monaghan 1986). Maltby (1998) reported employees winning 14.9 percent of their cases in 1994. A study of federal district court cases decided in 1992–1994 found that only 8 percent of the cases filed went to trial. On the other hand, where there was a disposition of the case, employees got "some recompense" 71 percent of the time. When the case went to trial, however, employees won only 28 percent of the time, although they did better when a jury decided the case, winning 38 percent of these cases (Howard 1995). A later study (Litras 2000) found that employees won 23.8 percent of the discrimination cases terminated by trial verdicts in 1990, and 35.5 percent in 1998. Research reported in the *Wall Street Journal* in 2001 found that employees won in federal district court in about 30 percent of discrimination cases (Bravin 2001).

There have been a few studies of outcomes in particular kinds of employment discrimination cases. An analysis of Age Discrimination in Employment Act cases found that employees won 25 percent of the time, and on appeal, the employer won 68 percent of the time (Eglit 1997). An American Bar Association study of Americans with Disabilities Act cases between 1992 and 1998 showed employees winning only 8 percent (Parry 1998).

The employee win percentages across the above-mentioned studies are summarized in Table 3.1. In general, studies have shown success rates to be somewhat higher in employment arbitration than in federal courts, but not state courts.

A publication called *Jury Verdict Research* (2001) provides interesting statistics on court cases. According to their data, in 2000 employees won 67 percent of the jury verdicts in *all types of employment cases*, up from 50 percent in 1994. In discrimination cases, employees won 65 percent in 2000, up from 46 percent in 1994. In federal district

Table 3.1 Studies of Employee Win Percentages in Employment Arbitration and State and Federal Courts

Employment Arbitration		State Courts	Federal Courts
General	Securities Industry		
68	43	68	24
18	55	70	28
63	48	64	14.9
52	41 (NYSE[a])		23.8
	24 (NASD[b])		35.5
63	38.46 (NYSE[a])		30
	32.57 (NASD[b])		
20.6			25 (ADEA[c])
			8 (ADA[d])

[a]Indicates New York Stock Exchange cases.
[b]Indicates National Association of Securities Dealers cases.
[c]Indicates Age Discrimination in Employment Act cases.
[d]Indicates Americans with Disabilities Act cases.
SOURCE: Authors' calculations from cited data.

courts in 2000, employees won 75 percent, up from 39 percent in 1994, and in state courts, the numbers were 60 percent in 2000 compared to 56 percent in 1994. In 2000, employees were most likely to win verdicts in age discrimination cases, being successful in 78 percent of these.

Of course, only a small proportion of the cases ever makes it to a jury. By far the greatest proportion are either settled or decided on a motion for summary judgment by a judge. One survey found that between 79 and 84 percent of the court cases were settled prior to final adjudication (Howard 1995). Settlements of arbitration cases were not as common—between 31 and 44 percent of the cases. It is believed that this is because arbitration is but the final step in a process in which most claims are resolved, which makes it likely that the possibilities for settlement have been fully explored prior to filing for arbitration (Howard 1995).

Litigation undertaken by the EEOC appears to have been more successful. These cases are selected for litigation because of their legal importance or magnitude. A study of the EEOC litigation program between 1997 and 2001 (EEOC 2002) found that, in the 1,963 suits filed by the EEOC during that period, a successful result (either by court decision or settlement) was obtained in 90.72 percent of the cases. Of the 83 trials conducted by the EEOC field legal units, there was a success rate of 60.24 percent. The EEOC was also generally successful in the appellate courts.

Another aspect of litigation in the federal court system is the role and actions of the courts of appeal when cases are appealed to them from the district courts. One study found bias against claimants in discrimination cases. In such cases, employers appealing adverse lower court decisions prevailed on appeal 44 percent of the time, compared to other defendants appealing from district court, who achieved reversals only 33 percent of the time. Employees appealing discrimination decisions were successful only 5.8 percent of the time. This compared to plaintiffs' appeals in other types of cases being granted 12 percent of the time (Bravin 2001).

Not taking into account settlements, and looking not just at jury verdicts but rather at dispositions of cases either by a judge or a jury, employee success rates in the federal district courts are quite low. In the latest year for which data were available (2000), employees were winning only 11 percent of their cases. As shown in Table 3.2, between 1996 and 2000 they averaged 12 percent (Federal District-Court Civil Cases 2001).

Judicial review of employment arbitration awards is a highly problematic area. One prime advantage of arbitration is finality, yet the courts have not always permitted the arbitrator's decision to be the last word. A study of judicial enforcement of employment arbitration awards between 1990 and 2001 (LeRoy and Feuille 2001) showed that 75.3 percent of the 33 court challenges were by employees. Federal district courts confirmed the full award in 85.3 percent of the cases, confirmed the award in part in 2.9 percent, and vacated the award in only 11.8 percent. It was the employer who won the largest proportion (67.6 percent) of the judicial challenges.

In addition to comparing employment arbitration to federal court outcomes, it is interesting to make a comparison to outcomes in labor arbitration. A 1987 study of 1,042 labor arbitration cases (Block and Stieber 1987) found that 57 percent of these discharge cases were decided in favor of the employee. The Block and Stieber criterion for an employee victory was an order of reinstatement, with or without back pay. These findings are consistent with the conventional wisdom among labor arbitrators, which holds that employees win about half the time.

One recent study compared decision outcomes under employment arbitration and labor arbitration. In this research, Bingham and Mesch (2000) took an approach similar to our procedure (described in Chapter 4). They used an experimental design, presenting different types of decision makers with a hypothetical case and asking them to decide it. The scenario was varied by gender of the grievant and by whether or not there was a collective bargaining agreement. Where there was no collective bargaining agreement, the subjects were directed to apply the standard of "good cause" contained in the Model Employment Termination Act, which has not been adopted by any state.

Bingham and Mesch's sample consisted of 743 subjects, including 161 arbitrators who were members of the National Academy of Arbitrators, 210 labor arbitrators who were not members of the National Academy of Arbitrators, 188 employment arbitrators, and 184 students. Each subject was given all four versions of the scenario. The dependent variables were reinstatement of the employee and the awarding of back pay.

Before the application of controls for other sources of variation, Bingham and Mesch found that employment arbitrators reinstated employees significantly less frequently than did any of the other groups. However, once they controlled for other variables, such as the profession of the arbitrator, decision-making groups did not have a significant effect, nor did the gender of the employee. All arbitrators reinstated more often under a collective bargaining agreement's just cause standard than under the Model Employment Termination Act good cause standard. Students were more likely to award back pay than the other groups.

Our Research

The data

In order to obtain information on employee win rates under the different procedural alternatives, it was necessary to utilize a variety of sources. We were fortunate to find a source of employment awards online (although this service has now been discontinued), and printed digests of these awards from the AAA. In addition, *Labor Arbitration Reports,* which is mainly an outlet for labor arbitration awards, does contain a small number (34) of employment arbitration awards, identified by having "Individual Grievant" as one of the parties. *Labor Arbitration Reports* furnished a large sample (580) of labor arbitration awards. Since many arbitration awards are not published, however, *Labor Arbitration Reports* does not provide a complete set of all existing arbitration awards, though it is by far the most commonly used research sample and consists of the awards that are most visible by virtue of their being published. Results of cases involving Title VII of the Civil Rights Act were gathered from an online Web site.

The analysis

Table 3.2 shows a simple cross-tabulation of our sample of employment arbitration cases and labor arbitration cases, along with the numbers of employee wins reported in federal district courts. One of us, who is both an arbitrator and a lawyer specializing in employment

Table 3.2 Employee/Employer Win Rates

Procedure	Percent employee wins	Percent employer wins
Employment arbitration[a] Overall $n = 216$	33	67
Federal discrimination statute involved $n = 59$	22	78
Employment contract $n = 52$	56	44
Burden of proof on employer $n = 57$	60	40
Labor arbitration[b] $n = 580$	52	48
Federal district court[c] 1996–2000 $n = 26,841$	12	88
1987–2000 $n = 53,248$	16	84

[a]SOURCE: Bureau of National Affairs (1994–2002); American Arbitration Association (1999–2001).
[b]SOURCE: Bureau of National Affairs (1994–2002).
[c]SOURCE: Federal District-Court Civil Cases (2001).

law, as well as a teacher of arbitration and employment law, read the employment arbitration and labor arbitration cases. The employment arbitration cases were analyzed in some depth, while the labor arbitration cases were viewed only in order to determine whether the employee won. All of the arbitration cases dealt with terminations. As in the Block and Stieber (1987) study, it was judged that an employee had won an arbitration case if he or she was reinstated to the job, with or without back pay. A back pay award without reinstatement (which is rare) was not judged to be an employee win.

Although the overall win rate of employees in employment arbitration compared to those in the other two procedural alternatives is of some interest, the most meaningful comparisons are between results in particular categories of employment arbitration cases and other systems. The pertinent comparison with court cases that involved claims of discrimination in violation of a federal statute is employment arbitration cases involving that same claim. Similarly, outcomes in labor arbitration discharge cases, which turn upon a claimed violation of a collective contract, should be compared to employment arbitration cases that involve a contract violation and/or have adopted the same rules as labor arbitration with respect to burden of proof.

In employment arbitration cases where a federal discrimination statute was involved, employees won 22 percent of the cases, which compares to only 12 percent in federal district courts in the most recent five-year period. Thus, the chances of an employee winning in employment arbitration would appear to be much greater than in court when the case goes to a final adjudication. As noted above, there have been studies that conclude that employee lawyers only accept 5 percent of the cases that come to them (Howard 1995), meaning that the cases going to federal court have gone through a rather rigorous screening process (St. Antoine 2001). It is unlikely that the employment arbitration cases are as carefully screened.

In labor arbitration cases under a collective bargaining contract, unlike court cases enforcing a federal statute, the employer has the burden of proving misconduct, and the propriety of the penalty. Usually the standard is proof by a preponderance of the evidence. However, for more serious cases, proof by clear and convincing evidence, or even proof beyond a reasonable doubt, may be required.

Employees won 56 percent of employment arbitration cases in which there was a claim of an employer violating an individual contract of employment. This compares favorably to the 52 percent win rate in labor arbitration cases enforcing a collective contract. Employees won 60 percent of the employment arbitration cases in which the arbitrator imposed the burden of proof on the employer. This also compares favorably to employees winning 52 percent of the termination cases heard by labor arbitrators.

COMPARING AMOUNTS RECOVERED

It is likely that the fear of large adverse verdicts is one of the prime motivators behind employers' desire to avoid going to court. Consequently, the amounts recovered by employees in employment arbitration cases is of interest. Unfortunately, like win/loss statistics, the numbers on this issue are not straightforward.

An early study (Summers 1992) of wrongful discharge litigation in state courts in California showed that most wrongfully discharged employees received inadequate awards, frequently less than half of the economic losses that they suffered. Even employees who obtained high jury verdicts often had these reduced on appeal, and the contingent attorney fees that they paid also reduced the amount of money that they actually received. So, even though high jury verdicts received a great deal of attention, the reality was that the successes of employees in these suits were quite modest. However, another early study of wrongful discharge cases in California (Jung and Harkness 1988), covering the years 1978–1987, found that employees won a median award of $124,150, and a mean award of $486,812.

Perhaps the most sophisticated analysis of this question was done by Maltby (1998). In addition to comparing mean awards in employment arbitration and federal district courts for a period, he analyzed these results in terms of the percentages of the amounts demanded that were awarded to all claimants. Maltby found that when he simply compared AAA 1993–1995 employment arbitration awards to 1994 federal district court decisions, the mean award in arbitration ($49,030) was considerably less than the mean award in court ($530,611). However, when he looked at what he called the "adjusted outcome" (the percent of the demand awarded to all plaintiffs, including those who recovered nothing), he found that employees received almost twice as great a share of their demand in arbitration (18 percent) than in court (10 percent).

In a 2001 article, Estreicher describes the results of several interesting studies, some of which were unpublished at this writing. These had to do with the median awards in employment arbitration. He cites data showing median employment arbitration awards of $52,737 prior to the adoption of the Due Process Protocol, and $39,279 thereafter (based on Bingham and Sarraf (2004)). He refers to another study of AAA awards in cases decided in 1999 and 2000 that found a median award of $34,733. Bingham (1998) found a mean award of $49,030 in a sample of 91 AAA cases decided during the period 1993–1995.

When one looks at awards by courts, the numbers do appear to be higher than in employment arbitration. It is worth noting that this may partly be a result of the longer period necessary to resolve court cases, leading to greater amounts of back pay owed (Sherwyn, Tracey, and Eigen 1999). A body of data on the federal district courts collected at Cornell University (Federal District-Court Civil Cases 2001) show a mean award in discrimination cases in 2000 of $885,640, while the median was $115,000. Table 3.3 shows the numbers of awards, and mean and median awards for the period 1987 to 2000.

As shown in Table 3.3, the median award has gone from $59,118 in 1987 to $115,000 in 2000. It is obvious from the lack of a pattern in the mean awards that a few extremely high settlements can strongly bias the statistics on mean awards. This might lead one to ignore this statistic in favor of the median. However, it may be precisely those extreme awards that bias the statistics that motivate employers to avoid going to court by adopting employment arbitration procedures.

Another source of data on outcomes of employment litigation is Jury Verdict Research (2001). They report median and mean awards for all employment practice liability cases, including both state and federal courts for the period 1994–2000. According to their statistics, the median award has increased from $93,000 to $218,000 during that period, and the mean from $300,799 to $712,636, with an overall me-

Table 3.3 Federal District Court Awards in Employment Cases, 1987–2000

Year	Cases terminated	Mean award[a]	Median award[a]
2000	22,553	885,640	115,000
1999	23,721	843,886	91,992
1998	23,606	1,202,072	100,852
1997	21,492	1,199,728	95,488
1996	19,381	1,271,245	90,394
1995	15,705	1,165,313	84,744
1994	12,833	622,460	67,064
1993	10,787	611,756	53,626
1992	11,318	1,178,720	68,119
1991	8,371	1,544,417	93,559
1990	8,459	2,134,309	192,358
1989	8,937	682,388	48,320
1988	9,055	748,011	45,475
1987	9,140	1,223,751	59,118

[a]Awards in 2000 dollars.
SOURCE: Federal District-Court Civil Cases 2001.

dian for the period of $150,000 and a mean of $519,116. For discrimination cases, which would be expected to be mainly decided in federal courts, they show an increase in the median award in that period from $78,592 to $218,000, and the mean from $236,232 to $783,926, with an overall median for the period of $150,000 and a mean of $531,780. The Federal District Court data collected at Cornell (shown in Table 3.2) yields an average annual median of $92,219 and a mean of $1,027,192 for the same period (1994–2000).

Jury Verdict Research also analyzed settlements. Over the period 1994–2000, for all employment practice cases, the median settlement was $62,000, with a mean of $1,863,406. For discrimination cases, the median was $60,000 and the mean was $2,157,563.

Although one must be concerned about the substantial differences in the numbers produced by Jury Verdict Research and the Cornell Federal District Court data, they still lead to the same conclusion. This is that litigants do recover larger amounts of money in court than they do in employment arbitration. However, this does not speak to the conclusion reached by Maltby (1998), noted above, that an analysis that takes into account the amounts demanded in court proceedings and employment arbitration might lead to a different determination. Ultimately, the only way to conclusively prove the existence of differences in outcome produced by differences in procedures is to pose to employment arbitrators and judges and/or jurors *exactly the same cases* and observe what, if any, differences in outcomes result.

COMPARISONS OF COST AND TIME

The alleged advantages of employment arbitration over litigation include its relative speed and low cost for both parties. This is often cited by advocates of arbitration as a positive feature for both employers and employees.

Cost

A thorough discussion of the issue of costs in employment arbitration versus those in court is contained in a recent article by LeRoy and Feuille (2002). These authors conclude that, although arbitration generally does have advantages in this regard, this may not be true in particular cases. Litigation has the advantage of the direct court costs being less expensive. Employment arbitrators charge an average of $2,000 per day, compared to zero cost for the time of a judge. AAA charges a filing fee of $500 and an administrative fee of $150 per day of hearing. Attorney's fees can also be substantial and employment arbitrators often deny employee's claims for their attorney's fees, even though this is provided for in the applicable statute. Offsetting these costs is the relative informality of arbitration, which may permit the employee to make do without a lawyer, thereby saving attorney's fees. Also, because discovery procedures are more limited in arbitration than in court, this very time-consuming (and therefore costly in terms of attorney's fees) phase of the court process can be reduced. Also, costly appeals through the court system are avoided by the rule that the decision of an arbitrator is final and binding and not subject to review by the courts except in extraordinary circumstances. However, in another paper, LeRoy and Feuille (2001) cite evidence that employment arbitration is much more expensive than labor arbitration in terms of arbitrators' fees.

In "Debunking the Myth of Employer Advantage from Using Mandatory Arbitration for Discrimination Claims," Green (2000) argues strenuously that employment arbitration does not save costs. He cites studies of ADR procedures in other settings that show that ADR can be quite expensive. One writer attributes this to the tendency of employer attorneys to work just as hard (and therefore put in just as many billable hours) in an arbitration case as in a court case. There are horror stories of cases, such as one involving Intel Corporation, that lasted seven years and cost $100 million.

A 2002 report claims that the cost of initiating arbitration is nearly always more expensive than filing a court suit. The example is given of the difference between a $221 filing fee in the Circuit Court of Cook County, Illinois, and a fee paid to the National Arbitration Forum of $10,925 for the same claim. The AAA would charge up to $6,650 and Judicial Arbitration and Mediation Services up to $7,950. In arbitration forums, there are also fees for such things as issuing a subpoena, requesting discovery, and having a continuance. For instance, it may require going to court to enforce a subpoena for a witness. If the employer refuses to comply with the award, it is necessary to go to court to enforce it (Public Citizen 2002).

On the other hand, it seems that attorney's fees are cheaper in employment arbitration than in court. As noted in Chapter 2, it is this hope that is a primary motivator for employers turning to arbitration (Bickner, Ver Ploeg, and Feigenbaum 1997). A Rand Institute study in the mid 1990s showed that the average cost of defending a wrongful discharge action in court had risen from $80,000 in 1988 to $124,000 in 1994. Another study (Howard 1995) found that the average cost of defense was $20,000 in arbitration compared to $96,000 in court. Clearly, the greater likelihood of a final resolution without going through an appeals process is financially attractive.

Time

There is very little evidence that permits a comparison between employment arbitration and court proceedings with respect to the length of time required to complete the process. Clearly, time saved is one of the traditional justifications of labor arbitration, and ADR generally.

In contradiction to the conventional wisdom, there are studies of ADR that find that it does not save time (see Green 2000). Nevertheless, it is quite clear that court proceedings can be quite lengthy. The early study by Summers (1992) mentioned previously found that courts in wrongful discharge cases frequently took three to five years after the employee's discharge to provide a remedy. The data on the Cornell University Web site (http://teddy.law.cornell.edu:8090) show that in 2000 it took, on average, nearly a year (355 days) from the time the case was filed in Federal District Court until it was decided. This was down slightly from the 368 days required in 1987, and was fairly typical for the period 1987–2000. One study (Litras 2000) found that, in 1998, the average time from filing to a verdict in trial was 18 months. Of course, a case that is appealed to a court of appeals takes much longer. Maltby (1998) estimated that it took about half the time to resolve a claim in arbitration than it did in court.

The literature on employment arbitration leaves a number of practical questions unanswered. These include the undocumented proportions of employees bringing claims that are professional or managerial employees, and are represented by counsel. There is also a question regarding the competence of their counsel. What is the extent of the use of discovery and how worthwhile is it? How are costs distributed? Who has the burden of proof, and what is the quantum of proof required? What is the quality of the arbitration process for employers and employees in terms of serving the interests of each? Is employment arbitration an efficient and effective mechanism for resolving disputes? We surveyed employment arbitrators in order to attempt to answer these questions.

SURVEY OF EMPLOYMENT ARBITRATORS

Over a period of several months in 2002 and 2003, we surveyed employment arbitrators. The sources of their names and addresses were 1) NAA members who identified themselves as practicing employment arbitration, 2) a list of employment arbitrators provided to us by the AAA, a supplier of employment arbitrators, and 3) arbitrators identified and located from information available on the website of Judicial Arbitration and Mediation Services, Inc. (JAMS), another supplier of arbitrators. The aim of the survey is to gain information on the practical workings of employment arbitration and to determine the perceptions of employment arbitrators as to the quality of the process. Questionnaires were sent to 807 employment arbitrators. We received 176 useable responses, for a response rate of 21.8 percent.

Table 3.4 describes the characteristics of the arbitrators included in the sample. Overall, the average respondent held a law degree or higher and had a considerable amount of prior experience serving as an arbitrator. The amount of experience as an arbitrator varied from 1 year to 39 years, with a median length of 9 years, and more than 95 percent of the respondents had 3 or more years of service. Similarly, there was significant variation in the number of cases heard, with two respondents reporting never hearing a case while the upper 25 percent reported hearing 30 or more cases. Not surprisingly, many (61 percent) reported prior experience serving as either a labor arbitrator or judge. Nearly half of all respondents reported prior experience as an advocate for employers.

Table 3.4 Respondent Characteristics

Average length of service as an arbitrator (years)	10.4
Average number of employment arbitration cases heard	39
Percentage of respondents who are/were also labor arbitrators	45.5
Average number of labor arbitration cases heard	516
Percentage of respondents who were judges	16
Average length of service (years)	10.3
Percentage of respondents who previously served as an advocate	
Employer	47.7
Employee	18.2
Graduate degree held (%)	
JD/LLB	90
Ph.D.	3
Other	3
n	176

SOURCE: Authors' calculations from survey data.

The types of cases heard by this sample of employment arbitrators was as follows: 1) statutory cases, 37.6 percent; 2) employment contract cases, 25.4 percent; 3) cases involving a nonbinding handbook or policy, 14.7 percent; 4) contractual issues other than cause for termination, 17.8 percent; and 5) other, 4.4 percent. Although statutory and employment contract cases make up the majority of cases, together they still amount to only 63 percent of the cases, a somewhat smaller proportion than we expected.

Fifty-five percent of the cases involved professional or managerial employees. In the majority of cases, therefore, the employee is one who would likely have the resources to pursue litigation, and whose salary would be high enough to warrant substantial damages being awarded if the employee prevailed. Such claims would be the ones that we would expect to be most attractive to a lawyer, meaning that for this 55 percent, obtaining counsel for a lawsuit would likely not be a problem.

As to the practical workings of the process, there are several issues of interest. First, employees were represented by attorneys in 80.9 percent of the cases. They represented themselves in only 10.6 percent of the cases, and were represented by a coworker or a friend in 8.5 percent. The employment arbitrators believed that representation was generally competent for both employees and employers. On a four-point scale (Never = 1, Rarely = 2, Sometimes = 3, Always = 4), the average arbitrator response was 3.2 for employees (standard deviation 0.47) and 3.6 for employers (standard deviation 0.53). The difference between employee representation and employer representation was statistically significant ($p = 0.005$). This suggests that employers tend to have competent representation more often than employees, which is what one would expect to find, given the greater resources and sophistication of employers in employing legal counsel. On the same four-point scale, the average score on our question regarding how frequently a policy or contract provided for the employee to have a representative prior to arbitration was 2.4 (standard deviation 0.89). This means that having a representative provided for in the early stages of a claim was somewhere between being a rare and occasional occurrence. In labor arbitration, the employee would almost always be represented by a union steward or other official at the very earliest stages of the grievance procedure.

Second, discovery took place in 80 percent of the cases. This evidences a very high rate of use for this procedure, the lack or inadequacy of which is one of the major criticisms of employment arbitration as compared to courtroom litigation. When asked whether discovery was worth the time and costs involved, on the same four-point scale the average response was 3.1 (standard deviation 0.65) in favor. This means that discovery was perceived to be only sometimes worth the time and costs.

Third, employees were found to have paid all of the costs of arbitration in 3.7 percent of the cases, a substantial share in 22.6 percent, a minimal portion in 30.8 percent, and none in 42.9 percent. This means that in about a quarter of the cases, the employee was assuming such a burden of costs that it is highly likely that a court would refuse to either compel arbitration or enforce the award (see *Cole v. Burns International Security Services* 1997, and discussion in Chapter 2).

Fourth, we gathered some data on the allocation of the burden of proof and the quantum of proof required by employment arbitrators. We found that 29 percent of employer contracts and policies expressly provided that the burden of proof to show a violation of his or her rights was placed upon the employee. In the absence of an express provision allocating the burden of proving the case, 70 percent of the employment arbitrators would place the burden on the employer and 30 percent on the employee ($n = 164$). This contrasts with labor arbitration, in which the burden would always be on the employer (Brand 1998), and court processes where the burden would always be on the employee. Of the employment arbitrators who have also served as labor arbitrators, 78 percent would place the burden on the employer, and 22 percent on the employee. Of those who have not served as labor arbitrators, only 64.5 percent would allocate the burden to the employer, and 35.5 percent to the employee (the difference between those with and those without labor arbitration experience is significant at the 0.10 level). As expected, experienced labor arbitrators are more likely to place the burden of proof on the employer. This is important, given our findings shown in Table 3.2 that employees win 60 percent of the cases in which the employer has the burden of proof, compared to only 33 percent overall.

Table 3.5 shows the decision rules used by employment arbitrators with respect to the quantum of proof required in their cases. There are two striking findings revealed in Table 3.5. First, a majority of employment arbitrators would *not* overturn a termination for violating a clearly unreasonable rule. In contrast, it is a nearly universal practice for labor arbitrators to overturn a termination that is based on an unreasonable rule (Brand 1998). Here, we see a majority of employment arbitrators behaving more like peer review committees than like labor arbitrators. Second, the fact that the employer acted in good faith would not be a defense in labor arbitration, yet a third of employment arbitrators said that they would uphold a termination, so long as there was good faith on the part of the employer.

Table 3.5 Employment Arbitrators' Decision Rules as to Quantum of Proof

Quanta	Yes (%)
Sometimes require proof beyond a reasonable doubt	5.2
Sometimes require proof by clear and convincing evidence	39.1
Overturn termination for violating clearly unreasonable rule	46.6
Uphold a termination if employer acted in good faith	33.3

NOTE: $n = 170$

The last portion of our questionnaire asked for employment arbitrators' perceptions as to the quality of employment arbitration from the respective standpoints of employers and employees. Table 3.6 sets out these results.

We find from Table 3.6 that employment arbitrators perceive employer interests to be served better than those of employees in all three types of cases. The difference, however, is smaller in cases involving employment contracts. Indeed, although it is statistically significant, the difference between 4.17 and 4.30, both indicating agreement that the respective interests are served in cases involving contracts, is probably too small to be practically significant. In contrast to these findings as to contract claims, the mean scores with respect to both statutory claims and cases involving handbooks or policies are under 4. This means that the score on these questions is not high enough to lead one to conclude that the employment arbitrators agreed that employee interests were well served. This is consistent our findings in Table 3.2, which shows employees winning 56 percent of the employment arbitration cases involving an employment contract, compared to only 22 percent where a statutory issue is involved.

When asked to what degree they agreed that the employment arbitration system is an efficient way to resolve employment disputes, the

Table 3.6 Employment Arbitrator Perceptions as to System Serving the Parties' Interests[a]

Employment arbitration does a good job protecting:[b]	Mean	Standard deviation
Employee statutory rights	3.87**	0.93
Employer rights in statutory cases	4.09	0.70
Employee rights under employment contracts	4.17**	0.76
Employer rights under employment contracts	4.30	0.58
Employee rights and interests under nonbinding handbooks and policies	3.67[†]	0.91
Employer rights and interests under nonbinding handbooks and policies	4.30	0.58

NOTE: ** Significant at 0.05 level; † significant at 0.005 level.
[a]$n = 170$, except as to the item regarding employee rights and interests under nonbinding handbooks and policies. For that item, $n = 166$.
[b]1 = Strongly disagree; 2 = Disagree; 3 = Neither agree nor disagree; 4 = Agree; 5 = Strongly agree.

employment arbitrators generally agreed that it was (mean = 4.34 on the five-point scale that went from Strongly disagree = 1 to Strongly agree = 5). A similar result was reached when they were asked about agreement that employment arbitration is better than the court system (mean = 4.21).

CONCLUSIONS

Win/loss rates, amounts recovered, and cost and time advantages are quite difficult to compare among the various dispute resolution procedures. This is especially true on the crucial question of win/loss ratios. Employees win a little better than half of the time in labor arbitration; in employment arbitration, they seem to do about as well, at least where the issues and burden of proof are similar; and in court cases, the question is a good deal more complicated.

There is evidence that those few employees who obtain legal counsel do reasonably well in the court system. Although they win only a small proportion of the cases decided in the Federal District-Court Civil Cases, there is anecdotal evidence that there is a substantial probability of a favorable settlement. When they go to a jury, they have a good chance of recovery.

Amounts recovered in court proceedings are substantially higher than in employment arbitration. Those employees who win often win big. This has been called a "lottery" (Summers 1992, p. 466), which is arguably unfair, yet the fear of a big jury verdict may serve to force employers to be careful to comply with the law—or seek an alternative. What makes one somewhat uncomfortable with employment arbitration is that it has the appearance of giving employers an alternative to complying with the law—adopting a process that doesn't have the same potential for extreme awards to employees. This would mean that the most beneficial effects of the law—stimulating lawful behavior by employers—would be removed. After all, it is not compensating the minority of employees whose rights are violated that should be the principal aim of employment discrimination laws. Instead, it should be ensuring lawful behavior toward the vast majority of employees who never find their way into a courtroom or arbitration hearing.

With the exception of the Bingham and Mesch (2000) study comparing labor and employment arbitration, the crucial question that is not answered by any of the extant studies is whether there are differences in results across different dispute resolution systems *in similar cases*. The cases going to court, employment arbitration, labor arbitration, peer review panels, or European labor courts may differ systematically. There may also be systematic differences among the parties and advocates involved in the cases arising across these systems (Ware 2001; Bingham 1997). As explained in Chapter 5, it is precisely this point with which our research attempts to deal.

From our survey of employment arbitrators, we find a predominant proportion of cases to be either statutory (37.6 percent) or contract (25.4 percent). However, the proportion of cases that are neither of these (22.2 percent) was higher than expected. Most of the debate in the literature has to do with statutory cases. While a substantial amount of employment arbitration deals with these issues, this does not represent anywhere near a majority of cases. Fifty-five percent of the cases involving professional and managerial employees is, perhaps, a lower percentage than we might expect. This means that employment arbitration involves a substantial number of lower level employees as well.

A very high proportion of employees (80.9 percent) have legal counsel representing them in employment arbitration. The representation of employees is generally judged to be competent, but employers are significantly more likely to have competent representation. An employee having a representative prior to arbitration is quite rare, which contrasts with labor arbitration, where union officers represent an employee at all steps of the process. This is surely one of the critical differences between labor and employment arbitration. Discovery was commonly used, but believed to be only sometimes worth the time and costs involved. In over a quarter (26.3 percent) of the cases, employees pay all or a substantial share of the costs of the case. This is an issue over which the courts continue to struggle, and a characteristic of an arbitration system that might well cause a court to either invalidate it or at least refuse to enforce that condition of it (see discussion in Chapter 2).

The allocation of the burden of proof is an interesting issue since, as noted above, employees have much greater success when the burden is on the employer to prove cause for termination. Employment arbitrators who also have experience as labor arbitrators are significantly more likely to impose the burden of proving misconduct on the employer.

As to what needs to be proved, as shown in Table 3.5, employment arbitration differs from labor arbitration in two respects. First, a majority of employment arbitrators would not overturn a termination for violating a clearly unreasonable rule. Second, a substantial proportion would uphold a termination if the employer showed that it acted in good faith. On both of these points, labor arbitrators would disagree.

Employment arbitrators, perhaps predictably, view employment arbitration favorably. They agree that it is an efficient system and that it is better than the courts in handling employment disputes.

Having looked at the evidence on the processes of employment arbitration in the United States, we will next turn to examining the processes on termination in other countries. Following that, we will compare substantive outcomes across different systems of reviewing termination of employment.

4
An International Perspective

Only in the United States, Austria, Belgium, Denmark, and Israel is there no general right for employees not to be terminated without a justifiable reason (Crotty et al. 2000), whereas in other countries employees have this general right. This means that in most industrialized countries, unlike the United States, there is a systematic body of law that deals specifically with termination of employment. This set of laws furnishes an interesting benchmark for analyzing and evaluating the American system of workplace justice without unions.

In international bodies, there has long raged an intense debate on termination of employment. This is because of what has been called the "dire economic consequences" to employees, and the view of employers that strict regulation of worker dismissal undermines the flexibility of management in such a manner as to render enterprises unproductive and inefficient (Crotty et al. 2000, p. 7).

The right not to be unjustifiably terminated has various justifications in both common law systems that follow the English model and civil law systems that follow the continental European model. Common law systems have based this right on such grounds as a concept of individual justice that resists arbitrary treatment of workers, and the promotion of employment security. Civil law systems often view this as a matter of basic human rights, even incorporating it into their constitutions (Crotty et al. 2000).

There have been numerous studies of the practical effects on employment levels of the regulation of employment termination, and the evidence is mixed. A 1999 study by the Organisation for Economic Co-operation and Development (OECD) found no evidence that overall employment levels were affected by regulation of termination. On the other hand, an International Labor Organization (ILO) report concluded that there is some evidence that "excessive regulation" may deter employers from hiring workers for fear of difficulty in getting rid of them (Crotty et al. 2000, p. 10). This would especially affect low-skill workers. There is some experience with countries (France, Spain,

Argentina) making their laws more flexible without improving employment levels (Crotty et al. 2000). As concluded by the OECD (1999), however, factors other than regulation of employee dismissal seem to be more important in determining unemployment rates.

In this chapter, we will discuss the law of termination of employment from an international perspective. We will start with a consideration of international standards on termination, and follow with a country-by-country summary description and analysis of law and practice in a sample of 11 countries from which we have been able to gather some data on actual practices. A narrative discussion of the laws in these countries can be found in Appendix A. Although mainly European, the sample includes Australia and countries from the Middle East, Asia, and Africa.

The country-by-country discussion in this chapter will include descriptive data on legal practices in termination cases in these 11 countries. These data were collected from judges who attended a meeting of mostly European labor court judges under the auspices of the ILO in Geneva, Switzerland, in December 2001. At least one judge from each of these countries filled out our questionnaire regarding the operation of their legal system with regard to the termination of employment.

INTERNATIONAL STANDARDS ON TERMINATION OF EMPLOYMENT

The most visible international standard is the Termination of Employment Convention, adopted by the ILO in 1982 (ILO 1982). As a tripartite body (employers, unions, governments) and one of the oldest United Nations agencies, the ILO speaks with authority in the field of labor.

The Termination of Employment Convention, like most other ILO conventions, has not been adopted by the U.S. government. Therefore, it does not have legal effect within the boundaries of the United States. However, it does reflect the views of the international labor, management, and government community as to what the law *should* be in all of the member countries of the ILO, including the United States.

The crucial language of the convention is found in Article 4:

> The employment of a worker shall not be terminated unless there is a valid reason for such termination connected with the capacity or conduct of the worker or based on the operational requirements of the undertaking.

By this standard, workers should be terminated only for a lack of ability to do the job, misconduct, or redundancy. The only exclusions are for employees under fixed-term contracts, on probation, or "engaged on a casual basis for a short period" (Article 2).

The convention goes on to list some specific reasons for termination that are not valid, which include 1) union membership or activity; 2) serving as a workers' representative or seeking such office; 3) participating in proceedings against an employer regarding an alleged violation of the law; 4) "race, color, sex, marital status, family responsibilities, pregnancy, religion, political opinion, national extraction or social origin;" or; 5) being absent from work for maternity leave (Article 5). Also, temporary absence from work due to sickness or injury is not a proper cause for discharge (Article 6).

The convention sets out some rudimentary procedural guarantees. A worker is to be given an opportunity to defend against allegations of misconduct against him/her before he/she is terminated; the worker has a right to appeal his/her termination to an impartial body; and the burden of proof is to be placed on the employer to establish alleged misconduct (Article 9).

A number of other international human rights instruments lend support to this convention. Two of the more important sources of these documents are the United Nations and the ILO. The right to work and to be protected against unemployment is included in the Universal Declaration of Human Rights of the United Nations (Article 23) (United Nations 1948). The right to pursue "material well being" with "economic security" is in the Constitution of the ILO in Declaration of Philadelphia, para. II (a), Annex to the Constitution of the ILO (ILO 1948).

It is clear that the American common law employment-at-will doctrine is at odds with the convention. U.S. law does cover by statute many of the specific examples of invalid reasons for termination (e.g., race, sex, union activity). However, as a broad proposition, the rights set out in the ILO Termination of Employment Convention do not exist in the United States.

TERMINATION OF EMPLOYMENT IN VARIOUS COUNTRIES

Although nearly all countries provide workers with a guarantee against unjust termination, they do this in a variety of ways. Some, such as France, Italy, and Germany, state this in very broad terms, while others, such as many Latin American countries, spell out the acceptable reasons in some detail. A number of countries specify procedural requirements that an employer must meet, including written notice of reasons for termination (e.g., Germany, Greece), an interview with the worker (France), or consultation with the works council (Germany) (Crotty et al. 2000).

In those countries that mandate notice of termination, this requirement applies only to contracts of employment of indefinite duration. Length of notice may depend on length of service, whether the employee is paid on a weekly or monthly basis, blue- or white-collar status, or age. An employer who fails to give proper notice will generally have to pay wages for the notice period (Crotty et al. 2000).

The bodies to which a worker can appeal his termination also vary considerably. A number of countries (e.g., Belgium, Germany, United Kingdom) have separate labor courts, while special labor magistrates exist in Spain and several other countries. The labor courts in some countries, including Germany and Belgium, are tripartite (Crotty et al. 2000), including both professional judges, and labor and management "wingmen" who are practitioners. This compares to the United States, which uses private labor arbitrators as well as ordinary courts and the NLRB.

The burden of proof in termination cases can rest on either the worker or the employer. In some countries it rests on neither, and it is simply the obligation of the tribunal to obtain the necessary information and make an impartial decision (Crotty et al. 2000).

There is little consistency across countries in regard to remedies. In the Termination of Employment Convention of the ILO, the remedy that is favored is reinstatement. Although reinstatement is provided for in many countries, lost wages are often awarded in lieu of putting the worker back on the job. Severance pay is sometimes awarded even where the employee is at fault (Crotty et al. 2000).

In the following section, we will examine the law and practice of termination of employment on a country-by-country basis. This will cover 11 countries: Australia, Finland, Germany, Israel, Italy, Malaysia, Norway, South Africa, Spain, Sweden, and the United Kingdom. We will deal chiefly with terminations arising from the capacity or conduct of the worker, as dismissals on the grounds of redundancy are beyond the scope of the present study.

All of the 11 countries are in compliance with international labor standards as set forth in the ILO's Termination of Employment Convention. That is, where there are no reasons for termination related to the operations of the firm, they guarantee workers against termination except for reasons related to their "capacity or conduct."

As we can see from Table 4.1, most of these countries guarantee fair treatment in dismissals by statute. Two countries (South Africa and Spain) also have constitutional provisions on this subject. Israel utilizes collective agreements. Malaysia generally relies upon common law principles, and generally exempts foreign companies and domestic firms in its export sector from the provisions of Malaysia's statutory labor laws (Kuruvilla 1995).

The standards that must be met to justify a termination often vary according to whether the termination is an ordinary one (which usually requires notice) or a summary dismissal. For summary dismissal, "grave misconduct" (Germany), "very grave misconduct" (Italy), "gross breach of duty" (Norway) or "culpable non-performance" (Spain) are among the standards used. Dismissal with notice can be for "justified reason" (Italy), be "objectively justified" (Norway), or for "objective reasons" (Spain). Some systems do not make such a distinction, requiring that the employer not be "harsh, unjust or unreasonable" (Australia), have an "empirically weighty reason" (Finland), a "valid reason" (Israel), "just cause" (Malaysia), "serious misconduct making continuation intolerable" (South Africa), that the dismissal be "materially justified" (Sweden), or that the employer acted as a "reasonable employer" (United Kingdom). However they express the rule, it appears that, across these countries, summary dismissal requires very serious misconduct on the part of the employee. For dismissal with notice, the standards vary somewhat. What is constant is the requirement of objective, provable grounds for dismissal.

Table 4.1 Summary of Termination of Employment Laws in Eleven Countries

Country	Source	Standard	Notice required	Notice length	Notice determined	Forum[a]	Remedies
Australia	Statute	Not harsh, unjust, or unreasonable	Yes, if not serious misconduct	1–6 weeks	Service, age	Industrial Commission, ordinary courts	Reinstatement, damages, 6 months' pay (monetary limit)
Finland	Statute	Especially weighty reason	Yes	1–6 months	Service	Ordinary courts, labor court	Normalized indemnity, 3–4 months' wages
Germany	Statute	Socially justifiable, grave misconduct (summary)	Yes (not for summary)	1–7 months	Service	Labor court	Reinstatement and up to 12 months' pay
Israel	Collective agreement	Valid reason	Yes	15–30 days	Service	Ordinary courts or labor courts	Damages
Italy	Statute	Justified reason (with notice), very grave misconduct (summary)	Yes	Varies by collective agreement	Collective agreement	Ordinary courts	Reinstatement and damages
Malaysia	Common law, statutes	Just cause	Yes, except misconduct	4–8 weeks	Service	Industrial court or labor court	Reinstatement and damages

Country	Source	Justification	Notice required	Notice period	Severance factors	Forum	Remedy
Norway	Statute	Objectively justified (with notice) gross breach of duty (summary)	Yes, except summary	1–3 months	Service, age	Ordinary courts (special procedures)	Reinstatement or compensation
South Africa	Constitution, statutes	Serious misconduct making continuation intolerable	Yes	1–4 weeks	Service	Commission for Conciliation Arbitration and Mediation; or labor court, ordinary courts	Reinstatement, up to 12 months' wages
Spain	Constitution, statutes	Objective reasons, culpable non-performance	Yes, for objective reasons	30 days	All same	Labor court	Reinstatement, lost wages, up to 42 months' pay
Sweden	Statute	Materially justified	Yes, unless immediate effect	2–6 months	Age	Labor court	Reinstatement or financial compensation
United Kingdom	Statute	Employer acted as a reasonable employer	Yes	½ week, unlimited	Service, age	Industrial Tribunal, arbitration, or ordinary courts	Reinstatement, awards up to monetary limits

aFor all cases except discrimination on prohibited grounds.

Where notice of termination is required, length of notice varies to a great degree across countries—it ranges from a few days to seven months. In a particular national system, the amount of notice to which an employee is entitled usually depends upon length of service, however, age is sometimes a factor.

Most, but not all, of these countries have specialized forums for hearing termination of employment cases. Remedies generally include reinstatement and compensation for lost wages, and sometimes other damages. One gets the impression that reinstatement is a remedy nearly universally available, but rarely used.

The practices in the courts in 9 of the 11 participating countries are summarized in Table 4.2. Here we see that proof of misconduct, or lack of capacity, proved by a preponderance of the evidence (or a balance of the probabilities, which is very similar), is the requirement in most of these countries. However, one country (Finland) requires clear and convincing evidence. It should be noted that the United Kingdom ultimately asks the question of whether the employer acted as a reasonable employer.

We see that the parties are generally competently represented in the tribunals that hear dismissal cases. However, there is some indication that competent representation may be more likely to be present in some countries (Italy, Malaysia, South Africa) for employers than for employees. Sufficient information for an informed decision seems to be generally present, and discovery processes appear to work reasonably well where they are available. Overall, the court systems are seen as being good for both employers and employees, except perhaps for employers in Italy. The systems are seen by these judges as being efficient in all of these countries except Italy and Malaysia. Specialized tribunals are viewed as being better than ordinary courts wherever they exist.

COMPARISON WITH U.S. EMPLOYMENT ARBITRATION

Because there are some parallels between the questionnaires sent to employment judges in other countries and American employment arbitrators, it is possible to make some rough comparisons between the U.S. system of employment arbitration and the systems in these coun-

Table 4.2 Court Practices in Nine Countries[a]

Country	Burden of proof	Employer competently represented	Employee competently represented	Sufficient information for decision	Worthwhile discovery process[b]	System good for employees	System good for employers	System efficient	Better than ordinary courts[c]
Australia	Preponderance	Usually	Usually	Usually	Sometimes	Agree	Agree	Agree	Agree
Finland	Clear and convincing	Usually	Usually	Usually	Always	Agree	Agree	Agree	Not applicable
Germany	Beyond reasonable doubt	Usually	Usually	Usually	Not applicable	Agree	Agree	Agree	Agree
Italy	Preponderance	Always	Usually	Usually	Not applicable	Agree	Neutral	Disagree	Not applicable
Malaysia	Preponderance	Usually	Sometimes	Usually	Usually	Agree	Agree	Neutral	Strongly agree
Norway	Preponderance	Always	Always	Always	Not applicable	Agree	Agree	No response	Not applicable
South Africa	Balance of probabilities	Usually	Sometimes	Usually	Usually	Agree	Agree	Agree	Strongly agree
Spain	Proof by employer	Usually	Usually	Usually	Usually	Agree	Agree	Agree	Strongly agree
Sweden	Preponderance	Usually	Usually	Always	Always	Strongly agree	Strongly agree	Strongly agree	Agree

[a]Israel and the United Kingdom are excluded from this table, owing to lack of agreement among the several respondents from these countries (see text discussions of these countries in Appendix A).

[b]"Worthwhile discovery process" is not applicable where there is no discovery process.

[c]"Better than ordinary courts" is not applicable where there is not a separate labor court system.

tries. This gives us an additional frame of reference within which to view employment arbitration.

When asked whether employers and employees have competent representation in their tribunals, foreign judges were generally positive as to representatives of both employers and employees. In the nine countries analyzed on this point, with respect to employers, judges from two countries said that representation was always competent, and those from seven countries said that it was usually the case. As to employee representatives, only one said that this was always the case, six said it was usually true, and two stated that this was only sometimes the case. Although these last results are not directly comparable because different scales were used on these items on the two questionnaires, as noted in Chapter 3, in U.S. employment arbitration the mean score on the questions regarding employer representation of 3.6, and for employee representation of 3.2 (on a four-point scale where 1 = Never, 2 = Rarely, 3 = Sometimes, 4 = Always), appears to be similar. That is, both by judges in other countries and U.S. employment arbitrators, representation for both sides was judged to be competent more than sometimes, but with the frequency of having competent counsel somewhat more common for employers than for employees.

Discovery was available in only six of the nine countries shown in Table 4.2. In comparison, as shown in Chapter 3, this is something that was used in about 80 percent of the U.S. employment arbitration cases. In those countries where discovery was available, it was perceived as being worth the time and cost either usually (three countries) or always (two countries) in five of the six countries. In only one was it judged to be only sometimes worth the time and cost. Again, because of a different scale, it is not possible to make a direct comparison with employment arbitrators' perceptions. However, it appears that discovery may be perceived as slightly more worthwhile by the judges in other countries than it is in American employment arbitration.

Regarding the quantum of proof required, of the nine countries in Table 4.2, in some cases only one country requires proof beyond a reasonable doubt and one requires proof by clear and convincing evidence. By comparison, as shown in Table 3.5, 5.2 percent of American employment arbitrators said that they would sometimes require proof beyond a reasonable doubt. Clear and convincing evidence would sometimes be required by 39.1 percent. It is difficult to compare these results, so perhaps the most that can be said is that the requirement of proof by a greater quantum than by a preponderance of the evidence (i.e., beyond a reasonable doubt or by clear and convincing evidence) is present both in some other countries and in American employment arbitration. In American labor arbitration, arbitrators are likely to use at least a clear and convincing evidence standard, or even proof beyond a reasonable doubt, in cases where it is alleged that the employee committed an offense involving moral turpitude such as theft or acts of violence (Brand 1998; Volz and Goggin 1997).

Both the judges from other countries and American employment arbitrators were surveyed regarding their views about the quality of their systems. As to the protection of the interests of both employees and employers, the judges generally either agreed or strongly agreed that the interests of both parties were well protected by their systems. The only exception is Italy, where the judges were neutral as to whether employer interests were well protected. As shown previously in Table 3.6, American employment arbitrators were reasonably positive as to the interests of both employers and employees. However, as to all types of cases, American employment arbitrators were more strongly in agreement that the rights of employers were protected. This difference was especially pronounced where nonbinding handbooks and policies are concerned.

As can be seen from Table 4.2, the judges from outside the United States largely agreed that their system was efficient, although the Italians disagreed with this, and the Malaysian judge was neutral on this point. As shown in Chapter 3, employment arbitrators in the United States were somewhat more approving of their system, with an average score of 4.34 (five-point scale with Agree = 4, Strongly agree = 5). On the other hand, the judges were more positive when asked whether their system worked better than using the ordinary courts. All who had a specialized system (six countries) either strongly agreed (three countries), or agreed (three countries) that this was so. American employment arbitrators were also reasonably positive on this question (4.21 on a five-point scale), but perhaps not quite as approving as the judges.

We conclude that there are no striking differences between the processes in other countries and employment arbitration in the respects in which we compared them. Both in U.S. employment arbitration and in the courts of other selected countries, both sides were believed to generally have competent representation, but that employers are more likely to have competent representation than employees. Discovery seems to be more favored in other countries than in employment arbitration, and practices as to quantum of proof are similar.

As to the system's effectiveness in protecting the rights of the parties, it would seem that American employment arbitrators are more likely to perceive employers as being better served than employees. It is notable that judges in one country—Italy—were neutral as to their system protecting the interests of employers. American employment arbitrators seem more likely to be approving of the efficiency of their system, but the judges are somewhat more likely to say that their system is better than the ordinary courts.

Having examined, in general terms, the laws and processes on termination of employment in international perspective as well as in the United States, we will now proceed to describe an empirical analysis of decision making in dismissal cases in the United States and several of these countries.

5
Judging the Merits of Terminations: Does It Matter Who Decides?

As discussed in earlier chapters, within the unionized sector, labor arbitration plays a critical role in determining what decisions are made with regard to employee termination. Furthermore, the norms and procedural elements governing labor arbitration have been extensively studied and are well understood by both labor and management (Cooper, Nolan, and Bales 2000). The joint role of unions and management in the arbitration process combined with clearly established just cause requirements imposes a particular, reasonably well-understood balance with regard to employee and employer rights (Werhane 1985). Knowledge of other forms of workplace justice that have emerged in association with the decline of unionization is not as far advanced, however (Ewing 1989). As noted earlier, in some nonunion organizations, peer review procedures have been introduced as a substitute for labor arbitration to help minimize the threat of unionization (Colvin 2003). In other firms, the HR function plays an increasingly important role in addressing whether a given termination is permissible (Kandel and Frumer 1994). In still other firms, employment arbitration systems have been introduced—a development expected to increase in light of the recent legal developments addressed in previous chapters. And in many other organizations, disputes that traditionally would have been resolved within labor arbitration now find their way into the judicial system (Bales 1997).

According to some arguments, the different institutional arrangements that have emerged over the last two decades for resolving disputes regarding termination will have few implications for actual outcomes. Decision makers (irrespective of institutional constraints) are expected to apply universal standards regarding fairness, and these norms of fairness will have a significant effect on outcomes—regardless of the rules and procedures governing the dispute resolution process (Wheeler, Klaas, and Rojot 1994). For example, while the primary task of juries in statutory cases is to determine whether there was illegal discrimination, jurors may be influenced by whether they believe the employee was treated justly—independent of the issue of illegal discrimination (Abbott 1993; MacCoun 1989). To the extent that these fairness norms dominate decision making, few differences are likely to be observed across different procedures for making decisions about whether a termination is justified.

However, it is important not to discount the significance of differences across institutional arrangements in the rules and procedures that govern how decisions about termination are to be made. Evidence suggests that, while fairness norms may affect a wide variety of decision makers, these individuals are still influenced by institution-specific rules regarding how decisions should be made (Klaas and Feldman 1994). More or less universal norms of fairness may well exist, but such norms are rather general and often offer insufficient practical guidance for decision makers. It is within this context, then, that differences in institutional norms and procedures may come to play a role in affecting decisions about terminations. For example, within labor arbitration, just cause standards inform arbitrators how they should judge the issue of fairness (Block and Steiber 1987). By contrast, peer review panelists judge fairness by determining whether the termination is consistent with company rules and procedures (Ewing 1989). While peer review deliberations may indirectly cause the modification of organizational rules, the fundamental focus of the peer review panel is to assess whether the termination is consistent with existing policies and procedures.

In addition to differences in the institutional procedures used to guide decision making, differences in the background, training, and interests of the decision maker exist across alternative forums. For example, while HR managers and peer review panelists may well have an interest in ensuring the fair treatment of employees, they also are likely to have an interest in ensuring the effective functioning of the firm (Klaas and Feldman 1993). This interest in protecting the firm may cause them to differ from third-party decision makers, whose concerns about the firm's success may not be as compelling. Similarly, differences may exist between labor and employment arbitrators in terms of their professional experience and training. For example, because labor arbitrators must be acceptable to both unions and management, the typical profile of a labor arbitrator may differ from the typical profile of an employment arbitrator (Bingham and Mesch 2000). Within employment arbitration, advocates (e.g., management-side employment lawyers or plaintiff-side employment lawyers) are permitted to serve on arbitration lists, which is not generally permitted within labor arbitration.

To understand how the decline in unionization affects workplace justice, it is appropriate to compare how decision makers from different institutional forums would respond to similar cases involving employee termination. With respect to labor arbitration, it should be noted that the effect of decision maker or case characteristics has previously been studied by analyzing actual decisions (using the written decision provided by the arbitrator). For example, the effect of decision maker or case characteristics on outcomes has been estimated, controlling for factors described within the written opinion of the arbitrator in Block and Steiber (1987). While examining actual cases offers some advantages, it is often difficult to ascertain from the arbitrator's written decision the exact nature of the offense, the evidence against the employee, and mitigating circumstances. As such, it is difficult to control for the severity of the offense or the available evidence—characteristics that might well be expected to differ across the different institutional forums being examined here. Further, detailed written decisions are not available from many of the alternative institutional forums that have grown in importance in association with the decline of unionization.

The approach taken here was to develop hypothetical cases regarding employee termination, and to ask different types of decision makers to indicate whether they would find in favor of the employee or the employer in light of the facts presented. Asking subjects to respond to paper and pencil scenarios is, of course, a common social science methodology. While questions have been raised about the degree to which subjects can anticipate how they would actually behave in response to the facts presented, evidence suggests that subjects who have made similar decisions in the past are typically capable of drawing on their experience in order to judge how they would behave if actually faced with the facts presented in the scenario (Locke 1986). Here, all subjects examined have had experience making decisions about whether to rule in favor of an employee in a termination case—either as a labor arbitrator, an employment arbitrator, a juror, a peer review panelist, or an HR manager.

It should be noted that while labor arbitrators, employment arbitrators, and HR managers all make decisions on an individual basis, peer review panelists and jurors make decisions as part of a group. By asking jurors and peer review panelists to respond as individuals, we are capturing how they would form their initial judgment about how to respond. It must be understood that such initial judgments could change as a result of group deliberations.

The overall approach taken here was rather straightforward. First, we drew upon theory and research to identify how and why decision makers within different institutional forums might respond differently to a variety of cases involving employee termination. Second, we developed written scenarios that are realistic termination cases. They vary in terms of salient characteristics such as evidence of discrimination, strength of the evidence, mitigating circumstances, and procedural compliance on the part of the employer. Third, we administered the scenarios to experienced decision makers from different institutional forums. Fourth, we systematically compared the responses to the scenarios from the different decision makers. We did this to determine whether the results show the differences that we expected to find, based on theory and previous research. And lastly, we addressed the implications of these results for our understanding of workplace justice.

In this chapter, after a brief discussion of the decision makers and the hypothetical cases with which they were presented, we outline our expectations for each group of decision makers. We then present the results of our analysis and the implications of these results. In Appendix B, we more fully describe the sample of decision makers that took part in this research, and how the data were gathered. In this appendix, we also set out in more detail summaries of the hypothetical cases that we posed to the decision makers.

THE DECISION MAKERS AND THE CASES

In this study, we are examining how the role of the decision maker affects decisions made regarding rulings in favor of an employee challenging a termination. We compare labor arbitrators; employment arbitrators instructed to evaluate claims of a statutory violation, as well as claims of a violation of a "for-cause" provision in the employment agreement; peer review panelists; HR managers operating within a nonunion environment; and jurors with experience in employment termination cases. Also included for comparison purposes is a small sample of judges from countries where "for-cause" standards exist and are enforceable in their court systems.

Before proceeding further, we would like to make one note regarding methodology. All subjects were asked to respond to a number of different termination cases. Although these decision makers are from different forums, it is reasonable to expect that the content of a case could be the same across forums. For example, within labor arbitration, emphasis is given to whether the employer has just cause for termination. Just cause tests do not directly pertain to issues raised in cases involving allegations of illegal discrimination. Thus, there might be questions about whether a labor arbitrator would even hear a case that is similar to what is heard by a jury. In response to such questions, it is important to note that it is often suggested that labor arbitrators may commonly hear cases that otherwise would have been translated into a case involving allegations of a statutory violation. For example, within labor arbitration, it is common for a claim to be made that the employer did not have cause for termination. Often, that substantive claim is combined with a contention about the actual motives of the employer—motives that might include allegations about discrimination on the basis of race, gender, age, or some other protected category. While the labor arbitrator may focus on the issue of whether there is cause for termination, claims made regarding discrimination are likely to be considered to the extent that they inform judgments about whether there is just cause (Cooper, Nolan, and Bales 2000). Further, in the absence of labor arbitration, it might well be that an employee would pursue his/her case within the judiciary system with the primary focus being upon the alleged discrimination. However, factors relating to evidence against the employee, procedural compliance, or the employee's work record would inevitably be addressed within judicial proceedings. Thus, the facts of the case would remain the same as they would be in labor arbitration. The differences observed across forums would revolve around different questions addressed by the decision maker, and in differences in emphasis with respect to various aspects of the case.

All of the cases that were posed to respondents to this study were designed to enable comparisons across the different dispute resolution forums.

The cases were developed by reviewing relevant cases from labor and employment arbitration. Cases were designed to be realistic for labor arbitrators, employment arbitrators evaluating statutory claims, employment arbitrators with for-cause requirements, peer review panelists, jurors, HR managers, and labor court judges. While the facts of each case remained constant across decision makers, we did vary the instructions provided. For example, labor arbitrators were informed that the contract contained a "just cause" requirement for termination, and employment arbitrators evaluating a statutory claim were told the employee was an at-will employee. Relevant material regarding the interpretation of the statute in question was included to ensure that the decision setting reflected information that would be present when the respondent was actually deciding such a case. As an additional example of how the instructions differed, peer review panelists were instructed that they should assess whether they would rule in favor of the employee if such a case appeared before them in their peer review system. Consistent with the structure of the peer review system in the organizations sampled, subjects were told that the peer review body had the authority to overturn management's action and that their ruling would be final and binding within the company. They were further instructed that their task was to determine whether the termination was consistent with the policies and procedures of the company. As one final example of how the cases varied in terms of the instructions given to the decision makers, labor court judges were from countries where the for-cause requirement is embedded in statute, common law, or collective bargaining agreements with near-universal coverage. Reference to employment-at-will was eliminated from instructions that they received. Judges were simply informed to make their determinations in accordance with norms that existed in their judicial system.

Before finalizing the scenarios, feedback on them was obtained from experienced labor arbitrators, employment arbitrators, HR managers in firms where peer review is used, and HR managers who have primary responsibility for authorizing termination.

Cases varied in terms of content and in terms of the degree to which a finding in favor of the employee would be expected. Our intention was to create scenarios where the case against the employee was strong but not incontrovertible, scenarios where there were substantial problems with the case against the employee, and scenarios where potential problems with the case against the employee were combined with other factors that might be seen by some as supporting a case for termination.

Table 5.1 summarizes how the 12 cases reviewed by the subjects varied across key dimensions. Further details regarding each case are provided in Appendix B. As can be seen in Table 5.1, the cases involve a number of different disciplinary offenses, ranging from absenteeism to theft. The cases also vary in terms of the degree of evidence against the employee. In some cases, the evidence against the employee is strong, whereas in other cases, questions could legitimately be raised about whether there is sufficient evidence to conclude that the employee is guilty. While some of the cases revolve solely around whether there is a violation of a "for-cause" requirement within an individual or collective contract, others contain allegations of illegal discrimination. For these latter cases, evidence of discrimination ranges from weak to substantial. The cases also vary in whether the rule allegedly violated by the employee might be viewed as unreasonable. Procedural compliance by the firm also varies: in 10 of the cases, the firm's actions are consistent with procedural requirements, while in 2 of the cases, questions could be raised about whether the firm's actions are consistent with its own procedural requirements. Finally, the cases vary in terms of whether there are mitigating or extenuating circumstances present, and whether there is any evidence that inappropriate behavior by the employee might have been provoked by his or her supervisor.

ARE THERE DIFFERENCES AMONG DECISION MAKERS?

Before launching into an extensive analysis of the differences in outcomes across our sample of decision makers, it is helpful to take an overview of our data to see whether there is any evidence that there are differences worth explaining. That this is the case is shown rather clearly by the analyses shown in Tables 5.2 through 5.5.

Table 5.1 Summary of the Characteristics and Strength of the Case against the Employee

Case	Nature of alleged offense	Strength of evidence against employee	Allegations of discrimination	Reasonableness of rule	Issues of procedural compliance	Mitigating or exacerbating circumstances	Provocation
1	Theft	Strong	None	Reasonable	None	Very short tenure (1 year)	None
2	Theft	Strong	Weak evidence of racial discrimination	Reasonable	None	Very short tenure (1 year)	None
3	Insubordination	Modest	Modest evidence of gender discrimination	Reasonable	Questionable noncompliance	Short tenure (4 years), highly productive	None
4	Theft	Strong	None	Possibly unreasonable	None	Very long tenure (20 years)	None
5	Fighting	Modest	None	Reasonable	None	Short tenure (4 years), negative work record	None
6	Absenteeism	Strong	None	Possibly unreasonable	None	Very long tenure (15 years), family problems	None

7	Poor performance and insubordination	Strong	Weak evidence of age discrimination	Reasonable	None	Short tenure (4 years), prior warnings	None
8	Poor performance and insubordination	Modest	Weak evidence of age discrimination	Reasonable	Clear non-compliance	Short tenure (1 year), poor work record	None
9	Poor performance and insubordination	Modest	Substantial evidence of age discrimination	Reasonable	None	Short tenure (4 years)	None
10	Poor performance and insubordination	Modest	Weak evidence of age discrimination	Reasonable	None	Short tenure (4 years), poor work record	Evidence of provocation
11	Poor performance and insubordination	Modest	Weak evidence of age discrimination	Reasonable	None	Very long tenure (22 years), poor work record	None
12	Poor performance and insubordination	Modest	Weak evidence of age discrimination	Reasonable	None	Short tenure (4 years), poor work record, family problems	None

We begin by providing descriptive statistics about the decision making on the 12 cases described in Appendix B. Table 5.2 shows the average ratings across all decision makers for each of the 12 cases rated. The results are anchored on a seven-point Likert-type scale, where a rating of 7 indicates the strongest likelihood of a ruling for the employee by overturning the termination, and a rating of 1 indicates the strongest likelihood of ruling against the employee by letting the termination stand. A higher rating favors the employee, while a lower rating favors the termination. The seven-point scale is constructed in such a way that a score of 5 or above reflects a decision to overturn the termination of the employee, while a score of 3 or below reflects a decision to confirm the termination. A rating at the midpoint (4) indicates that the rater is uncertain about the outcome.

As can be seen from Table 5.2, the likelihood of a ruling in favor of the employee was lowest for Case 7, followed closely by Case 2 and Case 1. This is to be expected because in all three of these cases, evidence against the employee was relatively strong, there was little evidence of discrimination, there was no evidence of procedural violations by the company, and with the exception of Case 7, there were no mitigating circumstances.

The likelihood of ruling in favor of the employee was highest in Case 3, followed closely by Cases 11 and 8. In all three cases, evidence

Table 5.2 Likelihood of Overturning Termination across Decision Maker Types: Means and Standard Deviations

Case number	Mean	Std. dev.
Case 1	2.82	1.53
Case 2	2.71	1.31
Case 3	5.00	1.38
Case 4	4.22	1.67
Case 5	3.77	1.49
Case 6	3.67	1.59
Case 7	2.32	1.43
Case 8	4.74	1.56
Case 9	4.35	1.65
Case 10	3.98	1.46
Case 11	4.97	1.56
Case 12	4.31	1.58

NOTE: Ratings were on a 1 to 7 scale, where 7 indicates a high likelihood of overturning the termination and 1 indicates a low likelihood of overturning the termination.

of employee wrongdoing was relatively modest, and this was combined with either procedural problems with the termination (Cases 3 and 8), or long tenure on the part of the employee (Case 11).

Table 5.3 shows the mean likelihood of a ruling in favor of the employee broken down by type of decision maker. As can be seen, employment arbitrators evaluating statutory claims were the least likely to rule in favor of the employee across all of the cases. Employment arbitrators with a for-cause requirement were the next least likely to rule in favor of the employee, followed by jurors, peer review panelists, HR managers, labor court judges, and labor arbitrators. Mean ratings ranged from a low of 3.38 (employment arbitrators evaluating statutory claims) to a high of 4.41 for labor arbitrators.

Another way of looking at this same issue can be seen in Table 5.4. Across all the cases, labor arbitrators indicated that they would be likely to rule in favor of the employee a minimum of 55 percent of the time. This can be contrasted with employment arbitrators evaluating statutory claims, who indicated that they would be likely to rule in favor of the employee a minimum of 25 percent of the time. Interestingly, even with the for-cause requirement, employment arbitrators indicated they would be likely to rule in favor of the employee only 33 percent of the time, which is still less than jurors (at 38 percent) who had no for-cause requirement. Decision makers from within the organization (peer review panelists and HR managers) fell between employment arbitrators and jurors at one end of the scale and labor arbitrators

Table 5.3 Likelihood of Overturning Termination across Cases: Means and Standard Deviations by Decision Maker

Decision maker type	Mean	Std. dev.
Labor arbitrator	4.41	1.55
Employment arbitrator (evaluating statutory claim)	3.38	1.49
Employment arbitrator (for-cause requirement)	3.70	1.42
Peer review panelist	3.99	1.70
Juror	3.82	1.75
HR manager	4.00	1.75
Labor court judge	4.37	1.76

NOTE: Ratings were on a 1 to 7 scale, where 7 indicates a high likelihood of overturning the termination and 1 indicates a low likelihood of overturning the termination.

Table 5.4 Percentage of Rulings Likely to be in Favor of the Employee across All Cases: by Decision Maker

Decision maker	% of cases where ruling in favor of employee is likely
Labor arbitrator	55
Employment arbitrator (statutory claims)	25
Employment arbitrator (for-cause requirement)	33
Peer review panelist	45
Juror	38
HR manager	46
Labor court judge	51

NOTE: A ruling was classified as likely to be in favor of the employee when a decision maker selected a response of 5 or higher on the 7-point response scale. A scale value 5 was anchored with "likely to rule in favor of the employee."

and labor court judges at the other end. These overall differences might well be expected in light of our prior discussion about differences in the decision task. One possible exception to this is for employment arbitrators that were assigned to the for-cause condition. Given the nature of the decision task, one might have expected jurors to have been less likely to rule in favor of the employee than employment arbitrators with the for-cause requirement. However, the overall difference might well be understood if one considers the differences in both the decision task and in the interest of the decision maker, as well as differences in tendencies to identify with one party versus another (jurors being more likely to identify with the employee).

These differences suggest that the role of the decision maker is likely to play a significant role in determining what decisions are made when employees challenge termination decisions. However, as noted earlier, we expect that differences between decision makers will vary across different types of disciplinary cases as well. Accordingly, we now turn to examining how the decision makers differed for each of the 12 cases examined here. Our goal is to perform all possible pairwise comparisons for each of the 12 cases examined. But before making these pairwise comparisons, it is necessary to examine whether decision maker type explains a significant amount of variance in each case.

As can be seen in Table 5.5, using analysis of variance procedures, we found that decision maker type accounted for a significant portion of the variance in outcomes for each of the 12 cases. While there is

Table 5.5 Effect of Role of the Decision Maker on Likelihood of Overturning Termination

Case number	F-value
Case 1	9.29**
Case 2	5.66**
Case 3	21.08**
Case 4	6.20**
Case 5	11.93**
Case 6	4.33**
Case 7	2.77*
Case 8	15.73**
Case 9	3.14**
Case 10	8.00**
Case 11	12.35**
Case 12	9.35**

NOTE: *$p < 0.05$; ** $p < 0.01$

variation in the level of significance across these cases, decision maker type played a significant role for each. This result justifies an examination of pairwise differences.

In the balance of this chapter we will present, for each compared pair of decision makers, our discussion regarding the results that we expect to find, why we expect those particular results, and the results, which will be presented in Tables 5.6 through 5.26.

PAIRWISE COMPARISONS OF DECISION MAKERS

Labor Arbitrators vs. Employment Arbitrators Evaluating Statutory Claims

Expectations

Many employment arbitration agreements specify that, while employees are required to submit claims regarding statutory violations to employment arbitration, the employee remains an "at will" employee. Under such agreements, the employment arbitrator's sole task is to determine if a statutory violation occurred (Bales 1997). In cases where a statutory claim is made by an employee, the employment arbitrator is likely to focus on factors that offer evidence as to whether illegal discrimination occurred. Under such agreements, the employment arbitrator (much like a juror or a judge) is not directed to assess the fairness of the termination for the employee or the wisdom of termination from the standpoint of the business.

In discrimination cases, both in the courts and (we would expect) in an employment arbitration tribunal, the initial burden of coming forward with the evidence, as well as the ultimate burden of persuasion, lay upon the employee. In cases of sex, race, natural origin, color, or religious discrimination, if the employee fails to show a *prima facie* case, the employer is not obligated to defend or justify its decision (Bennett-Alexander and Hartman 2001). Thus, absent credible evidence of discrimination or of circumstances giving rise to an inference of it, employment arbitrators are unlikely to reach questions regarding procedural fairness or the quality of the evidence against the employee. In indirect evidence cases where the employee has not provided direct evidence of discrimination but only circumstances giving rise to an inference of discrimination, the employer can prevail by merely articulating (not proving) a legitimate nondiscriminatory reason for its action. If the employer does this, the employee can prevail only by showing that the articulated reason is a mere pretext (Bennett-Alexander and Hartman 2004). It is only at this point that general considerations of fairness come into play. In mixed-motive cases, once the employee has shown that a discriminatory motive played a part in its action, the employer will be found to have violated the law. However, if the employer can demonstrate to the court that the employee would have been terminated in the absence of the discriminatory motive, the employer will be excused from paying any damages (Bennett-Alexander and Hartman 2004; *Ragsdale v. Wolverine World Wide, Inc.* 2002). We would expect an employment arbitrator to adopt this same kind of analysis. Therefore, at the point of showing pretext, or the employer attempting to demonstrate that the employee would have been terminated in the absence of discrimination, there would be an opportunity for the employee to argue the inherent unfairness of the employer's decision. In cases of age discrimination a similar analysis applies, except that in mixed motive cases the employer will not be found to be in violation of the law if the employee was terminated for cause (Bennett-Alexander and Hartman 2004).

Similarly, at least in the absence of a *prima facie* case of discrimination, little consideration is likely to be given by an employment arbitrator to the employee's work history or mitigating circumstances that might limit the degree of blame or indicate that the misconduct would be unlikely to reoccur. By contrast, these same factors are likely to be highly relevant to labor arbitrators. Application of just cause standards would require that consideration be given to such factors, regardless of claims relating to illegal discrimination (Cooper, Nolan, and Bales 2000). Thus, labor arbitrators are more likely than employment arbitrators to find for the employee where there is only a moderate amount (less than a preponderance) of evidence of both discrimination and of misconduct that provides a just cause for termination. This difference derives from the fact that the employee must prove discrimination, while it is the employer who must show that there is just cause for termination (Bennett-Alexander and Hartman 2004; Bales 1997). So long as the employer is unable to affirmatively establish just cause, the labor arbitrator will find for the employee.

Questions might be raised about likely differences between employment arbitrators and labor arbitrators when there is both substantial evidence of discrimination and of a possible violation of the just cause standard by the employer. The differences that will be observed will likely depend on the degree to which the evidence of discrimination is conclusive (rather than being plausible but inconclusive). When evidence of discrimination is conclusive, employment arbitrators are likely to find little reason to doubt whether a statutory violation occurred. For labor arbitrators, conclusive evidence of discrimination is likely to give rise to questions about the employer's accusations against the employee, leading to concerns about whether there is just cause for termination.

However, differences between employment arbitration and labor arbitration are still likely to be observed when the evidence of discrimination is plausible but inconclusive. While norms regarding burden of proof are not clearly established within employment arbitration, within the judicial system the employee has the initial burden of proof and the ultimate burden of persuasion (Bales 1997). To the extent that this norm is followed within employment arbitration, it is likely that there will sometimes be hesitation to conclude that the employee met the burden of proof if evidence of discrimination is not conclusive. Moreover, this hesitation is unlikely to be mitigated by the presence of possible problems with the termination that we call "just cause violations" by the employer, unless these violations inform the arbitrator's judgment about whether discrimination occurred. By "just cause violations" we refer to *both* 1) substantive problems of lack of evidence of wrongdoing, and of ignoring mitigating circumstances; and 2) procedural problems of the company acting in a manner that is inconsistent with its own policy, and of procedural irregularities in the manner of the termination.

In labor arbitration, the arbitrator is not required to determine whether or not the employee can show evidence of discrimination. While such evidence may inform the arbitrator's judgment about whether there is just cause, the employee does not have to prove this in order to prevail. Thus, in cases where there is a potential violation of a just cause standard by the employer, labor arbitrators may readily rule in favor of the employee if the evidence of discrimination falls into the category of "plausible but inconclusive."

Questions might also be asked about whether differences between labor and employment arbitrators would be observed when the employee's case is weak on multiple dimensions. For example, consider a case where the employee claims that termination is not justified and that a prohibited form of discrimination may be the real reason for the termination. However, evidence of discrimination is lacking, and furthermore, no violations of the employer's just cause obligation are apparent. Evidence of employee wrongdoing is substantial, termination for the offense is justified under organizational policy, there are no procedural violations, and there are no mitigating circumstances. While one might argue that no differences between employment and labor arbitrators would be observed under such conditions, we argue that differences might still be observed. A key assumption behind this argument is that at least some ambiguity remains regarding the evidence of wrongdoing or the severity of the offense. Where there is such ambiguity, some decision makers are likely to be affected by a fairly natural reluctance to terminate an employee. This reluctance to take severe or harsh action against the accused or a "deviant" has been observed across a number of settings and circumstances when some ambiguity remains as to the justification or need for harsh action (Feldman 1984). This reluctance is likely to be heightened in instances where the decision maker identifies psychologically with the employee (Tajfel 1979, 1981). Under such circumstances, concern about the consequences of job loss for the individual could result in decision makers requiring high levels of certainty and justification before taking severe action.

We argue that this reluctance to terminate is less likely to affect decisions made by employment arbitrators. In order for an employment arbitrator to rule in favor of the employee, he or she must find that the employer engaged in illegal discrimination. Any reluctance to terminate may well be offset by a reluctance to declare that the employer discriminated—particularly if there is limited evidence in this regard. By contrast, a labor arbitrator can rule in favor of an employee by declaring that the employer failed to show just cause. In addition, it should be noted that within employment arbitration, advocates are allowed to serve as arbitrators. In fact, data reported here previously suggest that a higher percentage of management-side advocates (compared to plaintiff-side advocates) serve as employment arbitrators. Having worked with management teams throughout their career, such individuals may come to identify with the management team involved in the case, therefore, they may be more sensitive to the costs for the management team of ruling that they engaged in illegal discrimination. Sensitivity to these costs may counteract any reluctance to terminate.

A final factor that may counter any reluctance to terminate is the cost to the employment arbitrator associated with ruling in favor of the employee when management's case is strong. In employment arbitration, employers (but not employees) may be seen as repeat players by the employment arbitrator (Bingham 1997). As such, ruling against the employer when the employer's case is strong (due to a reluctance to use termination) is likely to strongly affect acceptability of the arbitrator within the employer community. While this same effect is likely within labor arbitration, the perceived costs may be less because labor unions also play a significant role in arbitrator selection. Therefore, the costs of damaging acceptability with the employer community may be seen as somewhat offset by increased acceptability with the other side. Taken together, these arguments suggest that employment arbitrators are more likely than labor arbitrators to rule in favor of the employer when the case against the employee is strong.

Findings

The mean rating in terms of the likelihood of overturning termination for both labor arbitrators and employment arbitrators examining statutory claims is shown in Table 5.6. Also, as will be the case with other tables in this chapter, *t*-values for the differences between the means are shown for each case, and tested for statistical significance to see whether the differences observed in our sample are sufficiently likely (at least 95 percent) to be present in the universe from which the sample is drawn.

Note that differences are not reported in Table 5.6 for Cases 1, 4, 5, and 6, in order to limit this comparison to labor arbitrators and employment arbitrators who were considering only a statutory claim. For these four cases that are not reported in Table 5.6, the employment arbitrators were instructed to respond as if there was a for-cause statement in the employment agreement. These four cases are reported in Table 5.7 (which is for employment arbitrators who received the for-cause condition).

The analysis in Table 5.6 compares—with the decisions of labor arbitrators—only the decisions of those employment arbitrators who were deciding whether there was a statutory violation. Of the eight

Table 5.6 Pairwise Comparisons: Mean Differences between Labor Arbitrators and Employment Arbitrators Evaluating Statutory Claims

Case number	Mean rating for labor arbitrators	Mean rating for employment arbitrators evaluating statutory claims	*t*-value for mean difference
Case 1	2.89	—	—
Case 2	3.00	2.39	3.60**
Case 3	5.92	4.29	10.02**
Case 4	5.05	—	—
Case 5	4.25	—	—
Case 6	4.06	—	—
Case 7	2.73	2.22	3.27**
Case 8	5.49	3.67	9.05**
Case 9	4.67	4.49	0.97
Case 10	4.57	3.32	6.62**
Case 11	5.56	4.05	7.47**
Case 12	4.70	3.50	5.84**

NOTE: Ratings were on a 1 to 7 scale, where 7 indicates a high likelihood of overturning the termination and 1 indicates a low likelihood of overturning the termination; — = not applicable; **$p < 0.01$.

cases analyzed in Table 5.6, significant differences were observed in all but one. For Case 9, while the difference was in the direction expected (i.e., labor arbitrators were more likely to rule in favor of the employee than employment arbitrators), the difference was not significant. It is important to note that Case 9 was the only case in which there was substantial evidence of discrimination. While we expected a difference in outcome in Case 9 because of differences in the burden of proof, and in the interests and identification patterns of the decision makers, these results did not significantly support this expectation.

It is also interesting to note that a significant difference was observed when the case against the employee was strong and there were no countervailing procedural problems or mitigating factors. This was true in Case 2 and Case 7. In both of these cases, a significant mean difference is observed, which is consistent with our argument that employment arbitrators have a stronger incentive to overcome any reluctance to terminate when there is a strong case against the employee. It should also be noted, however, that the mean difference for Case 2 and Case 7 is substantially smaller than for cases where there are potential violations of the just cause standard. This suggests, consistent with differences in how the decision task is structured, that differences between employment and labor arbitrators will increase when potential employer just cause violations are present.

Labor Arbitrators vs. Employment Arbitrators with "For-Cause" Requirements

Expectations

Fewer differences are likely to be observed between labor arbitrators and those employment arbitrators who are required to apply a "for-cause" standard. When the employment agreement specifies that termination must be "for-cause," employment arbitrators can find for the employee even if they fail to find evidence of discrimination. Accordingly, factors such as evidence of employee wrongdoing and lack of compliance with proper procedures on the part of the employer are likely to play a more significant role, making it easier for the employment arbitrator to rule in favor of the employee. However, some research indicates that employment arbitrators are less likely to rule in favor of the employee, even where a "for-cause" standard exists (Bingham and Mesch 2000).

What is less clear is why such differences exist. One possible explanation is that, relative to labor arbitrators, employment arbitrators consider a smaller set of factors when determining whether there is just cause. In labor arbitration, strong norms exist regarding the determinants of just cause. These norms may give emphasis to factors that might be deemed less relevant when judging a case from the standpoint of traditional contract law requirements (Cooper, Nolan, and Bales 2000). It is possible, for example, that employment arbitrators would give less emphasis to mitigating and extenuating factors, which have traditionally been considered by labor arbitrators. Where such mitigating circumstances are present, we would expect that labor arbitrators would be more reluctant to rule in favor of the employer than would employment arbitrators. This prediction is likely to depend, however, on the background of the employment arbitrator. Some employment arbitrators have worked extensively in labor arbitration. It may well be that they would utilize norms from labor arbitration when judging "for-cause" cases. So, while a sample of employment arbitrators is likely to behave differently from a sample of labor arbitrators, there is likely to be variation across employment arbitrators as to the degree to which any such difference is observed.

Clearly, however, it is likely that some factors relevant in labor arbitration from a just cause standpoint would be of equal relevance when evaluating—from a more narrow framework—whether there is cause for termination. For example, evidence of employee wrongdoing and employer compliance (with its written policies and procedures) are likely to be critical in employment arbitration when a "for-cause" requirement exists in the employment agreement (Cooper, Nolan, and Bales 2000). Because such factors would be relevant in both employment and labor arbitration, one might expect little difference in outcomes when a termination case centers around a lack of evidence and/or clear employer procedural violations.

It was argued earlier that employment arbitrators assessing whether there is a statutory violation would be less likely than labor arbitrators to rule in favor of the employee when there is weak evidence of both discrimination and just cause for termination. One reason that was offered for this expected difference is that while there is a natural reluctance to support termination, this reluctance might be more limited among employment arbitrators because they could find for the employee only by concluding there was illegal discrimination—a significant accusation. Where a "for-cause" standard exists, employment arbitrators can—like labor arbitrators—find for the employee by simply declaring that evidence of cause was not shown. As such, the difference between employment and labor arbitrators might be less significant in instances where the case against the employee is strong if a "for-cause" standard exists. However, differences might still be expected. The repeat-player argument (Bingham 1997) still applies, as does the argument that suggests that employment arbitrators (to the extent that they have served as management-side advocates) may identify psychologically with the management team. Both arguments suggest factors that would counter the natural reluctance to terminate which would otherwise be expected among decision makers.

Findings

Table 5.7 compares decisions made by employment arbitrators, when a for-cause standard exists in the employment arbitration agreement to decisions made by labor arbitrators. As can be seen in Table 5.7, the likelihood of a ruling in favor of the employee was higher for labor arbitrators than for employment arbitrators with a for-cause requirement for all of the cases analyzed, and significantly so for all cases except Cases 5 and 9. With Case 5, there is only modest evidence against the employee. No other just cause violations by the employer were present. The lack of a difference between labor and employment arbitrators with this case is understandable since strength of the evidence is likely to be a for-cause factor considered heavily by both labor and employment arbitrators. With Case 9, there were two possible problems with management's case against the employee. First, there was substantial evidence of discrimination. Second, the evidence of the employee's misconduct was modest at best. These are factors that would be expected to be relevant to employment arbitrators with a for-cause requirement and, as such, it is understandable that no difference was observed between employment and labor arbitrators in this case.

It is interesting to note that Cases 4, 6, 8, 10, 11, and 12 contained possible just cause concerns relating to the reasonableness of the rule,

Table 5.7 Pairwise Comparisons: Mean Differences between Labor Arbitrators and Employment Arbitrators with For-Cause Requirements

Case number	Mean rating for labor arbitrators	Mean rating for employment arbitrators with for-cause requirements	*t*-value for mean difference
Case 1	2.89	2.22	3.52**
Case 2	3.00	—	—
Case 3	5.92	—	—
Case 4	5.05	4.12	4.27**
Case 5	4.25	4.05	1.24
Case 6	4.06	3.27	3.85**
Case 7	2.73	2.33	2.42*
Case 8	5.49	4.59	5.31**
Case 9	4.67	4.38	1.57
Case 10	4.57	3.71	4.71**
Case 11	5.56	4.26	7.26**
Case 12	4.70	3.62	5.44**

NOTE: Ratings were on a 1 to 7 scale, where 7 indicates a high likelihood of overturning the termination and 1 indicates a low likelihood of overturning the termination; — = not applicable; $*p < 0.05$; $**p < 0.01$.

mitigating circumstances, or procedural compliance by the employer. The significant difference between labor and employment arbitrators for these cases could be explained by the argument that employment arbitrators are less likely to consider some of these factors that are traditionally a part of just cause determinations in labor arbitration, even where a for-cause requirement exists. For example, we argued earlier that reasonableness of the rule and employee work history might be less relevant to employment arbitrators. While we expected that procedural compliance on the part of the employer would be equally relevant to both employment arbitrators with a for-cause requirement and labor arbitrators, the labor arbitrators were significantly more likely to rule for the employee where procedural compliance was questionable.

As with employment arbitrators evaluating statutory claims, employment arbitrators with a for-cause requirement were less likely than labor arbitrators to overturn terminations when the case against the employee was relatively strong and there were no obvious just cause violations on the part of the employer (Cases 1 and 7). It is difficult to attribute this to differences in how the decision task is structured. As such, it might be argued, consistent with points made earlier, that a difference in the interests of the decision makers may be a relevant explanatory factor.

Labor Arbitrators vs. Peer Review Panelists

Expectations

In thinking about how peer review panelists might differ from labor arbitrators, it is important to consider differences in the way the decision task is structured, as well as the interests and backgrounds of the panelists. With regard to how the decision task is structured, peer review panelists are asked to determine whether a termination is consistent with disciplinary rules and procedures established by the firm (Ewing 1989). In many ways, this is a narrower test of "cause" than just cause standards applied within labor arbitration, and may produce differences between labor arbitrators and peer review panelists in certain types of cases. For example, to the extent that peer review panelists adhere to their guidelines, they would be less likely than labor arbitrators to consider the reasonableness of the company rule.

With regard to differing interests, one must consider that peer review panelists are reviewing a termination decision made by their employer. Permitting a problem employee to continue with the firm may well be seen by them to be a threat to the safe and productive operation of the firm. Thus, where the firm is able to offer substantial evidence of wrongdoing, peers may feel that it is in their interest to support the termination. This tendency among peers would be likely to check any reluctance to terminate that might otherwise be present among decision makers when the case against the employee is strong but not incontrovertible (Klaas and Feldman 1993). Further, while some might argue that peers will identify psychologically with the employee who has been terminated, that sense of identification might be limited if the organization can provide evidence of wrongdoing. Peer review panelists are not randomly drawn from the population. Both self-selection and organizational selection (if only through past disciplinary and dismissal decisions) are likely to create a pool of individuals that have experienced the consequences of working with deficient employees within their own work group (Ewing 1989). As a result of this experience, peer review panelists might well identify more with the managers who initiated the termination than with the accused employee. This tendency to identify with the manager bringing charges (rather than the accused employee) may be even greater where it can be shown that the employee has a history of problem behavior, and thus is increasingly seen by productive members of the group as a "deviant" (Feldman 1984). Further, when employees are asked to serve on a peer review panel, they are being asked to participate in a management function—further increasing the tendency to identify with the management team rather than the employee labeled as a "deviant" (Turner 1984; Tajfel 1979).

Exceptions to the expected tendency to favor management may exist, however. Where the problem behavior cited by management is seen as an aberration—caused by something largely beyond the employee's control—peers may well be inclined to identify with the employee rather than management. Further, as members of the same social organization as the employee, peers are likely to implicitly calculate the employee's idiosyncrasy credits (Hollander 1958; Feldman 1984). Where the employee has accumulated credits through a long history of effective contribution, peers are likely to tolerate some level of idiosyncrasy if it can be attributed to an aberration beyond the employee's control. This suggests that peers would be expected to be more likely to rule in favor of the employer than labor arbitrators, unless the employee has accumulated idiosyncrasy credits and the employee's deficiency can be treated as an aberration caused by events beyond his or her control.

In sum, differences might be expected between peers and labor arbitrators—with labor arbitrators expected to be more likely than peers to rule in favor of the employee. Exceptions to this are expected, however, when the employee's deficiency can both be attributed to an external cause and is inconsistent with a history of effective contribution.

Findings

Table 5.8 displays the pairwise comparisons between labor arbitrators and peer review panelists. As was expected, based on differences

Table 5.8 Pairwise Comparisons: Mean Differences between Labor Arbitrators and Peer Review Panelists

Case number	Mean rating for labor arbitrators	Mean rating for peer review panelists	t-value for mean difference
Case 1	2.89	3.45	2.30*
Case 2	3.00	3.19	0.86
Case 3	5.92	5.44	2.72**
Case 4	5.05	3.88	4.62**
Case 5	4.25	3.01	5.48**
Case 6	4.06	3.96	0.40
Case 7	2.73	2.23	3.23**
Case 8	5.49	4.78	3.98**
Case 9	4.67	4.03	3.49**
Case 10	4.57	4.21	1.84*
Case 11	5.56	5.11	2.40**
Case 12	4.70	4.53	0.80

NOTE: Ratings were on a 1 to 7 scale, where 7 indicates a high likelihood of overturning the termination and 1 indicates a low likelihood of overturning the termination; * $p < 0.05$; ** $p < 0.01$.

in the decision task, interests, and identification tendencies, the likelihood of ruling in favor of the employee was significantly higher for labor arbitrators in 8 of the 12 cases examined. In one case (Case 1), peers were significantly more likely to rule in favor of the employee. No significant difference was observed between peers and labor arbitrators in Cases 2, 6, and 12. One possible explanation for the lack of significance in Cases 6 and 12 is that both cases addressed situations where the employee's poor performance could easily be attributed to personal problems that were beyond the employee's control and were unlikely to continue to be a problem in the future. While termination may be consistent with company policy in such a circumstance, the extenuating circumstances may have preempted any labeling of the employee as a "deviant," making it more likely that peers would identify with the employee. Further, in Case 6, the employee had long tenure and no significant problems with his or her work record, which suggests that peers (as members of the same social group) might have been more willing to grant the employee idiosyncrasy credits when making their decision.

While we expected labor arbitrators to be at least as likely as peers to rule in favor of employees when the case against the employee was strong, the results were mixed in this regard. Cases 1 and 2 presented strong cases against the employee. In Case 1, peers were significantly more likely to rule in favor of employees. In Case 2, the same result was present in the sample, although the results were not significant. What these cases have in common is that, in both cases, the employee's case was based entirely on unsupported, self-serving assertions that someone else was at fault. It may be that these lay judges are more likely to give credence to such contentions than are professionals.

Where issues such as reasonableness of the rule, procedural compliance, mitigating factors relating to the employee's work history, and evidence of discrimination were present in the case, labor arbitrators were more likely than peers to rule in favor of the employee (Cases 3, 4, 5, 8, 9, 10, and 11). This might suggest, consistent with differences in the way the decision task is structured, that labor arbitrators consider a broader range of factors when determining whether termination is justified.

Labor Arbitrators vs. Jurors

Expectations

Labor arbitrators and jurors are both third parties. Unlike peers, jurors are not dependent on the employer. Further, neither self-selection nor organizational selection (through past discipline and dismissal decisions) affect participation on the jury panel. Moreover, unlike peers, jurors are not being asked by management to assist with an important management function. These points make it less likely that jurors would identify with the management team. Indeed, anecdotally, it is often suggested that jurors tend to identify with the plaintiff (Abbott 1993). As such, some of the factors that are thought to create differences between labor arbitrators and peer review panelists might not be operative with regard to jurors. However, we would argue that the structure of the decision task would result in jurors being less likely to rule in favor of the employee across a number of different types of cases.

In discrimination cases, jurors are asked to evaluate whether there was illegal discrimination—not whether the termination was fair or just. Judicial instructions typically emphasize what factors jurors are to consider when making their determination, and these factors differ from what is typically considered in labor arbitration. Accordingly, in termination cases where the employee claims that termination is not justified and that there was illegal discrimination, labor arbitrators will be more likely than jurors to find for the employee if there is little evidence of discrimination but some evidence of a just cause violation on the part of the employer. However, differences are not likely to be observed between labor arbitrators and jurors when there is evidence of discrimination. While labor arbitration is not typically viewed as a forum for addressing statutory cases where the employee claims a failure to show just cause, plausible evidence of discrimination is likely to call into question evidence of wrongdoing by the employee. As such, differences would not be expected between jurors and labor arbitrators when plausible evidence of discrimination is present.

It should be noted that differences exist between jurors and labor arbitrators in terms of burden of proof. As is the case with employment arbitration judging claims of a statutory violation, with juries the plaintiff must provide the initial evidence of discrimination (Bennett-Alexander and Hartman 2001). But with labor arbitration, the employer bears the burden of proving just cause. We argued previously that, as a result, labor arbitrators would be more likely than employment arbitrators to find for the employee in cases where there is plausible but inconclusive evidence of discrimination and some indication of a just cause violation by the employer. We do not argue, however, that such a difference will be observed with jurors. This argument is premised on the assumption that jurors would be more likely to identify with the plaintiff and that they have no personal interest in the outcome. As such, jurors are unlikely to be affected by the higher burden of proof standard where plausible but inconclusive evidence of discrimination exists.

However, we would expect that the difference in the burden of proof would affect decisions in cases where there is weak evidence of discrimination and the case against the employee is substantial but not incontrovertible. Under such circumstances, there would be little basis for concluding that the employee met his/her burden of providing evidence of discrimination. However, when there is still some ambiguity about whether the employee committed the offense alleged, it is at least plausible to conclude that the employer failed to demonstrate just cause. While we are not suggesting that labor arbitrators would—on average—be likely to rule in favor of the employee, we are suggesting that labor arbitrators—as a group—would be more likely to rule in favor of the employee than would jurors.

Not all jury cases revolve around issues of discrimination; some cases revolve around contract issues. Where there is an employment agreement that stipulates that termination will be for-cause, we would expect fewer differences between jurors and labor arbitrators.

In sum, we expect that labor arbitrators will be more likely than jurors to rule in favor of the employee under different conditions. These conditions include 1) when there is little evidence of discrimination, combined with some evidence of a just cause violation by the employer, and 2) when there is weak evidence of discrimination, in combination with substantial but inconclusive evidence of a just cause for the termination. However, no difference would be expected when there is plausible but inconclusive evidence of discrimination, and fewer differences would be expected in cases that revolve around contractual issues relating to for-cause provisions.

Findings

Table 5.9 presents the pairwise comparisons for labor arbitrators and jurors. In 8 of the 12 cases, labor arbitrators indicated that they were significantly more likely than jurors to rule in favor of the employee. Interestingly, and contrary to what we expected, labor arbitrators indicated that they would be more likely than jurors to rule in favor of the employee, even when there was substantial evidence of discrimination (Case 9). However, consistent with what was suggested earlier, labor arbitrators were significantly more likely to overturn terminations in a number of instances where a possible just cause violation by the employer was present (Cases 3, 8, and 10). A similar difference is observed in only one of the two cases where there was weak or no evidence of discrimination, no lack of evidence of employee wrongdoing, and no other obvious just cause violations (Case 7). It was suggested that labor arbitrators might be more willing to rule in favor of the employee under such conditions because of differences in the burden of proof. The support for this is mixed, at best.

In those cases where both the jurors and labor arbitrators were deciding whether there was a violation of an employment agreement

Table 5.9 Pairwise Comparisons: Mean Differences between Labor Arbitrators and Jurors from Employment Discrimination Cases

Case number	Mean rating for labor arbitrators	Mean rating for jurors	t-value for mean difference
Case 1	2.89	3.15	1.10
Case 2	3.00	2.43	3.05**
Case 3	5.92	4.58	6.33**
Case 4	5.05	3.78	5.39**
Case 5	4.25	3.96	1.28
Case 6	4.06	3.40	2.67**
Case 7	2.73	2.28	2.22*
Case 8	5.49	4.60	4.80**
Case 9	4.67	4.07	2.83**
Case 10	4.57	3.70	4.32**
Case 11	5.56	5.36	0.90
Case 12	4.70	4.57	0.54

NOTE: Ratings were on a 1 to 7 scale, where 7 indicates a high likelihood of overturning the termination and 1 indicates a low likelihood of overturning the termination; $*p < 0.05$; $**p < 0.01$.

that promised that terminations would be only for-cause (Cases 1, 4, 5, and 6), labor arbitrators were more likely to rule for the employee in two of the four cases—Case 4 (where reasonableness of the rule is in question) and Case 6 (where personal problems were a possible mitigating factor). In Cases 1 and 5, the employees had short tenure. Also, jurors, like their fellow nonprofessional peer review panelists, score relatively high (3.15) on overturning the termination in Case 1, where the only fact in the employee's favor is an unsupported claim that others are at fault.

Labor Arbitrators vs. HR Managers

Expectations

In many nonunion organizations, those performing the HR function play a key role in determining whether a termination is approved. The HR role stems from a desire to ensure consistency across the organization and to prevent possible legal action against the organization. In some cases, HR managers are assigned this role to help promote effective employee relations, and thus maintain a nonunion status (Klaas and Feldman 1993). The HR manager is clearly part of the management team, and therefore may identify with the needs and interests of managers bringing disciplinary action (Tajfel 1981). Further, as agents of management, they have an interest (as do peer review panelists) in ensuring the safe and effective operation of the workforce. However, HR managers also have an interest in avoiding legal action against the firm and remaining nonunion. Indeed, given the visibility and salience of both legal action and union organizing drives (and the degree to which they would be held personally accountable for such events), HR managers are likely to be motivated to prevent terminations if there is a significant risk of successful legal action or damage to employee relations.

As a group, then, we would expect that HR managers would likely be influenced by the presence of evidence regarding illegal discrimination. Where plausible but inconclusive evidence exists regarding discrimination, we would expect that HR managers would be motivated to avoid legal risks (Colvin 2003). In such cases, we would expect that HR managers would be as likely as labor arbitrators to find for the employee. Similarly, where there are significant just cause violations by the employer, we would expect that concern for effective employee relations would motivate HR managers to discourage termination, taking positions very similar to those of labor arbitrators.

We would, however, expect some differences between HR managers and labor arbitrators. Where the case against the employee is strong (with no potential just cause violation by the employer and little evidence of discrimination), we would expect that HR managers would have a stronger incentive to terminate. When termination poses few risks to the organization, we would expect that HR managers— motivated by a desire to ensure the safe and effective operation of the firm—would be more likely to overcome any reluctance to terminate that might be present among other decision makers. We also would expect that HR managers—as agents of management—would be more likely to rule against the employee when the employee's work history creates concerns about the employee's impact on the safe and effective operation of the firm—even if there were concerns about the way management handled the case procedurally. This same tendency would also be predicted if HR managers—as part of the same social organization as the employee—are more likely to apply the logic of idiosyncrasy credits (Hollander 1958). To repeat what was suggested in the discussion of peer review panelists, the idiosyncrasy credits argument holds that persons may grant others in the same social organization credits for past contributions. By the same token, where past difficulties create a deficit status for idiosyncrasy credits, such decision makers may take harsher action than would otherwise be expected.

Overall, then, while we expect some similarity between decisions made by labor arbitrators and those made by HR managers, we expect HR managers to be more willing to terminate when the case against the employee is strong. We also expect HR managers to be more willing to overlook procedural just cause violations when there is no lack of evidence against the employee, and a negative work history.

Findings

Table 5.10 presents the results of the pairwise comparisons between labor arbitrators and HR managers. Here, we expected few differences when there was plausible evidence of discrimination. Consistent with this, no difference was observed in Case 9, the case

Table 5.10 Pairwise Comparisons: Mean Differences between Labor Arbitrators and HR Managers

Case number	Mean rating for labor arbitrators	Mean rating for HR managers	t-value for mean difference
Case 1	2.89	2.75	0.56
Case 2	3.00	2.71	1.21
Case 3	5.92	5.19	3.47**
Case 4	5.05	4.43	2.36**
Case 5	4.25	3.15	4.64
Case 6	4.06	3.92	0.50
Case 7	2.73	2.07	4.06**
Case 8	5.49	5.19	1.64
Case 9	4.67	4.50	0.79
Case 10	4.57	4.19	1.73*
Case 11	5.56	5.17	1.93*
Case 12	4.70	4.80	0.45

NOTE: Ratings were on a 1 to 7 scale, where 7 indicates a high likelihood of overturning the termination and 1 indicates a low likelihood of overturning the termination; $*p < 0.05$; $**p < 0.01$.

where there was substantial evidence of discrimination. Both groups were likely to overturn the termination. We also expected labor arbitrators to be more likely to rule for the employee when the case against the employee was strong, and there was little or no evidence of illegal discrimination by the firm. While this was supported by Case 7, significant differences were not observed in Cases 1 or 2. Differences were observed in Case 3, where there was modest evidence of discrimination, modest evidence against the employee, procedural problems, and a positive employee work record. Even where statistically significant differences existed, however, labor arbitrators and HR managers tended to agree with respect to overturning the termination decision (Cases 3 and 11), supporting the termination decision (Case 7), or being uncertain (Case 10). Similarly, in Case 4, where the case revolved around the reasonableness of the rule, labor arbitrators were more willing to rule in favor of the employee. Finally, labor arbitrators were more willing to rule in favor of the employee in Case 10, where modest evidence against the employee is combined with provocation by management, and Case 11, where modest evidence against the employee is combined with long tenure. It appears, then, at least to some degree, that labor arbitrators were more likely to consider possible just cause violations by the employer, and long tenure on the part of the employee, than were HR managers. While the differences were not large, they were statistically significant.

Employment Arbitrators Evaluating Statutory Claims vs. Employment Arbitrators with "For-Cause" Requirements

Expectations

We would expect no difference in the interests, background, or experience of employment arbitrators evaluating statutory claims and those evaluating a case where a "for-cause" requirement exists in the employment agreement. The primary difference would lie in terms of how the decision task is structured. Where statutory claims are being assessed, we would expect that the primary focus would be on evidence regarding discrimination. Other factors may sometimes be seen as relevant, but only to the extent that they inform judgments regarding the presence or absence of discrimination. Thus, we would expect employment arbitrators with for-cause requirements to be more likely to rule in favor of the employee when there is little evidence of discrimination, but questionable evidence of employee wrongdoing and/or evidence that the firm failed to comply with its own policies and procedures. The increased willingness to find in favor of the employee should be heightened by the fact that where for-cause requirements exist, the arbitrator can find for the employee by making the less controversial finding that there was a lack of cause (rather than that there was discrimination).

As discussed above, while there are other just cause tests used in labor arbitration, such as requiring that actions be consistent with company policy and taking into account mitigating circumstances, it is unclear whether these other tests would be used in employment arbitration where for-cause requirements exist (Cooper, Nolan, and Bales 2000). While such tests might actually be used by those who have experience as a labor arbitrator, the focus may be more restricted for those with a background as a judge or an advocate. Accordingly, we propose that differences due to the for-cause requirement will be observed only when the case revolves around problems with evidence against the employee or a lack of procedural compliance on the part of the employer.

Findings

Table 5.11 presents the comparison between employment arbitrators who received the statutory claim instructions and employment arbitrators who received the for-cause instructions (for Cases 7 through 12). Of the six cases examined here, significant differences were found in two cases (Cases 8 and 10), with employment arbitrators in the for-cause condition being more likely to overturn termination. The primary reason for expecting differences here are the differences in the way that their decision tasks are structured. No difference was expected for Case 7 (because there was a strong case against the employee) or in Case 9 (where the presence of substantial evidence of discrimination would mean that both sets of arbitrators would have had justification to rule in favor of the employee). Differences were observed, however, with employment arbitrators operating under the just cause requirement being more likely to find in favor of the employee when only modest

Table 5.11 Pairwise Comparisons: Mean Differences between Employment Arbitrators Evaluating Statutory Claims and Employment Arbitrators with For-Cause Requirements

Case number	Mean rating for employment arbitrators evaluating statutory claims	Mean rating for employment arbitrators with for-cause requirements	t-value for mean difference
Case 1	—	2.22	—
Case 2	2.39	—	—
Case 3	4.29	—	—
Case 4	—	4.12	—
Case 5	—	4.05	—
Case 6	—	3.27	—
Case 7	2.22	2.33	0.75
Case 8	3.67	4.59	4.09**
Case 9	4.49	4.38	0.53
Case 10	3.32	3.71	1.82*
Case 11	4.05	4.26	0.86
Case 12	3.50	3.62	0.59

NOTE: Ratings were on a 1 to 7 scale, where 7 indicates a high likelihood of overturning the termination and 1 indicates a low likelihood of overturning the termination; — = not applicable; $*p < 0.05$; $**p < 0.01$.

evidence against the employee was combined with procedural problems (Case 8), and when modest evidence against the employee was combined with provocation by management (Case 10). These findings provide some evidence that a for-cause requirement affects decisions by encouraging the consideration of possible just cause violations on the part of the employer.

Employment Arbitrators Evaluating Statutory Claims vs. Peer Review Panelists

Expectations

Differences between employment arbitrators evaluating statutory claims and peer review panelists would be expected because of differences in how their decision tasks are structured. It is the difference between a decision maker who is asked to determine whether a statutory violation has occurred and a decision maker who is asked to determine if the termination is consistent with company policy and procedures. Assessing whether a termination is consistent with company policy and procedures is likely to require that decision makers give consideration only to whether the firm complied with its own procedures and whether there is evidence that supports the allegations against the employee (Ewing 1989). However, these issues—by themselves—are less likely to be relevant in determining whether a statutory violation occurred. We would therefore expect that peer review panelists would be more likely to find for the employee when there is some evidence of discrimination and weak evidence of employee wrongdoing and/or evidence of a lack of procedural compliance by the employer.

While employment arbitrators and peer review panelists have different interest profiles, backgrounds, and reasons for identifying with different parties to the termination case, in many instances these differences will result in similar evaluation tendencies. For example, the repeat-player argument (Bingham 1997) suggests that employment arbitrators have an incentive to avoid ruling for the employee simply out of sympathy. Similarly, as employees of the firm, peers have an incentive to make decisions that support the safe and effective operation of the firm (Klaas and Feldman 1993), and thus, an incentive to take harsh action if evidence suggests a pattern of behavior problems.

Having said this, different types of decisions might still be expected under specific circumstances, because of differences in interests, backgrounds, and reasons for identifying with the parties to the termination. First, as noted above, as members of the same social organization as the employee, peers are likely to implicitly calculate idiosyncrasy credits (Hollander 1958; Feldman 1984). Where an employee has accumulated credits through an effective work history, peers may be more lenient toward the employee if it appears that the recently observed problems are likely to be corrected or are due to an external cause. Second, following this same logic, where idiosyncrasy credits are in deficit status, particularly where no external attribution is possible, peers may be more likely to terminate an employee even if there is some other problem with management's case against the employee. Whereas employment arbitrators may focus more tightly on whether there is evidence of discrimination, as members of the same social organization as the employee, peers may give weight to idiosyncrasy credits and thus arrive at decisions that differ—in some cases—from employment arbitrators.

Findings

Table 5.12 compares the decisions made by employment arbitrators evaluating statutory claims to those made by peer review panelists. As expected, in light of the way the decision task is structured, peer review panelists were significantly more likely to rule in favor of the employee in six of the eight cases analyzed, all of which are summarized in Table 5.1. Interestingly, the mean rating for employment arbitrators was significantly higher in Case 9, where there was substantial evidence of discrimination combined with modest evidence against the employee, who also had a short tenure. This result might well be expected if

Table 5.12 Pairwise Comparisons: Mean Differences between Employment Arbitrators Evaluating Statutory Claims and Peer Review Panelists

Case number	Mean rating for employment arbitrators evaluating statutory claims	Mean rating for peer review panelist	t-value for mean difference
Case 1	—	3.45	—
Case 2	2.39	3.19	4.37**
Case 3	4.29	5.44	7.08**
Case 4	—	3.88	—
Case 5	—	3.01	—
Case 6	—	3.96	—
Case 7	2.22	2.23	0.02
Case 8	3.67	4.78	5.00**
Case 9	4.49	4.03	2.33*
Case 10	3.32	4.21	4.11**
Case 11	4.05	5.11	4.67**
Case 12	3.50	4.53	4.66**

NOTE: Ratings were on a 1 to 7 scale, where 7 indicates a high likelihood of overturning the termination and 1 indicates a low likelihood of overturning the termination; — = not applicable; *$p < 0.05$; **$p < 0.01$.

indeed peers implicitly use the logic of idiosyncrasy credits to a greater degree than employment arbitrators, taking the short tenure into account more strongly than did the employment arbitrators. Both sets of decision makers were equally negative on the employee's case in Case 7, where there was strong evidence against the employee and a history of prior warnings.

Employment Arbitrators Evaluating Statutory Claims vs. Jurors

Expectations

The decision tasks for employment arbitrators evaluating statutory claims and jurors are, in essence, the same. As such, no differences in outcomes would be expected on this basis. There might, however, be differences in interests, backgrounds, and psychological identification tendencies. For example, some decision makers—when asked to determine whether there is a statutory violation—might be influenced by whether they believed the termination was fair (independent of evidence of discrimination). With employment arbitrators, however, there are factors that might limit this tendency. First, their legal backgrounds may make evidence of discrimination (or the lack thereof) more salient to their decision process. Second, it is unlikely to be in their interest to rule in favor of the employee if there is no evidence of discrimination. The repeat-player argument (Bingham 1997) would suggest that arbitrators may face personal costs (in terms of acceptability by the employer community) if they do anything other than assess whether or not there was a statutory violation. As such, we might expect that jurors would be more likely than employment arbitrators to find for the employee in cases where there was a significant just cause violation by the employer. While jury instructions may limit the degree to which attention is given to such factors (MacCoun 1989), the incentives and backgrounds of employment arbitrators lead us to believe that they will be less likely than jurors to be influenced by the presence of possible just cause violations by the employer.

Differences might also be observed when there is plausible but inconclusive evidence of discrimination. Judgment would be required to determine whether the employee met the burden of proof. It may be that jurors would be more likely to err on the side of the employee than would the employment arbitrator. This difference would be expected if, in fact, jurors would be more likely than employment arbitrators to psychologically identify with the plaintiff (Turner 1984) and/or if there is some legitimacy to the repeat-player argument.

Findings

Table 5.13 presents the differences between employment arbitrators evaluating statutory claims and jurors. Of the eight cases where comparisons are possible, jurors were significantly more likely to rule in favor of the employee in four instances. These were instances where there were mitigating conditions (procedural noncompliance, long tenure, or the employee had family problems) or provocation present. A significant difference in the other direction is observed in the case (Case 9) where there was substantial evidence of discrimination. These results suggest that jurors may have been more likely to pay attention to

Table 5.13 Pairwise Comparisons: Mean Differences between Employment Arbitrators Evaluating Statutory Claims and Jurors from Employment Discrimination Cases

Case number	Mean rating for employment arbitrators evaluating statutory claims	Mean rating for jurors	t-value for mean difference
Case 1	—	3.15	—
Case 2	2.39	2.43	0.22
Case 3	4.29	4.58	1.45
Case 4	—	3.78	—
Case 5	—	3.96	—
Case 6	—	3.40	—
Case 7	2.22	2.28	0.32
Case 8	3.67	4.60	3.99**
Case 9	4.49	4.07	1.83*
Case 10	3.32	3.70	1.67*
Case 11	4.05	5.36	5.05**
Case 12	3.50	4.57	4.31**

NOTE: Ratings were on a 1 to 7 scale, where 7 indicates a high likelihood of overturning the termination and 1 indicates a low likelihood of overturning the termination; — = not applicable; $*p < 0.05$; $**p < 0.01$.

issues other than simply whether there was evidence of discrimination. Given that the decision task is structured similarly for both employment arbitrators evaluating statutory claims and jurors, the differences observed may be due to differences in interests and tendencies regarding identification processes (with jurors being more likely to identify with the employee, and employment arbitrators being more likely to identify with the employer).

Employment Arbitrators Evaluating Statutory Claims vs. HR Managers

Expectations

Because of differences in the way their decision tasks are structured, we would expect that HR managers would be more likely to rule in favor of the employee in cases where there is little evidence of discrimination if there are questions about evidence of wrongdoing or compliance with organizational policies and procedures. Concern about maintaining effective employee relations and consistency would be likely to cause the HR manager to give weight to at least some just cause considerations (Klaas and Feldman 1993). Differences might also stem from the likelihood that HR managers (as part of the same social organization as the employee) will apply the logic of idiosyncrasy credits. As such, they may give more weight to a positive work history. Where there is evidence of discrimination, however, no differences are expected. Similarly, where the evidence against the employee is strong and there is no evidence of discrimination, no difference is expected between employment arbitrators evaluating statutory claims and HR managers.

Findings

Table 5.14 displays the differences between employment arbitrators evaluating statutory claims and HR managers. As can be seen, significantly higher ratings were observed for HR managers in five of the eight cases (summarized in Table 5.1) where comparisons were possible. The only exceptions were two cases in which the employee's case was very weak (Cases 2 and 7), in which both sets of decision makers supported the termination, and in the case where there was

Table 5.14 Pairwise Comparisons: Mean Differences between Employment Arbitrators Evaluating Statutory Claims and HR Managers

Case number	Mean rating for employment arbitrators evaluating statutory claims	Mean rating for HR managers	t-value for mean difference
Case 1	—	2.75	—
Case 2	2.39	2.71	1.60
Case 3	4.29	5.19	4.48**
Case 4	—	4.43	—
Case 5	—	3.15	—
Case 6	—	3.92	—
Case 7	2.22	2.07	1.16
Case 8	3.67	5.19	4.09**
Case 9	4.49	4.50	0.03
Case 10	3.32	4.19	3.48**
Case 11	4.05	5.17	4.34**
Case 12	3.50	4.80	5.24**

NOTE: Ratings were on a 1 to 7 scale, where 7 indicates a high likelihood of overturning the termination and 1 indicates a low likelihood of overturning the termination; — = not applicable; $*p < 0.05$; $**p < 0.01$.

substantial evidence of discrimination (Case 9), in which both groups favored the employee. This suggests that HR managers are more likely to consider factors relating to potential just cause violations. This pattern is consistent with what was predicted in light of differences in the decision task, and also differences in interests and identification tendencies.

Employment Arbitrators with "For-Cause" Requirements vs. Peer Review Panelists

Expectations

Few differences would be expected between employment arbitrators with a for-cause requirement and peer review panelists. Both are instructed to consider factors that go beyond the issue of a statutory violation, and as such, both would give consideration to whether there was evidence of employee wrongdoing and whether there was procedural compliance by the employer. Further, decision maker interests and identification processes would be likely to create similar evaluation tendencies. Two exceptions might be expected: First, as argued previously, as members of the same social organization as the employee, peers are likely to implicitly calculate idiosyncrasy credits (Hollander 1958). Where an employee has accumulated credits through an effective work history, peers may be more lenient toward the employee if it appears that the problems recently observed are likely to be corrected or are due to an external cause. Second, following this same logic, where idiosyncrasy credits are in deficit status, particularly where no external attribution is possible, peers may be more likely to terminate an employee even if there is some evidence of discrimination (Feldman 1984). Whereas evidence of discrimination is likely to be highly salient to employment arbitrators (regardless of whether the case is an at-will or a for-cause case), since peers are part of the same social organization as the employee, they may give more weight to idiosyncrasy credits (or the lack thereof). As such, in some specific cases, employment arbitrators with a for-cause requirement may arrive at decisions that would deviate from decisions that would be made by peers.

Findings

Table 5.15 displays the pairwise comparisons for employment arbitrators with for-cause requirements and peer review panelists. Significant differences are observed in the mean rating for likelihood of ruling for the employee in 7 of the 10 cases. In 2 of these 7 cases (Cases 5 and 9), peer review panelists were less likely to rule in favor of the employee. Case 9 is the only case that contains substantial evidence of discrimination, which suggests that employment arbitrators were more highly influenced by the presence or absence of this evidence. The salience of this information for employment arbitrators is not surprising, given that employment arbitration is used as a substitute for judicial proceedings, and given the legal background and training of the arbitrators. Case 5 is a case in which there is both short tenure and a negative work record. The weight given by peers to both short tenure and a negative work record is consistent with what might be expected if peers are more likely to make implicit use of idiosyncrasy credits.

Table 5.15 Pairwise Comparisons: Mean Differences between Employment Arbitrators with For-Cause Requirements and Peer Review Panelists

Case number	Mean rating for employment arbitrators with for-cause requirements	Mean rating for peer review panelists	*t*-value for mean difference
Case 1	2.22	3.45	6.13**
Case 2	—	3.19	—
Case 3	—	5.44	—
Case 4	4.12	3.88	1.00
Case 5	4.05	3.01	5.44**
Case 6	3.27	3.96	3.34**
Case 7	2.33	2.23	0.70
Case 8	4.59	4.78	0.94
Case 9	4.38	4.03	1.82*
Case 10	3.71	4.21	2.35**
Case 11	4.26	5.11	4.03**
Case 12	3.62	4.53	4.18**

NOTE: Ratings were on a 1 to 7 scale, where 7 indicates a high likelihood of overturning the termination and 1 indicates a low likelihood of overturning the termination; — = not applicable; *$p < 0.05$; **$p < 0.01$.

Consistent with the use of idiosyncrasy credits, peers were more likely to rule in favor of the employee in Case 11 (where very long tenure was a possible mitigating factor), Case 6 (where there is a long tenure in combination with facts suggesting an external attribution for the problem behavior), and Case 12 (where there were facts suggesting an external attribution for the problem behavior). While not expected, peers were also more likely to rule in favor of the employee in Case 1 (where the case against the employee was strong, with the basis for the employee's case being an unsupported accusation by others) and Case 10 (where there was evidence of provocation).

Employment Arbitrators with "For-Cause" Requirements vs. Jurors

Expectations

The decision task for employment arbitrators in assessing whether there is cause for termination is quite different from the task of jurors in discrimination cases. Based upon differences in the structure of the decision task, we would expect employment arbitrators to be more likely to rule for the employee when there is no evidence of discrimination, even where there is only weak evidence of misconduct against the employee and/or a procedural violation by the employer. Instructions typically provided to jurors direct them to limit their focus only to factors relevant to determining if there was a statutory violation. We are not suggesting that such instructions are likely to be completely effective in limiting the focus of jurors; however, instructions are likely to have some effect on their verdicts (MacCoun 1989). While we expect differences in the structure of the decision task to have a significant effect, the likely magnitude of this impact might be limited by differences between jurors and employment arbitrators with regard to whom they are most likely to identify with in the case. We argued earlier that jurors might be expected to exhibit a tendency to identify with the employee, whereas the opposite might be expected among some employment arbitrators. Where such tendencies exist, jurors may sometimes be willing to consider factors relating to the overall fairness of the termination (Guinther and Walter 1988), whereas employment arbitrators may impose more lenient standards with regard to evidence of wrongdoing or procedural compliance by the employer.

Differences might also be observed where there is plausible but inconclusive evidence of discrimination. Judgment would be required to determine whether the employee met the burden of proof, and it may be that jurors would be more likely to err on the side of the employee than would the employment arbitrator. This difference would be expected if, in fact, jurors are more likely than employment arbitrators to psychologically identify with the employee (MacCoun 1989), or if there is some legitimacy to the repeat-player argument.

When the case heard by the jury allows them to consider whether a contractual obligation requiring cause for termination was violated, we might expect jurors to be more likely to rule in favor of the employee. In such a situation, the decision task would be similar to that for the employment arbitrator. This may allow for differences in interests and evaluation tendencies to play a more significant role, resulting in jurors being more likely to find for the employee.

Findings

Table 5.16 displays the pairwise comparisons for employment arbitrators with a for-cause requirement and jurors. We suggested earlier that jurors might be more likely to rule in favor of the employee when there was substantial evidence of discrimination. This was not supported, however, as no significant difference was observed for Case 9. We also suggested that employment arbitrators would be more likely to rule for the employee in cases where evidence of discrimination is modest but there are problems with the case in terms of evidence of employee wrongdoing or procedural compliance. No evidence of this was observed. A significant difference between employment arbitrators with a just cause requirement and jurors was observed for only three cases, and in each instance it was the jurors who were more likely to rule in favor of the employee (Cases 1, 11, and 12). Here again, the nonprofessionals were more likely to give credit to an employee's unsupported assertions (Case 1). In Case 11, the employee had long ten-

Table 5.16 Pairwise Comparisons: Mean Differences between Employment Arbitrators with For-Cause Requirements and Jurors from Employment Discrimination Cases

Case number	Mean rating for employment arbitrators with for-cause requirements	Mean rating for jurors	t-value for mean difference
Case 1	2.22	3.15	4.69**
Case 2	—	2.43	—
Case 3	—	4.58	—
Case 4	4.12	3.78	1.46
Case 5	4.05	3.96	0.44
Case 6	3.27	3.40	0.63
Case 7	2.33	2.28	0.24
Case 8	4.59	4.60	0.02
Case 9	4.38	4.07	1.37
Case 10	3.71	3.70	0.04
Case 11	4.26	5.36	4.47**
Case 12	3.62	4.57	3.86**

NOTE: Ratings were on a 1 to 7 scale, where 7 indicates a high likelihood of overturning the termination and 1 indicates a low likelihood of overturning the termination; — = not applicable; *$p < 0.05$; **$p < 0.01$.

ure, and in Case 12, there were family problems with which the jurors might be more inclined to sympathize.

Employment Arbitrators with "For-Cause" Requirements vs. HR Managers

Expectations

Few differences are expected between employment arbitrators with "for-cause" requirements and HR managers. Both would be expected to give consideration to obvious violations of the for-cause standard. While employment arbitrators would do so to comply with contract requirements, HR managers would do so to maintain effective employee relations and ensure consistent application of disciplinary procedures. Both would be expected to give substantial weight to evidence of discrimination. Further, decision maker interests would typically be served by the same type of outcome, and both types of decision makers would be expected to be similar in their tendencies to identify with the employer.

As with peer review panelists, some differences between HR managers and employment arbitrators are likely to be observed, owing to the fact that HR managers are part of the organization in question. Just as is the case with peers, HR managers are part of the same social organization as the employee and, as such, are likely to implicitly calculate idiosyncrasy credits (Hollander 1958). Employees with a strong work history will be treated as having earned credits, particularly if it appears that the problems recently observed are likely to be corrected or are due to an external cause. Following this same logic, where idiosyncrasy credits are in deficit status, particularly where no external attribution is possible, HR managers may be more likely to support termination even if there is some other problem with the case against the employee (e.g., where there is a lack of procedural compliance on the part of the employer). However, HR managers are unlikely to tolerate problems with the case that revolve around evidence of discrimination. Given that HR managers are personally accountable for such matters, evidence of discrimination is likely to be highly salient for them, regardless of idiosyncrasy credits.

Findings

Table 5.17 displays the pairwise comparison between employment arbitrators with for-cause requirements and HR managers. A possible source of difference between employment arbitrators with for-cause requirements and HR managers relates to idiosyncrasy credits and the resulting importance of the employee's work record for the HR manager. Some support for this argument is found. For example, employment arbitrators were significantly more favorable to the employee in Case 5, where a negative work record was present. In the contrary direction, Cases 6 and 11, where long tenure suggests an accumulation of idiosyncrasy credits, HR managers were significantly more favorably disposed toward the employee's case.

However, other significant differences were found. For example, HR managers were more likely to rule in favor of the employee in Case 1 (where the case against the employee was strong, with the employee's case being based upon unsupported allegations against others). In

Table 5.17 Pairwise Comparisons: Mean Differences between Employment Arbitrators with For-Cause Requirements and HR Managers

Case number	Mean rating for employment arbitrators with for-cause requirements	Mean rating for HR managers	t-value for mean difference
Case 1	2.22	2.75	2.37**
Case 2	—	2.71	—
Case 3	—	5.19	—
Case 4	4.12	4.43	1.13
Case 5	4.05	3.15	4.43**
Case 6	3.27	3.92	2.66**
Case 7	2.33	2.07	1.80*
Case 8	4.59	5.19	2.86**
Case 9	4.38	4.50	0.49
Case 10	3.71	4.19	1.98*
Case 11	4.26	5.17	3.93**
Case 12	3.62	4.80	4.94**

NOTE: Ratings were on a 1 to 7 scale, where 7 indicates a high likelihood of overturning the termination and 1 indicates a low likelihood of overturning the termination; — = not applicable; *$p < 0.05$; **$p < 0.01$.

Case 7, which is similar to Case 1, with the exception of some (albeit weak) evidence of discrimination, employment arbitrators were more likely to find for the employee. However, in Case 7, both groups were unlikely to overturn the termination. HR managers were also more likely to rule in favor of the employee in Case 8 (where there were procedural problems) and Case 10 (where there was evidence of provocation by management). These differences suggest that HR managers may be more willing to consider a broader range of just cause violations, and that they may be more reluctant than employment arbitrators to support termination, even when the case against the employee is relatively strong.

Peer Review Panelists vs. Jurors

Expectations

As stated previously, jurors are assigned a more narrowly restricted decision task, focusing primarily on whether there is evidence to support claims of a violation of the law. This differs from peer review panelists, who are instructed to examine a broader range of issues relating to whether termination is consistent with organizational policy and procedures. While it is sometimes argued that jurors show tendencies to identify with the employee and that such identification increases the willingness of jurors to consider the overall fairness of the termination (Abbott 1993), we would expect peers (given the structure of their decision task) to be more likely to rule in favor of the employee in discrimination cases where there is little evidence of discrimination, and either questionable evidence against the employee or a lack of procedural compliance by the employer. This argument is based on the idea that strong manipulation of the decision task (as is the case when juries receive instructions from a judge regarding how to make decisions) will have a more significant effect than tendencies to identify with one side versus the other (MacCoun 1989).

Additionally, differences between peers and jurors might be expected because peers are part of the organization from which the employee is being terminated. This is relevant for two reasons: First, peers have a greater incentive than jurors to protect the organization from employees who may pose a threat to the safe and effective operation of the firm. Second, the firm is a social organization and members of the same social grouping are thought to apply the logic of idiosyncrasy credits. These differences would make it more likely that peers would support termination if there were evidence of poor performance and as well as a negative work history—even if there were some other problem with the case (e.g., evidence of discrimination). By contrast, peers may be more likely to overlook performance problems if the employee has built up idiosyncrasy credits and if the problems can be attributed to an external cause or event. Under such conditions, then, peers may be more likely than jurors to rule in favor of the employee.

If we are correct in arguing that peers have an interest in protecting the firm and may identify more with the management team than someone labeled as a problem employee, it is possible that peers will also be more likely to favor termination when there is little evidence of discrimination but a strong case against the employee. While we would expect that jurors would be as likely—on average—to support termination, there is less incentive for jurors to overcome any natural reluctance to terminate an employee. Differences might also be observed when evidence of discrimination is plausible but inconclusive. Differences in interests and in identification tendencies may make it more likely that jurors would find for the employee. These same differences in interests and identification tendencies may also lead to differences when jurors are considering a case where the employer is alleged to have violated a for-cause provision in an employment agreement. Under such circumstances, peers would be more likely than jurors to rule in favor of the employer when the case against the employee is strong, and also when the employee in question has a negative work history.

Findings

Table 5.18 displays the pairwise comparisons for peer review panelists and jurors. Differences were expected between these two groups because the decision task allows peers to consider a broader set of factors when making their decision (at least for cases involving violations of discrimination statutes). Accordingly, we might expect that, in instances where evidence of discrimination is weak, peers would be more likely to rule in favor of the employee when obvious problems

Table 5.18 Pairwise Comparisons: Mean Differences between Peer Review Panelists and Jurors from Employment Discrimination Cases

Case number	Mean rating for peer review panelists	Mean rating for jurors	t-value for mean difference
Case 1	3.45	3.15	1.18
Case 2	3.19	2.43	3.62**
Case 3	5.44	4.58	4.12**
Case 4	3.88	3.78	0.36
Case 5	3.01	3.96	3.76**
Case 6	3.96	3.40	2.23*
Case 7	2.23	2.28	0.75
Case 8	4.78	4.60	0.90
Case 9	4.03	4.07	0.19
Case 10	4.21	3.70	2.23*
Case 11	5.11	5.36	1.19
Case 12	4.53	4.57	0.17

NOTE: Ratings were on a 1 to 7 scale, where 7 indicates a high likelihood of overturning the termination and 1 indicates a low likelihood of overturning the termination; $*p < 0.05$; $**p < 0.01$.

exist with the firm's case against the employee. Some limited support was found for this in Cases 3 and 10, where significant differences were observed (with peers being more likely to rule in favor of the employee). In both of these cases, evidence of discrimination was modest or weak, and questions existed regarding either procedural compliance (Case 3) or provocation by management (Case 10).

It was also suggested that peers would be more likely to be influenced by the work record of the employee. Some support for this is found in Case 5, where peers were less likely to rule for the employee because he or she had a negative work record. Support is also found in Case 6, where very long tenure was combined with a family situation that might have been a cause of the current performance problems. However, we did not find support for this argument in Case 11, where no significant difference is found.

Peers were also significantly more likely to rule for the employee in Case 2, where the employee's case is based entirely on accusations of wrongdoing by others. A similar but nonsignificant result is found in Case 1, which shares this characteristic with Case 2. Thus, even compared to jurors, who are themselves likely to give weight to the employee's unsupported statements, peer review panelists tend to be more highly inclined to find for the employee.

Peer Review Panelists vs. HR Managers

Expectations

We would expect few differences between peer review panelists and HR managers, because the decision tasks are largely similar and there is similarity in terms of interests and identification patterns. Both are part of the same social organization, and thus are likely to be influenced by the logic of idiosyncrasy credits, so we would expect little difference between these types of decision makers.

Findings

Table 5.19 displays the pairwise comparisons for peer review panelists and HR managers. Few differences were expected for these groups. In two cases, peer review panelists were significantly more

Table 5.19 Pairwise Comparisons: Mean Differences between Peer Review Panelists and HR Managers

Case number	Mean rating for peer review panelists	Mean rating for HR managers	t-value for mean difference
Case 1	3.45	2.75	2.48**
Case 2	3.19	2.71	1.81*
Case 3	5.44	5.19	1.17
Case 4	3.88	4.43	1.72*
Case 5	3.01	3.15	0.52
Case 6	3.96	3.92	0.15
Case 7	2.23	2.07	1.12
Case 8	4.78	5.19	1.87*
Case 9	4.03	4.50	2.04*
Case 10	4.21	4.19	0.09
Case 11	5.11	5.17	0.25
Case 12	4.53	4.80	1.08

NOTE: Ratings were on a 1 to 7 scale, where 7 indicates a high likelihood of overturning the termination and 1 indicates a low likelihood of overturning the termination; *$p < 0.05$; **$p < 0.01$.

likely to find for the employee than were HR managers (Cases 1 and 2). In both cases, there was little basis for challenging the case against the employee. It should be noted, however, that no significant difference was observed in Case 7, where the employee also had a weak case. In three cases, HR managers were significantly more likely to rule in favor of the employee. A significant difference was observed in Case 4 (where reasonableness of the rule was at issue), Case 8 (where procedural compliance was at issue), and Case 9 (where there was substantial evidence of discrimination).

Jurors vs. HR Managers

Expectations

Because of differences in how the decision task is structured, we would expect that HR managers would be more likely to decide in favor of the employee in cases where there is little evidence of discrimination, combined with either limited evidence against the employee or a lack of procedural compliance on the part of the employer. In addition, HR managers are part of the same social organization as the employee, and they—like peers—may be likely to apply the logic of idiosyncrasy credits. As such, they also may be more heavily influenced by the employee's work history when determining whether termination is justified. As noted above, we think it is likely that jurors will sometimes ignore the law and find for the employee if they believe that the employee was treated unfairly. However, we would not expect this tendency to be sufficient to overcome the differences created by how the decision task is structured.

We would not expect differences when there is plausible but inconclusive evidence of discrimination. While jurors may be more likely than HR managers to identify with the employee, HR managers are likely to see themselves as being personally accountable for legal action taken against the firm (Colvin 2003). As such, their self-interest may affect how they evaluate evidence and, in turn, make it difficult for them to discount evidence of discrimination—even when the employee in question has exhibited problems with his/her work for an extended period.

When the jury case involves contract law issues (due to for-cause requirements in the employment agreement), fewer differences between jurors and HR managers are likely to be observed when the case against the employee is questionable. If differences are to be found, it is likely to be when the case against the employee is strong. Under such a circumstance, HR managers (as an agent of management) have an incentive to overcome any natural reluctance to terminate. However, that same incentive does not exist for jurors, who would be more likely to favor the employee.

Findings

Table 5.20 presents the pairwise comparisons for jurors and HR managers. As noted above, because of differences in the decision task, we would expect HR managers to consider a broader range of factors than jurors in a case in which the employee is alleging a violation of a statute prohibiting discrimination. HR managers are also likely to be influenced by both the need for consistency within the firm, as well as employee relations concerns. Some support was found for this, in that HR managers were significantly more likely to rule in favor of the employee in cases where evidence of discrimination was modest or weak, and where other types of challenges could be made to the em-

Table 5.20 Pairwise Comparisons: Mean Differences between Jurors from Employment Discrimination Cases and HR Managers

Case number	Mean rating for jurors	Mean rating for HR managers	t-value for mean difference
Case 1	3.15	2.75	1.48
Case 2	2.43	2.71	1.29
Case 3	4.58	5.19	2.36**
Case 4	3.78	4.43	2.18*
Case 5	3.96	3.15	2.90**
Case 6	3.40	3.92	1.77*
Case 7	2.28	2.07	1.11
Case 8	4.60	5.19	2.60**
Case 9	4.07	4.50	1.61
Case 10	3.70	4.19	1.89*
Case 11	5.36	5.17	0.69
Case 12	4.57	4.80	0.82

NOTE: Ratings were on a 1 to 7 scale, where 7 indicates a high likelihood of overturning the termination and 1 indicates a low likelihood of overturning the termination; $*p < 0.05$; $**p < 0.01$.

ployer's case (Cases 3, 8, and 10). This general argument is also supported by the significant difference observed with regard to Cases 4 and 6. While these cases involved contract issues rather than discrimination, the differences observed suggest a greater willingness by HR managers to consider a broader range of factors (in these cases, reasonableness of the rule) when determining the appropriate outcome.

There were significant differences observed in Case 5 (short tenure and a reasonable rule), where the HR managers were less favorable to the employee, and Case 6 (possibly unreasonable rule and long tenure), where the HR manager was more favorable to the employee. These results support the idea that HR managers (as members of the same social organization) are more likely to implicitly apply the logic of idiosyncrasy credits, and thus place greater emphasis on the employee's work history when making determinations.

Labor Court Judges: A Comparison Group

For the purpose of a cross-cultural comparison, we examined decisions made by labor court judges and compared these decisions to those made by labor arbitrators, employment arbitrators evaluating statutory claims, employment arbitrators with for-cause requirements, peer review panelists, jurors, and HR managers.

It should be noted that labor court judges are required to decide whether there is cause for termination, so their focus is not limited to determining whether a statutory violation has occurred. It should also be noted that labor court judges are less dependent upon maintaining their acceptability to either party to a case, since they are not selected by the parties. Consideration should also be given to the fact that labor court judges are not part of the organization involved with the case, and that they (like labor and employment arbitrators) have significant legal training and experience (Keller and Darby 2002). What is less clear when looking across the multiple countries where labor court judges are used is what role ideology (and therefore the willingness to identify with management versus the employee) plays in the appointment or selection of labor court judges. Thus, it is difficult to predict how labor court judges might compare with different types of decision makers in the United States. Therefore, while we will compare labor court judges with different types of decision makers within the United

States, we posit no expectations regarding the nature of these differences.

Table 5.21 presents the results of the comparison between labor arbitrators and labor court judges. Few differences were observed between labor arbitrators and labor court judges. Significant differences were observed only for Case 1, where the case against the employee was very strong, and labor arbitrators were more likely to rule in favor of the employee, and in Case 5, where the evidence against the employee was more modest, and labor court judges were more likely to rule in favor of the employee. In Case 1, however, both would be likely to uphold the termination, and in Case 5, both would be likely to overturn it.

Table 5.22 presents differences between employment arbitrators evaluating statutory claims and labor court judges. Labor court judges had significantly higher ratings for the likelihood of ruling in favor of the employee than did employment arbitrators in 5 of the 8 cases examined. This is not surprising, given differences in how the decision tasks are structured for the two groups. Significant differences were not observed in those cases where the employee's case was particularly weak (Cases 2 and 7), or where it was particularly strong (Case 9). The two

Table 5.21 Pairwise Comparisons: Mean Differences between Labor Arbitrators and Labor Court Judges

Case number	Mean rating for labor arbitrators	Mean rating for labor court judges	t-value for mean difference
Case 1	2.89	1.71	2.21*
Case 2	3.00	2.62	1.06
Case 3	5.92	5.35	1.58
Case 4	5.05	4.57	0.72
Case 5	4.25	5.25	2.14*
Case 6	4.06	4.25	0.33
Case 7	2.73	2.54	0.22
Case 8	5.49	5.75	0.52
Case 9	4.67	5.14	1.07
Case 10	4.57	5.00	0.95
Case 11	5.56	5.57	0.03
Case 12	4.70	4.42	0.56

NOTE: Ratings were on a 1 to 7 scale, where 7 indicates a high likelihood of overturning the termination and 1 indicates a low likelihood of overturning the termination; *$p < 0.05$.

Table 5.22 Pairwise Comparisons: Mean Differences between Employment Arbitrators Evaluating Statutory Claims and Labor Court Judges

Case number	Mean rating for employment arbitrators evaluating statutory claims	Mean rating for labor court judges	t-value for mean difference
Case 1	—	1.71	—
Case 2	2.39	2.62	0.58
Case 3	4.29	5.35	2.56**
Case 4	—	4.57	—
Case 5	—	5.25	—
Case 6	—	4.25	—
Case 7	2.22	2.54	0.50
Case 8	3.67	5.75	3.90**
Case 9	4.49	5.14	1.39
Case 10	3.32	5.00	3.42**
Case 11	4.05	5.57	2.70**
Case 12	3.50	4.42	1.81*

NOTE: Ratings were on a 1 to 7 scale, where 7 indicates a high likelihood of overturning the termination and 1 indicates a low likelihood of overturning the termination; — = not applicable; $*p < 0.05$; $**p < 0.01$.

sets of decision makers in the sample were in agreement as to whether the termination should be upheld in those cases.

Table 5.23 displays the results of the comparison between employment arbitrators with a for-cause requirement and labor court judges. As can be seen from the table, significant differences were observed in 7 of the 10 cases where comparisons were possible. In all 7 cases, the labor court judges were more likely to rule in favor of the employee. It should be noted that there were no significant differences in the two cases where there was no problem with the case against the employee (Cases 1 and 7).

Table 5.24 presents the results for the pairwise comparison between peer review panelists and labor court judges. In one case (Case 1), where the employee's case was based on unsupported assertions, peer review panelists were significantly more likely to find for the employee. In three cases (Cases 4, 8, and 9), labor court judges were significantly more likely to find for the employee. In Cases 4 and 8,

Table 5.23 Pairwise Comparisons: Mean Differences between Employment Arbitrators with For-Cause Requirements and Labor Court Judges

Case number	Mean rating for employment arbitrators with for-cause requirements	Mean rating for labor court judges	t-value for mean difference
Case 1	2.22	1.71	1.06
Case 2	—	2.62	—
Case 3	—	5.35	—
Case 4	4.12	4.57	0.71
Case 5	4.05	5.25	2.83**
Case 6	3.27	4.25	1.92*
Case 7	2.33	2.54	0.58
Case 8	4.59	5.75	2.90**
Case 9	4.38	5.14	1.76*
Case 10	3.71	5.00	2.84**
Case 11	4.26	5.57	2.85**
Case 12	3.62	4.42	1.75*

NOTE: Ratings were on a 1 to 7 scale, where 7 indicates a high likelihood of overturning the termination and 1 indicates a low likelihood of overturning the termination; — = not applicable; $*p < 0.05$; $**p < 0.01$.

there are issues, respectively, with unreasonableness of the employer's rule, and the employer failing to comply with its own procedures. In Case 9, there is substantial evidence of discrimination.

As can be seen in Table 5.25, there were significant differences between jurors and labor court judges in five of the cases examined. In Case 1 (one of the cases where the employee's case is based upon unsupported allegations), labor court judges were significantly less likely to rule in favor of the employee. However, in Cases 5, 8, 9 and 10, labor court judges were significantly more likely to rule in favor of the employee. Case 5 is one where it would seem that the employee would have a relatively high chance of prevailing before either a jury or a labor court. We are unable to explain why the jurors were not as favorable to the employee in this case. Case 8 is one in which a legal mind might be inclined to give greater weight to the failure of the employer to comply with proper procedures, and in Case 9, substantial evidence of discrimination is present. Perhaps the short tenure of the employee influenced the peers to a greater degree than it did the labor

Table 5.24 Pairwise Comparisons: Mean Differences between Peer Review Panelists and Labor Court Judges

Case number	Mean rating for peer review panelists	Mean rating for labor court judges	t-value for mean difference
Case 1	3.45	1.71	2.71**
Case 2	3.19	2.62	1.00
Case 3	5.44	5.35	0.17
Case 4	3.88	4.57	1.72*
Case 5	3.01	5.25	0.94
Case 6	3.96	4.25	3.78
Case 7	2.23	2.54	0.46
Case 8	4.78	5.75	2.04*
Case 9	4.03	5.14	2.27*
Case 10	4.21	5.00	1.44
Case 11	5.11	5.57	0.87
Case 12	4.53	4.42	0.19

NOTE: Ratings were on a 1 to 7 scale, where 7 indicates a high likelihood of overturning the termination and 1 indicates a low likelihood of overturning the termination; $*p < 0.05$; $**p < 0.01$.

Table 5.25 Pairwise Comparisons: Mean Differences between Jurors from Employment Discrimination Cases and Labor Court Judges

Case number	Mean rating for jurors	Mean rating for labor court judges	t-value for mean difference
Case 1	3.15	1.71	2.44**
Case 2	2.43	2.62	0.49
Case 3	4.58	5.35	1.42
Case 4	3.78	4.57	1.22
Case 5	3.96	5.25	2.15*
Case 6	3.40	4.25	1.42
Case 7	2.28	2.54	0.49
Case 8	4.60	5.75	2.33*
Case 9	4.07	5.14	1.80*
Case 10	3.70	5.00	2.29*
Case 11	5.36	5.57	0.33
Case 12	4.57	4.42	0.22

NOTE: Ratings were on a 1 to 7 scale, where 7 indicates a high likelihood of overturning the termination and 1 indicates a low likelihood of overturning the termination; $* p < 0.05$, $** p < 0.01$.

Table 5.26 Pairwise Comparisons: Mean Differences between HR Managers and Labor Court Judges

Case number	Mean rating for HR managers	Mean rating for labor court judges	t-value for mean difference
Case 1	2.75	1.71	1.76*
Case 2	2.71	2.62	0.17
Case 3	5.19	5.35	0.37
Case 4	4.43	4.57	0.21
Case 5	3.15	5.25	3.87**
Case 6	3.92	4.25	0.50
Case 7	2.07	2.54	1.29
Case 8	5.19	5.75	1.29
Case 9	4.50	5.14	1.15
Case 10	4.19	5.00	1.39
Case 11	5.17	5.57	0.76
Case 12	4.80	4.42	0.64

NOTE: Ratings were on a 1 to 7 scale, where 7 indicates a high likelihood of overturning the termination and 1 indicates a low likelihood of overturning the termination; $*p < 0.05$; $**p < 0.01$.

court judges. In Case 10, the labor court judges may have been willing to give substantially greater weight to the presence of provocation.

Our final pairwise comparison is between HR managers and labor court judges. It is shown in Table 5.26, where only two statistically significant differences are observed. In Case 1, where the employee has a weak case on substantive merits, the labor court judges were less likely to rule in favor of the employee. The reverse is true for Case 5, where modest evidence against the employee is combined with short tenure and a negative work record. Here again, the idiosyncrasy credit explanation may work against an employee with short tenure and a bad record, causing a member of the employee's own organization to be more negative toward his or her case.

Summary of Decisions by Type of Decision Maker

Table 5.27 presents a summary view of how the seven types of decision makers varied across the 12 cases examined. We coded ratings greater than four on the original response scale as an indication of a likely ruling in favor of the employee. In Table 5.27, we report the

Table 5.27 Percentage of Rulings Likely to be in Favor of the Employee, by Case and Decision Maker

Decision maker	Case 1	Case 2	Case 3	Case 4	Case 5	Case 6	Case 7	Case 8	Case 9	Case 10	Case 11	Case 12
Labor arbitration	14	13	92	79	48	47	8	88	62	58	90	65
Employment arbitrator (statutory claims)	—	3	41	—	—	—	0	33	51	17	46	21
Employment arbitrator (for-cause requirement)	4	—	—	51	33	21	2	58	55	30	48	23
Peer review panelist	30	20	88	48	22	46	3	67	42	43	77	50
Juror	21	4	58	35	42	31	7	58	48	28	75	54
HR manager	17	13	85	58	23	38	2	75	63	48	75	57
Labor court judge	0	0	88	50	75	50	25	88	50	63	75	50

NOTE: A ruling was classified as likely to be in favor of the employee when a decision maker selected a response of 5 or higher on the 7-point response scale. Scale value 5 was anchored with "likely to rule in favor of the employee." — = not applicable.

percentage of rulings likely to be in favor of the employee, broken down by case and decision maker type. This summary view offers some insights—largely consistent with what was suggested by the pair-wise comparisons—about how decision makers differed.

For example, when looking at Case 7—a discrimination case where there is little basis for the employee's challenge to the employer's action—one can see that employment arbitrators (both statutory claims and for-cause), HR managers, and peer review panelists were rarely willing to rule in favor of the employee. A small (but somewhat higher) percentage of labor arbitrators and jurors were willing to rule in favor of the employee, while the labor court judges were the most favorable to the employee's case.

Cases 8 through 12 are similar to case 7, except that they contain some substantial basis for challenging the case against the employee. For employment arbitrators evaluating statutory claims, a ruling in favor of the employee was most frequent in Case 9 (51 percent), where there was substantial evidence of discrimination, and Case 11 (46 percent), where the employee had very long tenure (22 years). In Case 8, where the employer failed to abide by its own procedures, the percentage was somewhat lower (33 percent). In Cases 10 and 12, involving provocation and family problems, respectively, these percentages did not approach what was seen for the other cases in this group. Among those considerations other than the strength of the proof of discrimination, only tenure seemed to have swayed these arbitrators. Even here, however, they—along with employment arbitrators in for-cause cases—are far less likely to base a decision on long tenure than are any of the other sets of decision makers.

Insights can also be gleaned from the analysis of employment arbitrators with for-cause requirements. Where there was weak evidence of discrimination, employment arbitrators with a for-cause requirement were much more likely to rule in favor of the employee if certain kinds of challenges to the case against the employee existed. For example, in Case 8, where there was both only modest evidence against the employee and procedural problems, the for-cause requirement seemed to affect how the case was decided. By contrast, in Cases 11 and 12, where work record and personal problems were crucial, the presence of a for-cause requirement did not seem to have as great an effect.

Comparisons between employment arbitrators and jurors are also instructive. Interestingly, in Case 9, where there is substantial evidence of discrimination, both employment arbitrator groups had a somewhat higher percentage of employee-favorable rulings than jurors. However, it appears that in some cases where factors not directly related to discrimination were the crucial challenges to the employer's case (Cases 11 and 12), jurors were more likely to rule in favor of the employee.

One might also argue that Table 5.27 suggests that both the structure of the decision task and characteristics of the decision maker affect how decisions are made. For example, labor arbitrators must apply just cause standards, and these standards involve giving importance to a number of factors in assessing whether there was just cause for termination. And quite clearly, a high percentage of labor arbitrators (in relative terms) were willing to rule in favor of the employee whenever one of these factors supported a challenge to the case against the employee. Cases 3 (procedural problems), 4 (lack of reasonableness of the rule), 10 (provocation), and 11 (long tenure) fit this description.

Characteristics of the decision maker groups also may have played a role. For example, in cases where work record and tenure were crucial factors, peer review panelists seemed to be influenced to a greater degree than when other factors related to just cause were at issue. And this is consistent with the argument that peers would be more likely to apply the logic of idiosyncrasy credits because of their membership in the same social group as the accused employee.

Looking at Table 5.27 suggests another interesting point: the powerful effect of long tenure. Case 11 is one which is distinguished primarily by this characteristic. Yet, among all of the decision makers but employment arbitrators, the percent of rulings likely to favor the employee in this case are quite high, ranging from 90 percent by labor arbitrators to 75 percent by jurors, HR managers, and labor court judges. Peer review panelists fall in the middle, at 77 percent. Even employment arbitrators would find for the employee in 46 percent of statutory cases or 48 percent of for-cause cases. This suggests that, in practice, there is recognition of something like a property right in the job, acquired over a long service with the employing firm. This is an idea that has become unfashionable in the management and industrial relations literatures, but may be very much alive in the real world.

The Nature of the Award

We asked jurors and employment arbitrators to indicate, in more detail, what rulings they would make if they decided in favor of the employee. This method was applied to Cases 7 through 12.

Jurors and employment arbitrators evaluating statutory claims were asked to choose between a finding: 1) for the employer, 2) of non-willful discrimination by the employer, and 3) of willful discrimination by the employer. These distinctions were explained to them, as were the financial implications of different findings for the employee and employer. Employment arbitrators with the for-cause requirement were given an additional option, namely, finding that the employer failed to show cause.

The results of our analysis of these awards are shown in Table 5.28. As can be seen from the table, jurors were over twice as willing to find that willful discrimination occurred than were employment arbitrators evaluating statutory claims, although the percentage remained modest in absolute amount (11 percent versus 5 percent). They were also somewhat more willing to find non-willful discrimination (36 percent versus 30 percent). This suggests that jurors would generally be more likely to find for the employee, and that they would also be more willing to find willful discrimination, which would result in more significant financial damages being awarded.

Table 5.28 Percentages of Jurors, Employment Arbitrators Evaluating Statutory Violations, and Employment Arbitrators with a For-Cause Requirement Issuing Different Findings

Finding	Jurors	Employment arbitrators evaluating statutory violations	Employment arbitrators with a for-cause requirement
Finding for employer	54	64	58
Finding of non-willfull discrimination	36	30	12
Finding of willful discrimination	11	5	4
Finding of contract violation and no finding of discrimination	—	—	27

NOTE: Only employment arbitrators with a for-cause requirement were allowed to choose the contract violation finding. Columns may not sum to 100 percent, due to rounding error. — = not applicable.

It is interesting to observe that when the for-cause requirement exists, employment arbitrators are somewhat more willing to find for the employee. Moreover, it appears that having the for-cause requirement reduces the likelihood of a finding of discrimination. Under the statutory claims condition, 30 percent of employment arbitrator decisions found non-willful discrimination. When the for-cause requirement exists, only 12 percent of employment arbitrators make such a ruling. This suggests that having the for-cause requirement may actually reduce findings of discrimination against the employer. It also suggests that where just cause requirements do not exist, employment arbitrators may find that there was discrimination even though they would rather say that there simply was a lack of cause. It is not clear whether this indicates that employment arbitrators sometimes use discrimination law to enforce a for-cause requirement, or that employment arbitrators find it more acceptable to rule that there was a lack of cause rather than discrimination.

CONCLUSIONS

The purpose of this chapter is to provide an empirical method to compare decisions of each category of decision maker. The result is 21 pairwise comparisons of seven separate categories of decision makers. In the broadest sense, it appears that the type of decision maker impacts the decision reached. This general finding can have consequences for employees who seek to resolve employment disputes in general, and disputes involving termination in particular. Employees with union representation are the most likely to achieve a favorable ruling in the well-established labor arbitration system. They can expect results that are akin to those achieved by employees subject to a labor court or similar system. According to our analysis, employees who are required to go through employment arbitration, on the other hand, are the least likely to have the case resolved in their favor. Outcomes for employees decided by peers, jurors, or HR managers fall in between.

Peer review and employment arbitration can be used by employers as mechanisms for attempts at union avoidance and suppression. Employment arbitration is credited with being less costly to employers, while at the same time providing timely and final resolution to disputes in a forum that is typically more private than a courtroom.

Considering that mandatory employment arbitration is primarily a substitute for litigation, it is fair to ask about the implications for workplace justice when disputes are resolved outside the judicial realm. The results presented here suggest that those employees who are, as a condition of employment, required to waive their legal rights to resolve employment disputes using litigation would expect to fare worse than those who are free to exercise that right and have their claim decided by a jury—if they are able to get to a jury. The results for employees are only slightly better when the employment arbitrator is operating under a just cause provision.

There is one important caveat to concluding that employees might be better off in court than before an employment arbitrator. As we noted in Chapter 3, the number of cases that actually make it to a jury is extremely small, with an estimated 80 percent of cases settled at an earlier stage (Howard 1995). What is more, it may be true that only a small proportion of potential claims are accepted by attorneys. Therefore, one should not conclude that employment arbitration is necessarily less favorable for employees than going to court. What is clear, however, is that labor arbitration offers employees the greatest advantages of any of the systems that we have studied. This is because it not only provides the best chance for an employee to win an adjudication of the case, it is also the final step in a complex and sophisticated process, whereby the union provides an advocate at the very earliest stage of the employee's grievance. This allows the facts of the case to be developed in a way that is not to the employee's disadvantage. Cases are systematically settled in the early stages of the process, with the employee having the assistance of a trained advocate.

Lastly, while HR managers, on average, had a lower likelihood of overturning a termination decision than labor arbitrators in the pairwise comparisons, the figures for the two groups of decision makers were remarkably close. In 10 of the 12 cases, HR managers agreed with labor arbitrators to either overturn or uphold the termination. Labor arbitrators did, however, rule in favor of the employee more frequently than their HR manager counterparts. Thus, while strong similarities exist, one should not necessarily surmise that decisions reached by HR managers are identical to those of labor arbitrators. Nevertheless, the relative consistency between their decisions warrants further empirical exploration.

6
Is Justice Weeping?

The main purpose of this book is to assess the degree to which workplace justice is present in the nonunion sector of the American employment relations system. That is, to what extent are employees free from arbitrary treatment? Also, how effective (for employees, employers, and society at large) are the processes that aim to provide protection to employees? To address these questions, we began with a review of the literature and data on the various systems of workplace justice for employees who are not protected by a collective bargaining agreement. In Chapter 5, we reported an empirical comparison of decision outcomes by persons who have been decision makers under various systems.

In our study, much attention has been given to employment arbitration—the most visible and controversial of nonunion systems. Our analysis has included a consideration of the literature on employment arbitration and the debates over its virtues and failings, as well as the state of the law on this subject. We concentrated on studies of the characteristics and effects of employment arbitration, and placed our inquiry into an international context. Finally, to better illustrate the comparative functions of available arbitration procedures, we systematically compared the results that would be reached in identical cases by employment arbitrators, labor arbitrators, jurors, managers, members of peer review panels, and labor court judges.

SUMMARY

The baseline of law from which we begin is the American rule of employment-at-will. This rule gives employers the unfettered right to act in an arbitrary fashion, not only in terminating employees, but also in otherwise disciplining and directing employees with the threat of termination always looming in the background. Almost alone among developed countries, the United States generally requires employees claiming unjust termination to assert and prove a violation of a specific law, such as Title VII of the Civil Rights Act. The courts have moderated this situation by developing, on a case-by-case basis, a law of unjust termination. Terminations judged to violate public policy, be abusive in manner, or violate either an implied-in-fact contract (usually an employee handbook) or implied-in-law contract term (the obligation of good faith and fair dealing) have been found by the courts to be actionable. Unions have extended protection to about 16 million workers against being terminated without just cause. This, however, leaves much room for "the command of persons, where secrecy and arbitrariness reign" (Wolterstorff 2001, p. 22).

Into this broad area of unfettered management flexibility, managers have inserted a number of management-initiated organizational systems of justice. Some of these are mere "soft" system—such as open-door policies, mediation, and ombudspersons—that do not produce outcomes that are legally binding on the employer. Some firms have gone beyond these to adopt "hard" systems—i.e., peer review panels and employment arbitration—capable of coming to conclusions that management is bound to accept, either by internal organizational justice rules or by external law.

In our work, we have concentrated mainly upon employment arbitration as a means to workplace justice. The literature on it consists mainly of legal analyses, debates about its pros and cons, and research on its characteristics and outcomes. The law on employment arbitration is clear in its major outlines, but highly unsettled as to its details. In *Circuit City Stores, Inc. v. Adams* (2001a), the U.S. Supreme Court plainly declared enforceable under the Federal Arbitration Act (FAA) agreements between an employer and an employee that claims, including those of a violation of the law, would be taken to arbitration. However, although a reading of the Federal Arbitration Act would lead one to believe that the right of employers to set up and operate employment arbitration structures is virtually unlimited, it appears that this is not the case. Even in the *Circuit City* case itself, the agreement was eventually set aside by the lower court on the grounds of "unconscionability." In 2004, the U.S. Supreme Court refused to review two other decisions ruling that Circuit City, Inc. arbitration clauses were unenforceable (*Circuit City Stores, Inc. v. Ingle* 2004; *Circuit City Stores, Inc. v. Mantor* 2004).

It is extremely difficult to say with any degree of certainty what the minimum requirements are for an employment arbitration structure to survive the scrutiny of the courts. It is clear that loading any substantial amount of the cost of arbitration on the employee will place the arbitration agreement in serious jeopardy. Literally as the finishing touches were being put on this study, the U.S. Supreme Court, in a case originating in South Carolina, has ruled that class-action suits may be brought in consumer arbitration cases if the arbitrator believes it to be appropriate (*Green Tree Financial Corp. v. Bazzle* 2003).

Also, it does seem that an arbitration system that complies with the Due Process Protocol will probably be found to be valid. The AAA procedures appear to meet these requirements, with the caveat that they do not include a requirement for limited judicial review. In our view, this is the most difficult standard for these systems to meet, yet it may be the most important for assuring that public policy is not relegated to private hands. Judicial review runs counter to the very nature of arbitration as it has developed in the unionized sector. Indeed, the lack of judicial review is one of the distinctive features of such arbitration, making it quicker and cheaper than court proceedings and insuring that expert arbitrators—rather than possibly inexpert judges—decide these cases.

When one sorts through the various arguments for and against employment arbitration from the standpoints of public policy, employers, and employees, a few stand out. The chief public policy concern appears to be the lessening of the workload of the federal courts. Federal judges see themselves as overwhelmed with a flood of employment litigation, and there is some basis for this perception. Employers would seem to benefit from the avoidance of juries and the high verdicts against them that may result from a jury trial, and they also stand to gain from the relative speed and low cost of employment arbitration. For employees, the chief advantages would appear to include a higher probability of having access to a remedial system, even if they earn only modest wages or have a case that is somewhat questionable. Employees also may have a higher probability of a successful outcome in arbitration than in court, which may encourage employers to comply with the law more strongly than the low probability of a large jury verdict. The low cost and speed of arbitration are advantageous to the employee as well as to the employer.

On the negative side, there are two main problems in terms of public policy. First, contrary to what is argued above, it may be the fear of high verdicts (and the high costs of attorneys' fees) that will most encourage employers to comply with the law, and removing that threat may eliminate such motivation. Second, the enforcement of federal and state law is being placed in the hands of unregulated employment arbitrators.

For the employer, there are several possible disadvantages of employment arbitration. One of these is the lower probability of winning in arbitration than in court, particularly when one takes into account the very large proportion of employee claims that will never even find legal counsel to pursue them in court. In the legal system, the employer has a significant advantage that may not be present in arbitration. While fears of large jury awards are somewhat unfounded, the hoped-for savings in cost and time to the employer may not be present in all cases. Finally, a point not usually considered is the possibility of the arbitrator converting employment-at-will into a "for-cause" relationship, which would take away the right of the employer to fire an employee without being required to show a cause for the dismissal.

For the employee, employment arbitration has many disadvantages. In the first place, it is a system created by the employer and imposed on the employee in an adhesive contract, and as such, the system may be carefully stacked against the employee. It may, as a practical matter, allow employers to "opt out" of Title VII and other antidiscrimination laws. The limits on the use of discovery may be a disadvantage to the employee, since the employer is generally in possession of most of the facts, and the employee needs this information. The right to a jury trial is lost, as is the right to meaningful judicial review. There are also concerns about the potential biases of arbitrators, which can be avoided in the union system. These potential problems have led states, such as California, to attempt to regulate employment arbitration providers such as AAA.

When one looks at the empirical studies of employment arbitration, the evidence on a number of issues is quite mixed. Data on, and studies of, win/loss rates in employment arbitration compared to other systems—e.g., the courts and labor arbitrators—are inconclusive. Our data do show employment arbitration faring reasonably well when compared to both labor arbitration and litigation in federal court; however, when employees win in court, they tend to get more money than they would if they had won an arbitration case.

Our survey results from 176 employment arbitrators show them to be relatively experienced and nearly always educated in the law. As expected, they hear mostly statutory, employment contract, and handbook cases, although other types of cases make up a greater proportion of their caseload (22.2 percent) than we expected. As expected, the majority of their cases involved managerial and professional employees. Counsel representing employers was judged by the arbitrators to be competent more often than lawyers representing employees. Although not highly popular with arbitrators, discovery procedures are more widely used.

A somewhat shocking finding was the frequency with which employees were paying either all of the costs (3.7 percent of the cases) or a substantial part of them (22.6 percent of the cases). These procedures would not be likely to stand up to a challenge in court. While 70 percent of the employment arbitrators would place the burden of proof on the employer to prove misconduct on the part of the employee, those arbitrators who had experience as arbitrators were significantly more likely to do this.

When asked about their decision rules, less than a majority (46.6 percent) of employment arbitrators would overturn a termination for violation of a clearly unreasonable rule, whereas virtually all labor arbitrators would do this. Also, a third of employment arbitrators would uphold a termination so long as the employer acted in good faith, while one would be hard-pressed to find a labor arbitrator who would use such a rule. Employment arbitrators' perceptions of how well the process protects employer and employee rights and interests were positive as to both sides; however, they generally viewed the process as better for employers than for employees. This was especially true with respect to cases involving nonbinding handbooks and policies.

When one places the American system in international context, it appears that the U.S. system is truly exceptional. We are among only a handful of countries in which employees do not have the protections against termination of employment required by international labor standards. The countries covered in depth in our study all require cause for termination. Generally, cause must be proved by the employer by a preponderance of the evidence or a similar standard, and the most common mechanism for this is statutory law. Most of these countries require notice of termination to the employee, and special courts, or special processes within ordinary courts, are common.

With respect to the operation of the courts in other countries compared to employment arbitration in the United States, there were some interesting differences and similarities. Both in the foreign courts and in U.S. employment arbitration, the representation by counsel of both sides was judged to be generally competent, but with the employer having some advantage. Discovery, although not uniformly available, was generally perceived somewhat more favorably by judges in other countries than by U.S. employment arbitrators. The requirement in some cases of a quantum of proof greater than a preponderance of the evidence is utilized both in other countries and in employment arbitration. However, this is less common in both of these processes than in American labor arbitration. A very high proportion of American labor arbitrators would be expected to use a higher standard (at least clear and convincing evidence) in the most serious cases.

American employment arbitrators were generally of the opinion that employers had their interests better protected than employees, especially where nonbinding handbooks were concerned. Judges from the other countries that were studied described the interests of both sides as being about equally well-represented, with the exception of Italy, where the judges felt that the interests of employers were not as well-served. Our survey found the judges from outside the United States to be not quite as approving of their systems as were the American employment arbitrators, yet these judges were somewhat more positive about the advantages of their specialized tribunals over ordinary courts than were American employment arbitrators.

One of the weaknesses of nearly all of the literature that attempts to evaluate different systems for resolving disputes over employment termination is the failure to address the question of how the decision makers in different systems would decide *the same cases*, as it is only when we know this that we can make a sound evaluation. It is on this ground that we believe our study may make its greatest contribution.

We examined here how decision makers from different institutional forums responded to situations where an employee was challenging a termination, either on the basis of statutory grounds or on the basis of a violation of contractual provisions, and clear differences were observed across a number of different types of disciplinary scenarios. Moreover, these differences raise provocative issues both from the standpoint of public policy and from the standpoint of organizations evaluating their approach to resolving workplace disputes.

CONCLUSIONS

While we believe the differences observed here raise important implications, it is important to stress that we are limited in our ability to draw normative conclusions regarding whether a particular type of institutional forum is better than another in balancing employee and employer rights. For example, we found that labor arbitrators tended to be more likely to make employee-favorable decisions than most other decision makers examined here (with the exception of labor court judges). By contrast, peer review panelists were less likely to make employee-favorable decisions, and employment arbitrators with for-cause requirements were even less likely to do so. But what normative conclusions can be drawn about these differences? How one views the tendency for peers or employment arbitrators to be less likely to make employee-favorable decisions may well depend on how much protection from unfair dismissal is afforded to employees and how much freedom management should have to direct and control its workforce. If one believes that it is critical that employers be allowed substantial discretion in managing its workforce—a discretion that has been unduly limited within many unionized organizations—the differences observed may be seen as an indication that new forums for resolving workplace disputes offer a more desirable balance between employee and employer rights. Alternatively, if one believes that the balance achieved between employee and employer rights within labor arbitration is appropriate, the differences observed might suggest a very different normative conclusion. In the broadest sense, then, we are limited in our ability to draw conclusions about the relative merits of the different forums for making decisions regarding workplace disputes.

That said, the differences observed here do address a number of very important issues from both the standpoint of public policy and organizational policy with regard to dispute resolution. To begin with, as discussed previously, with the decline of unionization, workplace disputes are increasingly being addressed within the judiciary system, often revolving around statutory claims. Any assessment of the changing face of workplace justice, then, would require that consideration be given to the difference in outcomes between labor arbitration, the jury system, and employment arbitration. As noted above, labor arbitrators found for the employee more frequently than did jurors or employment arbitrators. These latter forums are not explicitly designed to address a broad spectrum of employment disputes, and it is not surprising that differences are observed—particularly when evidence of a statutory violation is more limited.

It has been suggested that jurors sometimes ignore the law and impose their own sense of what is fair when making determinations. If true, this would suggest that juries apply some form of a just cause standard—regardless of whether they are permitted to do so under the law. The pattern of differences observed here suggests that jurors may sometimes consider factors that speak to the issue of fairness rather than to the more narrow issue of whether there is evidence of a legal violation. However, the pattern of differences also suggests that there are significant limits on the degree to which jurors are willing to ignore the law in favor of an implicit for-cause standard. As such, as one might expect, access to the judicial system offers a more narrow set of protections than does the labor arbitration system or the labor court systems in countries where for-cause standards are enforceable. Admittedly, the potential for juries to issue significant awards against an employer may constrain employer behavior in some instances, encouraging them to carefully consider their ability to justify the termination of an employee. However, our data do not suggest that juries apply—in any consistent fashion—a cause standard that is similar to what is employed within labor arbitration.

Another issue raised by our findings relates to the trend toward using employment arbitration as a substitute for the court system. For many, this trend has raised questions about whether employee rights are being limited in some fashion. While previous studies comparing employment arbitration and the courts (summarized in Table 3.1) are believed by us to be inconclusive, our own data on overall employee win rates (shown in Table 3.2) show employment arbitration in a rather favorable light. However, the results of our comparison of decision makers' reactions to the same cases (Chapter 5) suggests that employment arbitrators are less likely to rule in favor of employees, particularly when there is only limited evidence of discrimination. Our research (summarized in Table 5.4) found that jurors were willing to rule for the employee in 38 percent of the cases, compared to only 25 percent of the time for employment arbitrators in statutory cases. The pattern of results also suggests that employment arbitrators (when evaluating statutory claims) are more likely than jurors to restrict their focus to factors more closely related to evidence of discrimination. Employment arbitrators were also less willing to find willful (as opposed to nonwillful) discrimination. This is consistent with our conclusions in Chapter 3 about higher awards coming from juries than employment arbitrators. It is also important to note that while employment arbitrators were less likely to rule for the employee than were jurors, employment arbitrator decisions more closely resembled (in terms of overall tendencies) those of jurors than they did those of peer review panelists, HR managers, labor arbitrators, or labor court judges.

While employment arbitrators were less likely to rule for the employee than were jurors across the range of cases examined, in considering the implications of this it is important to recognize that a judge must first allow a case to go before a jury. And given that many of the cases examined here had relatively little evidence of discrimination, it is unclear what percentage of cases would actually have been heard by a jury. By contrast, employment arbitrators would have heard any of the cases that an employee chose to pursue. As such, while employment arbitrators are less likely than a juror to find for the employee, it is questionable whether significant differences in outcomes would have been observed between employment arbitrators and the judicial system taken as a whole. Further, in assessing the difference between jurors and employment arbitrators, it is important to consider that in statutory cases, differences appeared to be smallest when there was substantial evidence of discrimination.

We noted above that, while jurors may have sometimes been influenced by an overall sense of fairness when making a determination, there clearly were limits on the degree to which they applied a for-cause standard. One possible interpretation of the difference between jurors and employment arbitrators is that employment arbitrators were perhaps even less likely to apply a for-cause standard when evaluating the merits of a case that revolved around statutory issues. And while this may affect the likelihood that an employee will receive a favorable decision, it is consistent with the decision task assigned to employment arbitrators.

Implications are also suggested by the differences observed between employment arbitrators evaluating statutory claims and those with a for-cause requirement. While the for-cause manipulation clearly had an effect, the effect was not as large as one might have expected. Employment arbitrators with a for-cause requirement resembled (in terms of overall evaluation tendencies) employment arbitrators who evaluate statutory claims far more than they did labor arbitrators or labor court judges. This raises intriguing questions in light of recent public policy debates regarding the issue of employment-at-will workplace justice. It has often been argued that society, organizations, and employees would all benefit from a uniform standard relating to the conditions under which termination would be permissible. Substituting for-cause standards for employment-at-will on a universal basis has been suggested as a way to reduce complex and costly litigation over discrimination, ensure basic standards of justice across a broad spectrum of employees, and reduce uncertainty and confusion for an employer as to the likely consequences of terminating an employee. However, the suggested requirement of a for-cause standard has gained little traction in terms of public policy. In part, this is driven by a concern that such a standard would reduce labor market flexibility and interfere with management's ability to operate in an efficient manner (i.e., the power of management). Our findings regarding the impact of the for-cause standard on employment arbitrators raises questions about these concerns. While employment arbitrators with a for-cause standard rule in favor of the employee more frequently than employment arbitrators in evaluating a statutory claim, the difference was modest in comparison to other differences observed in this study. Employment arbitrators with a for-cause requirement still ruled for the employee less frequently than did jurors, peers, HR managers, labor arbitrators, and labor court judges. This suggests that the impact of a for-cause standard will depend on who is interpreting the standard and the institutional structure surrounding the interpretation of the cause requirement. One plausible interpretation of our findings is that it might be possible to have for-cause standards that offered some basic protection from unfair treatment, that offered clarity to employers regarding what is acceptable, that reduced the uncertainty often associated with cases that work their way into a legal system, and that do not unduly interfere with management's ability to direct and control its workforce.

Quite clearly, everything involves trade-offs to one degree or another. Implicit in our argument is that there may be institutional structures that would allow for a cause standard that would impose fewer restrictions than those that result from labor arbitration. While some might view this lessening of restrictions as an unfortunate reduction in employee rights, it may increase the feasibility that a cause standard could be applied more generally within the workforce.

A comparison of the outcomes under the systems of workplace justice without unions, particularly peer review panels and employment arbitration, to the process—labor arbitration—that exists in the unionized sector is of particular interest to this study. As we have noted, employment arbitration is currently the more visible of the two main nonunion sector systems. Policymakers as well as judges and academic scholars, managers, and labor spokespersons are engaged in a hot debate over the relative merits of the nonunion systems compared to the unionized one. Although our analysis in Chapter 3 comparing data on labor and employment arbitration awards would lead one to believe that the results under the two systems are quite similar, particularly when employment arbitrators are applying a just cause standard, our decision-making research leads to a different conclusion.

In our decision-making analysis, across all cases, labor arbitrators scored an average of 4.41, whereas employment arbitrators operating in the for-cause condition averaged only 3.70 (Table 5.3). Labor arbitrators would rule in favor of the employee in 53 percent of the same cases in which employment arbitrators with a for-cause condition would rule in favor of the employee only 33 percent of the time. As might be expected, this tendency is even greater when one compares labor arbitrators' decisions with those of employment arbitrators in deciding statutory claims. There was an overall average score of 4.41 for labor arbitrators versus a 3.38 score for employment arbitrators under this condition. Labor arbitrators decided in favor of employees 55 percent of the time, while employment arbitrators in statutory cases decided in the employee's favor only 25 percent of the time (Table 5.4).

It is worth repeating in our concluding chapter that labor arbitration is only the last step in a grievance process. In a unionized setting, the employee has an advocate at the very earliest stages of the process. Among other things, this means that the facts of the case develop in a way that can work to the employee's advantage. The union is required by law to take meritorious cases to arbitration, and to pay the costs of the arbitration. It is true that the case becomes that of the union rather than that of the employee, so the employee loses some control. However, with this loss of control comes the benefits of collective representation. The employee is not limited, in the words of the old union organizing song, to "the feeble strength of one."

Implications are also suggested by the differences observed between labor arbitration and both peer review panelists and HR managers. For example, peer review is sometimes seen as part of a union avoidance strategy and, thus, the differences observed may well be relevant to any assessment of peer review. Our results suggest that while peer review panelists and HR managers rule in favor of the employee less frequently than labor arbitrators and labor court judges (45 percent for peer review panelists compared to 55 percent for labor arbitrators and 51 percent for labor court judges), they rule in favor of the employee more frequently than jurors (38 percent) or employment arbitrators (33 or 25 percent). This suggests that these internal systems of justice (while less codified) may offer employees more protection than would be available through the judiciary system or even through employment arbitration (both where employment-at-will exists and where for-cause requirements exist). While their decisions sometimes appeared to be influenced by their membership within the organization, it does appear that peers and HR managers offer a middle position in terms of the balance between employee and employer rights.

It is also worth noting that it is often recommended that peer review be utilized by firms who make use of employment arbitration (with the associated waiver of the right to sue). Given this recommendation, it is important to consider how the balance of employee and employer rights shifts when this particular combination is used. Relative to firms where the only alternative is to pursue concerns regarding termination in court, our data might suggest that the balance shifts toward the employee in at least some instances. In peer review, panelists indicated a greater willingness to find for the employee across a broad range of cases—even when there was limited evidence of discrimination. Peers seemed, to a greater degree, to be utilizing some form of a for-cause standard—at least implicitly. And if an employee received a favorable ruling from the peer review panel, no need would exist for the matter to be considered within employment arbitration. If the employee received an unfavorable ruling, employment arbitration would still be available to ensure that the decision to terminate was consistent with existing statute. One might argue that employment arbitration would offer a more effective review of peer review if a for-cause standard existed. But regardless, employment arbitration would at least offer some review of the peer review process to ensure compliance with the law. The results obtained here suggest that such a process may well produce more favorable rulings for employees than would systems dependent on the jurors—at least for cases similar to those examined here. This possibility should be considered in light of two additional considerations. First, our results suggest that jurors were more likely to find willful discrimination and, thus, are more likely to provide for greater damages. Thus, while more employee-favorable outcomes might be expected under systems that combine peer review and employment arbitration, it is also likely that there will be fewer significant payouts for those employees who do obtain a favorable ruling. Second, as was noted above, the fact remains that there is no judicial review of employment arbitration rulings. While this might well be seen as a necessary tradeoff, it remains a significant departure from what is available through the judicial system. One interesting finding of our decision maker comparisons is the tendency of peer review panelists and jurors to be more likely than the professionals to find for an employee whose case is based entirely on an unsupported, self-serving claim that someone else is at fault. This is shown by the results of the analysis in Chapter 5 of Case 1, where the employee claims other employees committed the offense, and Case 2, where the employee claims that racially biased statements were made. An employee with a weak case based on such evidence might be better off before nonprofessionals such as peers or jurors.

Some might well argue that such a combination of peer review and employment arbitration offers at least a reasonable balance in terms of employee and employer rights. It might also be argued that the willingness of some firms to adapt such systems in the absence of unions offers promise regarding the likelihood of a move toward a system where there is some balance between employee and employer rights.

However, it is clear that such systems depend on the willingness of employers to adopt them. While such systems may be efficient for many employers and contribute to the development of a world-class workforce, it is likely that many employers will remain skeptical regarding the compatibility between formally protecting employee rights and maintaining a competitive advantage.

When unions were a more dominant influence within the private sector economy, organizing nonunion firms led to the increased use of labor arbitration as a system of justice. Where firms paid too little heed to the balance between employee and employer rights, organizing efforts offered some prospect that—through unionization—labor arbitration would become the mechanism for resolving disputes. Moreover, many argue that organizationally based justice systems were introduced to avoid such unionization.

Where the threat of unionization is minimal, then, one wonders how frequently employees will have access to well-developed systems that combine peer review and employment arbitration. When unions played a more dominant role, their efforts and their existence fostered the spread of workplace justice systems. As unions have declined in their presence within the private sector economy, however, what mechanisms exist to ensure the diffusion of systems that seem to offer at least some balance between employee and employer rights? Some might argue that market pressure will force such efforts—building a world-class workforce depends on committed employees, which in turn depends on finding an appropriate balance between employee and employer rights. However, few informed observers argue that the market is an efficient mechanism for enforcing the utilization of effective HR practices. Some might argue then, that the threat of legal action will encourage employers to develop effective systems. However, firms solely concerned about legal challenges might simply introduce employment arbitration with an associated waiver of the right to sue. In sum, while systems of justice may have emerged that offer some balance between employee and employer rights, it is unclear through what mechanism one might expect to see widespread diffusion of these systems of justice.

Related to this, questions might also be raised about workplace justice involving smaller employers where even the protections afforded by statutes prohibiting discrimination do not apply. Particularly in the secondary economy, where the link between human capital and competitive advantage may be less obvious, concerns might exist regarding the balance between employee and employer rights for the smaller employer. Indeed, the differences between systems such as peer review and labor arbitration may pale in comparison to the difference between firms that have some formal workplace justice system and those that are neither bound by statutes such as Title VII (because of size), nor have any formal system in place to protect employee rights.

Additional implications are suggested by the comparison between peer review panelists and HR managers. While there may well be reluctance to utilize peer review for fear that peers will be more lenient than managers, it is interesting to note that peer review panelists actually issued employee-favorable rulings less frequently than did HR managers. This may be due to HR managers being more risk averse since they may be held personally accountable if legal or employee relations problems resulted from a termination, but it may also be that peers were more likely to consider negative information about the employee's work history or other factors that indicate that the employee is not fully contributing. But regardless of the reason, the data reported here does call into question assumptions sometimes made about whether peer review panels are unduly lenient relative to the management team.

With the decline of unionization has come significant changes in workplace justice within this country. Here, we have examined how outcomes might differ across varying institutional forums for resolving disputes regarding employee terminations. We believe that some of the differences observed raise provocative issues, both in terms of public policy and in terms of issues to be addressed by organizations in evaluating the appropriate design of workplace justice systems.

It is important to keep in mind that, from the standpoint of employees, all of the nonunion systems fail to stack up to labor arbitration, which offers the best chance for workplace justice. Justice is least likely to weep where there is a union. We are also inclined to believe that this system works reasonably well for employers, and is consistent with the kind of public policy that should prevail in a democratic society.

We might note that the broad sphere of workplace justice is currently a fluid area in the United States, with much opportunity for experimentation and innovation. Indeed, some might argue that with rapid moves toward globalization and a knowledge-based economy, experimentation and innovation are necessary in striking an acceptable balance between employee and employer rights. Achieving such a balance has critical implications for the performance of our economy, the success of individual organizations, and the well-being of individual employees and their families.

Appendix A
Data from 11 Countries

This appendix consists of a summary of the laws of termination of employment in 11 countries: Australia, Finland, Germany, Israel, Italy, Malaysia, Norway, South Africa, Spain, Sweden, and the United Kingdom.

AUSTRALIA

Most Australian employees are covered by the Workplace Relations Act of 1996, as supplemented by the Workplace Relations Regulations of 1996. This legislation provides protection against unjust termination by mandating that, in order to terminate an employee, the employer must give the notice set out in the contract of employment or, if there is none specified, reasonable notice. Certain classes of employees, including casual employees, trainees, and workers earning more than a particular annual salary, are excluded from the coverage of this national legislation. All of the states but one have unfair dismissal legislation, and all have antidiscrimination laws.

For a dismissal to be valid under the Workplace Relations Act, the employer must ensure that it is not "harsh, unjust or unreasonable," that it is not on a prohibited ground, and that notice periods are complied with. Prohibited grounds include temporary absence from work because of illness or injury, membership or nonmembership in a union, acting as an employee representative, participating in proceedings against an employer, absence for parental leave, race, color, sex, sexual preference, age, disability, marital status, family responsibilities, pregnancy, religion, political opinion, national extraction or social origin, and refusal to consent to a workplace agreement.

Notice, or payment in lieu of it, need not be given if the employee is dismissed on grounds of "serious misconduct." Where required, the period of notice ranges from one to six weeks. This depends on length of service and age (greater when the worker is over 45 years old).

In reviewing a termination, the Industrial Relations Commission must follow the standards set out in the ILO Termination of Employment Convention. That is, it must decide whether the termination is for a reason based on the capacity or conduct of the employee or the needs of the employer. It must further consider whether, if the reason relates to the employee's capacity or conduct, the employee was notified of the reason and given an opportunity to respond to the charges. For terminations based on poor performance, it must inquire whether the employee was warned about the employer's dissatisfaction in advance of being terminated.

Charges of harsh, unjust, or unreasonable dismissal are heard by the commission. A claim of discrimination or breach of notice obligations goes to a federal court. If the case involves both, it is up to the employee to choose the forum.

Remedies for harsh, unjust, or unreasonable dismissal granted by the commission can include reinstatement, damages in lieu of reinstatement, or compensation for lost pay. Compensation for lost pay can be six months' pay or A$32,000, whichever is the lesser. If a termination is found to be discriminatory, the court may reinstate the employee, award compensation, or assess damages (Crotty et al. 2000).

Practice in the Courts

According to the Australian judge in our sample, proof of employee misconduct must be shown by a preponderance of the evidence rather than by clear or convincing evidence or proof beyond a reasonable doubt. Prior to the case coming to a hearing, there would have been both an attempt at conciliation by the court and a review by management initiated by the union, with the threat of possible collective action.

As to the quality of practice in Australian courts, this judge said that both the employer and the employee are usually competently represented. He also was of the opinion that the court usually had sufficient information upon which to base a decision, and that pretrial discovery proceedings, when used, were only sometimes worthwhile. He agreed that the Australian system generally does a good job in protecting both employee and employer rights, is an efficient way of resolving workplace disputes, and is better at this than if there were not specialized courts. The most important advantage of the labor court system in Australia, according to him, is that it provides an objective and respected third party who resolves the dispute in a relatively timely way. It is worth noting that he listed no disadvantages of this system.

FINLAND

Under the Finnish Employment Contracts Act, an employment contract that is not binding for a fixed period can only be terminated by either side by giving proper notice. This period may be set by contract, but must not be longer than six months, or longer for the employee than for the employer. If no express term of notice is set by contract, it is set by statute—ranging (for employers) from one month for employees with up to 1 year of service to six months for employees with 15 or more years of service.

An employer cannot give notice of termination of employment, except in the situations mentioned in the Employment Contracts Act (or the Seaman's Act). This can be only for "an especially weighty reason," and this must be connected either with the capacity or conduct of the employee. It cannot be for any of the following reasons: 1) illness, so long as it has not caused a substantial and permanent reduction of the employee's capacity to work; 2) participation in a strike; or 3) the employee's political or religious views or participation in the activities of an association. It is also prohibited to terminate an employee because of her pregnancy. A union shop steward, or a member of a labor protection committee, can only be terminated with the consent of employees or if the work that he/she performs is totally eliminated. If a steward is wrongly dismissed, an employer is subject to a fine in addition to the "normalized indemnity" (discussed below) (Suviranta 1999). There are also restrictions on collective terminations.

The contract of employment can be rescinded by either the employer or the employee if the other "has misled the other party in any material respect at the conclusion of the contract or if one of the parties through his carelessness jeopardizes safety at the workplace or assaults the other party or grossly insults him" (Suviranta 1999, p. 112). The contract of employment cannot be rescinded because of a strike or lockout, unless it is in violation of legal provisions for mediation of disputes, the Collective Agreements Act, or a collective agreement. If an employee is absent from work for one week without presenting an acceptable excuse within that time, the employer may consider the contract rescinded. If a rescission is found to be without a sufficient reason, the relationship is nevertheless ended, but the wronged party may sue for damages (Suviranta 1999).

In individual termination cases, an employee must be given an opportunity to be heard, and told the reasons for the termination, before being fired. The employee is entitled to have someone with him at a meeting with the employer. Notice of termination has to be served on the employee within a reasonable time after the grounds for it are known to the employer. On demand, the employer must furnish to the employee the reasons for the termination and the date upon which employment will end (Suviranta 1999).

Ordinary courts of the first instance handle disputes over individual employment contracts, and disputes over matters that are not tried by the labor court. The labor court handles matters connected with collective agreements. Generally, claims arising under the Employment Contracts Act are heard by general courts.

If an individual termination is found to be unlawful, the employee is entitled to a "normalized indemnity" of at least three, and at most four, months' wages. The employer may be given the option to reinstate the employee or withdraw the termination. The remedies available may be varied by a collective agreement.

Practice in the Courts

According to the judge who responded to our questionnaire, he would place on the employer the burden of proving cause for termination by clear and convincing evidence. Prior to coming to court, there is usually a grievance procedure that consists of meetings at both the local and federation levels.

As to the quality of the proceedings, our respondent is of the opinion that both parties are usually competently represented, the court usually has sufficient information upon which to base its decision, there is always pretrial discovery, and it is always worth the time and costs involved.

The Finnish judge agreed that the Finnish court systems do a good job of protecting both employee and employer rights. He agreed that the system is an efficient way of resolving workplace disputes, but was neutral as to whether it was better at this than ordinary courts would be.

In Finland, the most important advantages of the labor court system, according to the judge, are its professionalism, the possibility of a quick result, and the trust that the parties have in the system. Its chief disadvantage is that it is not open to workers who are unorganized.

GERMANY

Under both the Civil Code (CC) and the Protection Against Dismissal Act (PADA), which was most recently amended in 1996, there is protection for German workers against both summary termination and ordinary termination with notice. To be protected under PADA, an employee must work for an employer with more than five employees, and have worked for the employer for six months. If there is a Works Council or Staff Council, the Works Commission Act or the Federal Staff Representation Act covers them as well. Fixed-term contracts, once quite restricted, are now (since the Employment Promotion Act of 1985) not strictly limited as to the types of work to which they apply (Crotty et al. 2000). Being on a fixed-term contract deprives the employee of protection against dismissal at the end of the term, while being a temporary employee means that termination can take place at any time (Kittner and Kohler 2000).

Under PADA, even a routine dismissal is considered *prima facie* socially unjustifiable and therefore unlawful. PADA sets out three reasons for a justifiable dismissal: 1) the person of the employee (personal incapability or ill health); 2) the conduct of the employee (breach of obligations, violation of plant regulations or collateral obligations, breach of confidence); and 3) redundancy. Even if dismissal is for one of these reasons, the termination is socially unjustifiable if the worker can be transferred to another job after reasonable training (Crotty et al. 2000; Kittner and Kohler 2000).

The CC, which covers small employers, provides that summary dismissal must be based on "grave misconduct of the employee or severe economic circumstances unrelated to the behavior of the employee" (Crotty et al. 2000, p. 154; Kittner and Kohler 2000). A summary dismissal is lawful only if is "intolerable" for the period of notice to be worked (Sec. 626, Civil Code). Examples of grave misconduct include committing a crime, persisting in refusal to perform the worker's duties in spite of warnings, and deceiving the employer as to job qualifications. For white-collar employees, a summary dismissal must take place within two weeks of the occurrence of the events giving rise to the termination (Sec. 27, White Collar Employees Act).

There is a body of court decisions from which a set of principles on termination can be derived. The first of these principles is that a termination must be justified by a "negative prognosis." That is, past events must show that a continuation of the misconduct is likely in the future. Second, there is the *ultima ratio* principle, which holds that termination is only a last resort, and is to be avoided if a lesser action, such as transfer, will solve the problem. These two principles have led to the rule that an employee must be warned before being terminated for a conduct-related reason. The third principle is that the interest of the employer in terminating the employee and the interest of the employee in keeping the job must be weighed. This involves considering the employee's age, seniority, and job market prospects (Kittner and Kohler 2000).

Dismissal is unlawful if it is because of participation in a trade union, or discriminatory on the basis of sex, race, origin, language, national origin, creed, religious and political beliefs, pregnancy and maternity, child care leave, or compulsory military or community service. Members of worker representative bodies (such as works councils), workers who have completed apprenticeship programs, and some groups privileged under collective bargaining agreements are accorded special protection (Crotty et al. 2000).

For ordinary dismissals, there is a statutory period of notice that is at least four weeks before the 15th of any calendar month. Longer notice is required after certain periods of service and after the worker's 25th birthday. For 2 years' service, one month's notice is required; for 5 years' service, two months; for 10 years, five months; and for 20 years, seven months. For probationary employees, the period of notice is two weeks (Crotty et al. 2000).

For summary dismissals, the employee must have been given notice that continuing the misconduct will result in dismissal. Notice of dismissal must be given within two weeks of the time that the employer had knowledge of the grounds for termination.

When a works council or staff council is present, the employer must consult with the council prior to either an ordinary or summary dismissal. In the case of ordinary dismissals, the council has one week to respond. As to summary dismissals, the council has three days to state its objections, with agreement being presumed if it does not respond. If the council states objections, the employer is required to give these to the employee at the same time that he/she is given a document effecting the dismissal (Crotty et al. 2000).

An employee can challenge a dismissal in a labor court, which may declare the termination to be invalid, dissolve the relationship, and order compensation for job loss. The amount of compensation is determined by the court but must not exceed 12 months' pay (18 months for employees over 55 years old). The amount of the award depends upon the worker's social status (marital status, dependents, health), prospects in the job market and economic situation, and the extent of unfairness of the dismissal. The employee can choose between keeping a new job and returning to the employer, and if he/she returns to the employer, he/she receives compensation for lost pay (Crotty et al. 2000).

Practice in the Courts

The German labor court judge said that the burden is placed on the employer to prove misconduct beyond a reasonable doubt. Prior to going to the trial of the case, there is a "special consideration" hearing held solely before the professional judge.

According to our German judge, both employers and employees usually have competent representation, the court usually has sufficient information upon which to base an adequately informed decision, and there is no pretrial discovery process.

The German labor court judge respondent agreed that the labor court system does a good job of protecting both employer and employee rights. He also agreed that the labor court system was efficient and was better than ordinary courts would be in handling workplace disputes.

The most important advantages of the labor court system were seen as being its autonomy, its being at the same level and having the same standards as other German courts, and its having both professional and lay judges. The principal disadvantage is that many professional judges do not have practical experience in industrial matters.

ISRAEL

In Israel, employment termination is mainly regulated by collective agreements. As in the United States, there is no general statute requiring that dismissals be for just cause. Only recently (2001) have some procedural requirements been adopted (Keller and Darby 2002). Except for these procedural requirements, an employee outside of a collective agreement is at-will, unless it can be shown that the employer violated the contract of employment or acted in bad faith. There is no regulation of fixed-term or temporary contracts (Crotty et al. 2000). However, given a union density of approximately 85 percent, the vast majority of Israeli employees have protection against unjust termination through collective agreements.

It is generally provided, in collective agreements, that an employee cannot be terminated without a valid reason in accordance with an established procedure. Reasons that justify a worker being dismissed include being incapable of doing the job, or engaging in any serious misconduct. There are statutory prohibitions against terminations for particular reasons, including pregnancy and maternity, sex, race, religion, and nationality. Trade union officials are given special protection.

It has long been customary for employers to give notice of termination to employees. This was incorporated into law in 2001 by the Law of Early Notice for Termination. Under the terms of this legislation, employers and employees are both required to give notice of termination of the employment relationship. Salaried employees are entitled to up to 15 days of notice during their first year of employment and up to 30 days after that. Hourly employees are entitled to up to 21 days of notice during their first three years of employment, and up to 30 days after three years of service. Employees must give the same amount of notice upon their resignation from employment (Keller and Darby 2002).

Collective agreements provide for workers to be informed of the grounds for their dismissal and to have an opportunity to defend themselves against allegations made against them. Severance pay is required for all but seasonal employees with at least one year of service. Seasonal employees are entitled to severance pay only after working for the employer for two seasons (Crotty et al. 2000).

Companies and unions have private arbitration processes that do not involve the courts. If an employee claims a breach of the employment contract, this goes to an ordinary law court. Damages may be awarded for breach of a contractual obligation. If the claim arises from an industrial dispute, the labor court has jurisdiction. The remedies available to the labor court do not include reinstatement of the employee (Crotty et al. 2000).

Practice in the Courts

Three Israeli labor court judges responded to our questionnaire, and there was some disagreement among them on a few issues. For example, one of them stated that he/she would favor finding for the employee if the employer failed to prove misconduct, while the other two said that they would find for the employer if the employer proved that the termination was made in good faith. They split three ways on the quantum of proof required: one said that misconduct had to be proved by a preponderance of the evidence, another said that clear and convincing evidence was required, and the third said that proof had to be beyond a reasonable doubt. There was also disagreement about the processes that take place before a case comes to labor court.

As to the quality of the process, there was also disagreement. Two judges said that employers usually have competent representation, while the other said that this was only true sometimes. As to employee representation, two said that there was competent representation only sometimes, while the other said that this was usually the case. There was agreement, however, between the two judges who responded to the question that the court usually has sufficient information to make an adequately informed decision. As to pretrial discovery, one answered that this was done always, one said usually, and one said sometimes.

Two judges agreed, and one strongly agreed, that employee rights were well protected; two agreed and one strongly agreed that employer rights were well protected; two strongly agreed and one agreed that the labor court system is an efficient way of resolving workplace disputes; and two strongly agreed and one agreed that the labor courts were better at this than ordinary courts.

The advantages of labor courts noted by these judges included the participation of lay judges from both sides, their specialized nature for the special problems of workplace relations, the court's experience in dealing with a wide range of workplace relations, and employees knowing that they have a place to apply for a remedy. Two of the judges listed as a disadvantage the court's lack of speed.

ITALY

Italy's workers have some of the strongest protections in the world, and these laws are the object of strong feelings on the part of workers and unions. Attempts to weaken these in 2002 led to both a general strike and the murder of a distinguished Italian labor law scholar, Marco Biagi, who was involved in work on legislative reform.

In Italy, contracts for employment are regulated by the Italian Civil Code (CC), including Act 604 (July 15, 1966)—the Act on Individual Dismissals, as amended by Act 108 (September 11, 1990), and Act 300—the Workers' Statute (May 20, 1970). Almost all employees are covered by industry-wide collective agreements that bind all employers and employees in the industry. Although employers are not parties to them, interunion agreements to codes of practice are treated as standards for practice by employers as well as by unions (Crotty et al. 2000).

The Individual Dismissals law (Act 108/1990) gives both manual and white-collar workers protection against dismissal. Domestic workers, executives, and workers over 60 years of age are excluded.

The definition of an employment contract set down in the CC is one in which a person engages himself to "cooperate for remuneration in an enterprise by working manually or intellectually under the direction of the entrepreneur" (Crotty et al. 2000, p. 191). Contracts of employment that are not both full time and of indefinite duration are labeled as "special." Fixed-term contracts are limited to seasonal work, replacement of employees who are ill or on maternity leave, or for extraordinary or casual work. Temporary employment is also limited. It can be used for replacing absent employees, or in other instances permitted by a collective agreement. Temporary work is not permitted for dangerous work, striker replacement, or where a firm sheds workers and hires temps to do their work. Work-training contracts can be entered into with young workers for up to two years. Probationary periods must be put in writing and can last between 12 days and six months, depending on the job involved (Crotty et al. 2000).

Termination of an employment contract of indefinite duration can only be for a "justified reason" and in compliance with the required period of notice, or for "just cause" without notice. Employers may terminate fixed-term contract employees before the end of the term only for "just cause." Termination at will is limited to employees in trial periods, domestic workers, workers who have reached retirement age, and directors. Grounds for dismissal are frequently spelled out in collective agreements. In all dismissals, the employer must pay severance pay (Crotty et al. 2000).

"Just cause," which is required for termination without notice, has been made specific by court decisions. In broad terms, the principle set out in the statute is that termination "requires very grave conduct which, when evaluated both subjectively and objectively, constitute a serious and irremediable breach of the contract of employment" (Crotty et al. 2000, p. 192). A court will determine whether such a breach has occurred, considering all the relevant facts. "Justified reason," which is required for termination with notice, is defined by statute as "the obvious failure of the employee to fulfill contractual obligations; or reasons inherent in the production process, the organization of the work or the smooth running of the undertaking" (Crotty et al. 2000, p. 193). Dismissals are considered unfair unless the employer shows that there was either just cause or justified reason.

A number of particular grounds are declared by statute to be unfair. These include political opinions, union membership, sex, race, language, pregnancy, marriage, and religious affiliation. Members of worker committees are given special protection.

Where dismissal is for just cause, no notice is required. Where it is for justified motive, however, there must be a notice in writing, and the employer must wait 5 days for the dismissal to be effective. During the 5-day period, the employee has the right to be heard by the employer. Within 15 days the worker can ask for the reason for the dismissal and the employer has seven days to provide it (Crotty et al. 2000).

Either party may terminate a contract of employment of unspecified duration by giving the notice contained in applicable regulations, or according to custom and practice or principles of equity, although the employer's right to do this is limited by the necessity to have a justified reason. A party failing to give the required notice is liable for pay for the prescribed period. The periods of notice are established by collective agreements at the national industry level, and vary across sectors and by type of employee and length of service (Crotty et al. 2000).

One of the defining features of employment protection in Italy is severance pay. An employee can request the maximum amount of severance pay after eight years of employment, so long as he has not made prior requests for other expenditures, such as the purchase of the employee's first residence. Employees are entitled to a year's salary divided by 13.5, plus 1.5 percent for each year of service, including compensation for inflation (Crotty et al. 2000). Not counting inflation, this would amount to approximately $2,500 for an employee with 10 years of service who makes an average of $30,000 per year. An employee is entitled to this payment regardless of the reason for the termination. An additional payment, called a seniority indemnity, is paid to the employee at termination (Crotty et al. 2000).

Within 60 days after notice of dismissal, the employee may challenge it in the ordinary courts. Conciliation and arbitration are provided for in establishments with less than 15 workers, or where the overall workforce is less than 60 employees. Also, a worker can request through his/her trade union that his/her case be heard through a conciliation or arbitration tribunal (Crotty et al. 2000). A special procedure exists for dismissals for union activity.

A judge may order reinstatement in cases of "unjustified, discriminatory or formally vitiated dismissal" (Crotty et al. 2000, p. 195). Employers with 15 or more employees in an establishment of 60 or more workers overall are liable for reinstatement and damages equal to a minimum of five months' wages. If the employer offers reinstatement and the employee fails to accept the offer within 30 days, the contract of employment is deemed automatically terminated. If the employer has less than 15 employees in the establishment and fewer than 60 overall, and the court concludes that the dismissal was unlawful, the employer will be required to reinstate the employee or pay damages in the amount of between 2½ months' and 14 months' pay. If the employer refuses to comply with a reinstatement order, it must continue to pay the employee the full amount of her wages until it complies with the reinstatement order (Crotty et al. 2000).

Practice in the Courts

From Italy, as was the case with Israel, there were three respondents, all of whom agreed that the employer had the burden of proving misconduct by a preponderance of the evidence. Prior to coming to court, the employee and employer must have gone through a conciliation process.

As to the quality of the process, the three judges agreed that both employees and employers always have competent representation, that courts usually have sufficient information upon which to base a decision, and that there is no pretrial discovery process.

The three Italian judges agreed that their system does a good job of protecting employee rights, but they were neutral as to whether it did the same thing for employer rights. They all shared the view that their court system was not an efficient way of resolving workplace disputes.

MALAYSIA

In Malaysia, there is no statutory prohibition of unfair dismissal, but the courts have developed the principle that dismissals cannot be without "just cause." Termination of employment is governed by common law, with some regulation by the Employment Ordinance of 1955, the Industrial Relations Act of 1967 (IRA), and the Employment Termination and Lay-Off Benefits Regulations of 1980. The EA covers all employees paid less than a specified rate and all laborers regardless of pay level, whereas the IRA covers all employees who have a contract of employment (Crotty et al. 2000).

Dismissals with notice can be made for operational reasons. Also, if an employee covered by the Employment Ordinance of 1955 is continuously absent for more than two days without leave or reasonable excuse, he can be terminated. Dismissals without notice on the grounds of misconduct are permitted after "due inquiry," and an employee cannot be dismissed for union activity or union membership (Crotty et al. 2000).

In Malaysia, statutory notice periods are enforced, except when the employee is discharged for misconduct. These range from four to eight weeks, depending on the employee's length of service. Employees dismissed for performance reasons must be given notice ranging in length from 10 to 20 days. In either event, there can be a payment to the employee in lieu of notice. Severance pay, the amount of which depends on years of service, must be paid for terminations for operational reasons or for employee performance (Crotty et al. 2000).

Fixed-term contracts are permitted, but they must be in writing and for less than six months. Nonrenewals are examined by the courts to insure that they are genuine and not just for purposes of circumventing the law. An employee can be terminated during a probationary period, unless it is shown that the employer acted out of malice (Crotty et al. 2000).

Employees covered by the IRA can complain to the Industrial Relations Department that a dismissal was not for just cause. If conciliation fails, the case will be referred to the Minister, who may send it to the Industrial Court. The Industrial Court may either award reinstatement or compensation which would include one month's wages for every year of service. In practice, it rarely awards reinstatement. A question of law can be taken to the Malaysian High Court, although alternative paths to a remedy may be taken by an employee by suing in civil court for damages for wrongful dismissal, or by suing for unpaid wages in the labor court (Crotty et al. 2000).

Practice in the Courts

The Malaysian judge said that the burden was on the employer to prove cause for termination by a preponderance of the evidence. Prior to coming to court, a matter will have been reviewed by several levels of management and handled by an agency of the court in a conciliation procedure.

As to the quality of the proceedings, the judge stated that the employer usually has competent representation, but that the employee only sometimes does. He claims that the court usually has adequate information upon which to base a decision, and that there is sometimes a pretrial discovery process which is usually worth the time and cost involved.

The judge agreed that the Malaysian system does a good job of protecting both employee and employer rights, but he was neutral as to whether the labor court system was an efficient way of resolving workplace disputes. He strongly agreed that it was better than the ordinary courts would be at this. The advantages of the labor court system were said to be the inexpensive and expeditious nature of the proceedings, as well as the fact that it is a specialized court.

NORWAY

Norway provides employees with statutory protections against unfair dismissal. The Norwegian Worker Protection and Working Environment Act (WEA) (2001) states that: "Employees shall not be dismissed unless this is objectively justified on the basis of matters connected with the establishment, the employer or the employee" (Sec. 60). Summary dismissal may be done where the employee is "guilty of a gross breach of duty or other serious breach of the contract of employment" (Sec. 66). There are court precedents holding that summary dismissal is lawful for drunkenness on the job, theft, insubordination, and constant tardiness (Schjoldager 1976), but an employee may not be discharged for absence from work because of illness for either 6 months or 12 months (depending on length of service), pregnancy, or military service.

Dismissal with notice is allowed where there are not grounds for summary dismissal, but nevertheless appropriate reasons for dismissal. In addition to rationalization of production, plant closings, and production cut-backs, dismissal with notice has been held to be appropriate for poor performance (Schjoldager 1976). In such a case, the employer is required, where possible, to discuss the matter with the employee and his elected representative before making the decision to terminate the employee. The notice is required to contain information on the employee's rights to negotiate with the employer, to demand legal proceedings, and to remain on the job (WEA, Sec. 57). Unless otherwise agreed to by the employer and employee, or provided for in a collective agreement, one month's notice must be given by either party before terminating the employment relationship. Periods of notice increase to two months after 5 years of service, and three months after 10 years of service. Employees 50 years of age and older are entitled to longer notice, while employees in trial periods are entitled to 14 days' notice (WEA, Sec. 58).

Temporary contracts of employment are permitted only under certain conditions. These include situations where the work is different from the work ordinarily done in the establishment, the employee is a trainee, there is a labor market scheme in place through the Ministry, the employee is a chief executive officer, there is an engagement for a fixed term with a foreign state or international organization, or the employee is an athlete or other worker in organized sports (WEA, Sec. 58A).

Where a summary dismissal has occurred, the employer is required, as in the case of ordinary dismissals, to discuss the matter with the employee and her representative prior to making the decision, where possible (WEA, Sec. 66). In a summary dismissal case, the employee is not entitled to remain at her post while the case is progressing, unless a court rules otherwise. If the summary dismissal is found to be unlawful, the court will declare it to be invalid (which would entitle the employee to reinstatement). However, in "special cases," the court may weigh the interests of both parties and determine that "it is clearly unreasonable that employment should continue" (Sec. 66). If the court finds the dismissal to be "objectively justified," it will declare the employment relationship to be terminated (Sec. 66). If it is unlawful, the employee will be awarded compensation in such amount as the court "considers reasonable in view of the financial loss, the circumstances of the employer and employee, and other facts of the case" (Sec. 66).

In the case of ordinary dismissals, if the matter is not settled by negotiation, the employee may institute legal proceedings. The employee may remain on the job until an enforceable judgment is handed down by a court. However, a court may find that it is "unreasonable that employment should continue while the case is in progress" and deny the employee this right (Sec. 61). If the court finds that the employee has been unfairly dismissed, upon demand by the employee the dismissal will be ruled "invalid." However, as in the case of summary termination, if the court finds that it is "clearly unreasonable that employment should continue" it will be held to be terminated. Compensation will be awarded in the same manner as for summary dismissal (Sec. 62).

Disputes involving termination of employment are heard by ordinary municipal or district courts, rather than in labor court. The Norwegian Labor Court hears only cases arising out of collective agreements (Evju, undated). However, the municipal courts have special procedures for dismissal cases. In each county there is a panel of lay judges who participate, along with professional judges, in deciding dismissal cases. At the lowest level, the professional judge will sit with two lay judges, and in the appeals court, there will normally be four lay judges involved (WEA, Secs. 61B, 61C).

Practice in the Courts

The Norwegian judge confirmed that the Norwegian courts require the employer to prove cause for termination by a preponderance of the evidence. Prior to going to court, there will have been consultation with the employee before the termination decision was made, and "dispute negotiation" afterwards.

As to the quality of the proceedings in Norwegian courts in termination cases, the judge was of the opinion that both the employer and the employee always have competent representation. He also said that the court always has sufficient information upon which to base a decision. Although there are no pretrial discovery proceedings, legal briefs that are exchanged prior to trial indicate the evidence that will be presented at trial, including documentary evidence.

The judge agreed that the Norwegian court system does a good job of protecting both employer and employee rights. As these cases are handled by special processes in the ordinary courts rather than the labor court, it is not possible to speak of labor court advantages or disadvantages. The judge did say that the cost of litigation that a non-unionized employee must bear can sometimes be very burdensome, particularly if the employee loses.

SOUTH AFRICA

In South Africa, workers have a constitutional right to fair labor practices, which includes the right not to be unfairly dismissed. Because the constitution requires the courts and arbitration tribunals to consider international law, South African courts have referred to the documents of the ILO, including the Termination of Employment Convention of 1982, in defining this right. The constitutional right not to be dismissed unfairly is effectuated by two statutes: The Labor Relations Act of 1995 (LRA) provides a remedy for unjust dismissal, while the Basic Conditions of Employment Act of 1997 provides for notice of termination and severance pay (for dismissals related to operational requirements of the employer). These two statutes cover most South African employees, but for those few who are not covered, there remains the constitutional right that can be enforced in court. Collective agreements provide alternative procedures for enforcing this right (Crotty et al. 2000).

The LRA distinguishes between "unfair dismissals" and "automatically unfair dismissals" (Crotty et al. 2000, p. 290). An other than automatically unfair dismissal exists whenever the employer fails to prove that the reason for a dismissal was a fair one. Fair reasons include those connected with the employee's conduct or capacity, or with the employer's operational requirements. For example, participation in an illegal strike can be considered a fair reason. Also, the dismissal must utilize a fair procedure in order to be considered fair (Crotty et al. 2000).

Dismissals are automatically unfair if they are for the following reasons: 1) union or workplace forum membership or participation; 2) an applicant for employment being requested to avoid or give up such membership or activity; 3) participation in a legal strike; 4) exercising a right under the LRA; 5) the employer compelling the employee to accept its demands on a subject of mutual interest; 6) race, color, ethnic or social origin, gender, marital status, family responsibilities, sexual orientation, religion, conscience, belief, political opinion, or disability (unless based on an inherent requirement of the job); 7) pregnancy or maternity; or 8) age, unless the employee has reached the normal or agreed retirement age (Crotty et al. 2000).

Dismissals must be with notice to the employee, and the standard notice period varies from one week of notice during the first four weeks of employment to four weeks' notice for service of more than one year. The employer may make a payment in lieu of notice. Notice cannot be given while the employee is on leave, and it must be in writing unless the employee is illiterate (Crotty et al. 2000).

As to misconduct, the statutory Code of Good Practice of Dismissal, contained in the LRA, requires that employers adopt disciplinary rules appropriate for the size and nature of their business. These should promote certainty and consistency, be clear, and be made available to employees. In deciding on a disciplinary penalty, the employer must take into account all relevant facts, including the employee's record of discipline, length of service, and personal situation. Although the discipline procedure does not have to be a formal one, the employee has a right to be informed of the charges against her and have a chance to respond to them. There is provision for the employee having the assistance of an employee representative (Crotty et al. 2000).

The Code of Good Practice provides that it is generally not appropriate to discharge an employee for a first offense. Usually, the employee should be given a written warning or, for more serious offenses, a final warning. Dismissal is only for cases of serious misconduct or repeated violations of rules that make a continuation of the employment relationship "intolerable" (Crotty et al. 2000, p. 292). Examples of serious misconduct include gross dishonesty, willful damage to property, willfully endangering others, assault, and gross insubordination. Disciplinary action cannot be taken against a trade union representative without first consulting with the union (Crotty et al. 2000).

When incapacity is used as a basis for dismissal, the LRA makes a distinction between poor performance and incapacity due to illness or injury. As to poor performance, during probation an employee must be given proper instruction, and dismissal must be preceded by the employee, with the assistance of her trade union representative, being given the opportunity to respond to the allegations of poor performance. After the probationary period, the employee cannot be dismissed for incapacity unless the employer has given him proper instruction, training, and counseling, and a reasonable time for improvement. The employer should make an investigation of the matter before firing the employee and should also consider any viable alternatives to dismissal (Crotty et al. 2000).

Where an employee is dismissed because of incapacity stemming from illness or injury, the employer's investigation must include determining the extent of the incapacity and the prognosis. Counseling and rehabilitation must be considered as an alternative to dismissal.

An employee claiming unfair dismissal can bring a case to the tripartite Commission for Conciliation, Mediation and Arbitration or to the labor court. Usually, the case goes to the commission, which first attempts to settle the matter through conciliation. If conciliation fails, the case is referred to arbitration where a final, unappealable, decision is made. Automatically unfair dismissal cases must be filed in the labor court. Also, the commission may refer a case to the labor court if it is claimed that the dismissal was for discriminatory reasons, the case is very complex, there are conflicting arbitration cases on the issue, it is believed by the commission to be in the public interest, or a question of law is involved. Decisions of the labor court can be appealed only to the labor appeal court, but no farther. A common law claim in ordinary civil court is also an option for a dismissed employee (Crotty et al. 2000).

The remedy that is favored by the LRA is reinstatement. Temporary reinstatement may also be given where the need for interim relief is urgent. As an alternative, the arbitrator or labor court may order compensation to be paid to the employee. The maximum amount available is the equivalent of 12 months' wages. The LRA leaves the door open for the employee to claim other damages based on law, contract, or collective agreement.

Practice in the Courts

The South African labor court judge stated that it was up to the employer to prove that there was cause for termination, and that it had to be shown that the "balance of probabilities" favored the employer's case. This would seem to be similar to the preponderance of evidence standard that is common in other countries. Cases usually go through a conciliation process before they come to trial.

As to the quality of the proceedings, the judge responded that the employer usually has competent representation, but that this is only sometimes the case for the employee. The court usually has sufficient information upon which to base an informed decision, and there is always pretrial discovery that is usually worth the time and cost involved.

The judge agreed that the South African system does a good job of protecting the rights of both employees and employers. He agreed that the specialized court system was an efficient way of resolving workplace disputes, and strongly agreed that it was better at this than the ordinary courts would be.

The advantages of the specialized tribunals are that the judges are experts in labor law, matters are generally dealt with expeditiously, employers and employees have a say in the appointment of judges, and the labor court system is credible. The disadvantages include the inability of a party who is not represented by a lawyer to force the other side to also do without a lawyer. Also, the formalism of a court is still present, as it is in other courts.

SPAIN

The Spanish Constitution (Art. 35) provides that all workers have both the duty and the right to work, free selection of career, advancement through their work, sufficient pay to satisfy their needs and those of their family, and freedom from sex discrimination. Rights specific to termination of employment are given in the Workers' Charter and the Labor Procedure Act (Crotty et al. 2000).

Under the Workers' Charter, the employer may terminate an employee's contract of employment for the following "objective reasons:" 1) lack of aptitude for the job, but if it is observed during a probationary period and not acted upon at that time, it cannot be asserted later; 2) failure to adapt to technical modifications of the job, if the changes are reasonable and the failure continues for two months after the adoption of the change; and 3) absence from work for 20 percent of the working days in two consecutive months, or 25 percent in any 4 months in a 12 month period, if the rate of absenteeism in the work force exceeds 5 percent during these periods (Workers' Charter, Sec. 54) (Crotty et al. 2000).

In addition, the employer may terminate the employee for disciplinary reasons that amount to "culpable non-performance" by the employee. These include the following: 1) repeated and unjustified absence or lateness; 2) indiscipline or disobedience; 3) verbal or physical offenses against the employer, employees, or members of their families living with them; 4) violation of "contractual goodwill, and abuse of confidence in the discharge of duties"; 5) intentional and continued reduction of output below normal or agreed levels; and 6) "habitual drunkenness or drug addiction if it adversely affects" work performance (Workers' Charter, Sec. 54) (Crotty et al. 2000, p. 296).

By provision of the Workers' Charter [Secs. 4 (2), 17 (1)], terminations are prohibited on the basis of sex, ethnic origin, marital status, race, social status, religious or political beliefs, membership or non-membership in a trade union, or language. Discharge on account of disability is prohibited in a separate statute (Crotty et al. 2000).

The protections of the Workers' Charter extend to workers who "voluntarily provide remunerated services" for an employer (Crotty et al. 2000, p. 294). Excluded are employees in government, civil, or community service; those who are giving advice to a corporation's governing body; workers performing work "in the name of friendship, benevolence or good neighborliness"; family workers; and persons engaged in trading operations on an employer's behalf (Crotty et al. 2000, p. 294).

Contracts of employment can be either of indefinite duration or for a fixed term. Contracts for a fixed term of over four weeks must be in writing. Fixed-term contracts, which have become increasingly prevalent in Spain, may be for the completion of a particular set of tasks or services, to meet market demands, to replace a worker temporarily, or for the launching of a new activity. It is permitted to have probationary periods that vary in length depending on whether the worker is skilled or unskilled (Crotty et al. 2000).

Where there is a termination for objective reasons, a written communication containing the reasons must be given to the employee. The employer must pay the employee an amount equal to 20 days' pay for each year of service up to a maximum of 12 months' pay. In addition, the employer must give the employee 30 days' notice [Workers' Charter, Sec. 53 (1)]. If the termination is a disciplinary dismissal for misconduct, there must be a written notice setting out the facts on which the dismissal is based, and stating the date on which employment is to end [Workers' Charter, Sec. 55 (1)] (Crotty et al. 2000).

If a dismissed worker is a member of a trade union and the employer knows about this, the employer must give a trade union representative an opportunity to be heard on the matter in advance of the termination. If the worker is a trade union officer, "formal adversarial proceedings" must be held in which both the worker and the trade union are entitled to be heard (Crotty et al. 2000, p. 297).

Workers properly dismissed are entitled to 20 days' severance pay for each year of service up to a maximum of 12 months' pay. This is prorated if the employee has been employed less than one year [Workers' Charter, Sec. 53 (1) (b)]. Workers who are unlawfully dismissed are entitled to 45 days' pay for each year of service up to a maximum of 42 months' pay. Here, also, there is proration if the employee has been employed less than one year. There will also be compensation for lost wages from the date of the dismissal to the date that the employer is notified that the dismissal is unlawful, or until the worker has found another job if this happened before the case was decided [Workers' Charter, Sec. 56 (1) (a), (b)] (Crotty et al. 2000).

An employee may seek redress before a labor court within 20 days of termination. In the case of dismissal for objective reasons (not disciplinary), if the employer fails to meet the requirements of notice and payment required by law [Workers' Charter, Sec. 53 (1)], the termination will be declared null and void and the employer will be require to pay compensation as if there had been an improper disciplinary dismissal. However, mere failure to give notice will not nullify the dismissal—it will only require the employer to pay wages for the notice period.

If a dismissal is declared unlawful, the employer will have five days to make a choice between reinstating the worker and paying compensation, but the option to elect compensation only exists where the employee was a trade union representative. If no option is selected, the court will order reinstatement. If a worker is found to have been dismissed in violation of antidiscrimination laws (sex, race, etc.), the dismissal will be null and void and the employer will be required to reinstate the employee or pay his wages indefinitely. The employer may also be subject to other civil liabilities (Crotty et al. 2000).

Practice in the Courts

The Spanish judge responded that, in order to be justly terminated, the worker had to be found guilty of serious noncompliance with the employment contract. In his response, the judge did not indicate what quantum of proof would be required. Prior to the matter going to trial, a conciliation proceeding would always take place.

As to the quality of the process, the judge responded that both the employer and the employee usually have competent representation. It was his opinion that the court usually has the information that it needs to make an informed decision. He said that there is always pretrial discovery, which he believed to be usually worth the time and cost involved.

The Spanish judge agreed that his country's system does a good job in protecting the rights of both employees and employers, and also agreed that the labor court system was an efficient means of resolving workplace disputes. He strongly agreed that labor courts did this better than ordinary courts would.

The advantages of the Spanish labor court system include specialization, speed, and judges who are knowledgeable about social realities, while a disadvantage is the routine nature of some cases.

SWEDEN

Under the Swedish Security of Employment Act of 1984, which covers virtually all private contracts of employment, dismissal of an employee is legal only if notice is given and there is a valid reason. The notice of dismissal must be "materially justified" (Crotty et al. 2000, p. 307). Valid reasons include: 1) reason related to the conduct of the employee—e.g., refusal to obey orders (which has been held to be a valid reason for summary dismissal), and lack of punctuality, but these offenses must be sufficiently serious to constitute just cause; 2) in small undertakings, failing to cooperate with the employee's fellow workers; 3) incapacity to do the work, although this ground is restricted after the probationary period has been completed; and 4) criminal offenses against the employer (Crotty et al. 2000).

In general, employment is required to be for an indefinite period. Exceptions are: 1) if the nature of the work justifies employment for a set period, season, or job; 2) temporary replacement as a trainee or a holiday worker; 3) for a period of up to 12 months over two years if the work accumulates in a temporary way; 4) up to the date an employee begins military or comparable service for more than 3 months;

and 5) work performed after an employee's retirement date (Crotty et al. 2000).

Dismissal can be with immediate effect, but "this form of dismissal is unusual because the courts consider such dismissal appropriate only in the event that no other solution is possible" (Crotty et al. 2000, p. 308). Dismissal with notice, which is more common, requires a notice period ranging from 2 months (if the employee is 25 years old) to 6 months (if the employee is 45 years old). The employee must be notified of the impending dismissal two weeks before the notice period begins to run, and the employer must notify the local union two weeks before taking steps to terminate an employee. The notice must be in writing and tell the employee about the procedure to be followed if he wishes to contest it. If the union and the employee wish to discuss the termination with the employer, the termination cannot occur until this discussion has taken place.

When the discussions with the employee and trade union fail to produce a settlement, a suit may be brought in the labor court. The employer must retain the employee on the job until the case is decided, and has the burden of proving that the reasons for termination are valid. This includes showing that the continuation of the employment relationship is untenable for the firm and that alternative employment cannot be offered (Crotty et al. 2000).

If the labor court finds the dismissal to be unjustified, it may order reinstatement or financial compensation. Damages take into account the employee's length of service, age, and capacity to find alternative employment. If an employer fails to comply with a reinstatement order, the employment relationship is terminated and the employee can claim additional compensation as follows: 16 months' wages for less than 5 years of employment; 24 months' wages for 5 to 10 years of employment; or 32 months' wages for 10 or more years of employment. The amount increases if the employee has reached the age of 60. If the employee has less than 6 months of service, the amount of compensation is 6 months' wages (Crotty et al. 2000).

Practice in the Courts

In Sweden, the labor court requires the employer to prove cause for termination by a preponderance of the evidence. Before coming to court, a worker who is a trade union member would be represented by a union, which has the duty to negotiate with the employer before filing suit in labor court. Other employees may file a suit in an ordinary court without first negotiating with the employer.

As to the quality of the process, the judge responded that both the employer and the employee usually have competent representation, the court always has sufficient information upon which to base an informed decision, and there is always pretrial discovery, which is always worth the time and money involved.

The judge strongly agreed that the labor court system does a good job of protecting both employee and employer rights, and that the labor court system is an efficient way of resolving workplace disputes. He agreed that it was better at this than ordinary courts would be.

The advantages of the Swedish labor court are the specialized nature of the judges—in particular the lay judges—and the swiftness of the procedure. Although there are no general disadvantages of the system cited in the study, it might be seen by some as a disadvantage that workers have legal security of employment (lack of flexibility for employers). Also, nonorganized employees and employers may not like to have their cases heard by lay judges selected by employer and worker organizations.

UNITED KINGDOM

Under the Employment Rights Act of 1996 (ERA), British employees are given the right not to be dismissed unfairly. The ERA protects workers with two years of service with their employer, or who have been employed for shorter periods if the dismissal is for union membership, health and safety activities, sex, or race. Excluded from its protection are persons of normal retirement age (65 if there is no normal age for that job), share fishermen, persons who work outside the United Kingdom or are not ordinarily resident in the United Kingdom, members of armed forces, police officers, and workers under fixed-term contracts for one year or more if they have waived their ERA protection in writing (Crotty et al. 2000).

Dismissals are fair if they are because of reasons set out in the ERA. These include aptitude, personal incapacity or ill health, conduct, taking part in an industrial action and not being rehired within three months, not having the legal capacity to meet the employer's needs (e.g., not having a driver's license), "dismissal for some other substantial reason" that justifies dismissal, and redundancy (Crotty et al. 2000, p. 333). The employer must show cause for termination, and the Industrial Tribunal will then decide whether, considering all the circumstances, the employer "acted as a reasonable employer" (Crotty et al. 2000, p. 333).

Some grounds for dismissal are "automatically unfair" (Crotty et al. 2000, p. 333). These include trade union membership or office; refusal to join a union; unfair selection to be made redundant; pregnancy and confinement; discrimination on the basis of race, sex, or disability; for raising health or safety questions; seeking enforcement of a statutory right pertaining to employment; transfer of the undertaking (unless justified); conviction of an offense or failure to disclose conviction where it is protected by law; to avoid threatened industrial action; refusal of Sunday work; and being a trustee of an occupational pension scheme (Crotty et al. 2000).

In all cases other than those that involve "automatically unfair" grounds for dismissal, the dismissal must be for a fair reason and be "reasonable" (Crotty et al. 2000, p. 334). An employer is allowed considerable discretion as to what is reasonable, and the Industrial Tribunal is loathe to substitute its judgment for that of the employer. The inquiry by the Tribunal will be whether the dismissal falls within the range of "reasonable responses which a reasonable employer might have adopted" (Crotty et al. 2000, p. 334).

Notice of termination must be given to employees who have been employed continuously by the employer for one month. The amount of notice is based on the employee's length of service and age. The employee is entitled to one and a half weeks' notice for each year of service that the employee was not below 41 years of age, one week's notice for each year of employment when the employee was not below 21 years of age, and a half week's notice for each year of employment not falling under either of the first two conditions.

An employee may bring a claim before the Industrial Tribunal within three months of his termination. In 2001, the Labour government proposed charging employees a fee, which could be as high as

£100, to file a case with the Industrial Tribunal (Bureau of National Affairs 2001b).

In the Industrial Tribunal, conciliation is first attempted. If this fails, the matter goes to a hearing before the Industrial Tribunal. The Employment Rights (Dispute Resolution) Act of 1998 provides for arbitration as an alternative to the Industrial Tribunal. Arbitration under the Advisory, Conciliation and Arbitration Service (ACAS) system has been seldom used (Neal 2001). An employee may also sue in civil court, and may ask for an injunction. In the Industrial Tribunal, the employer must establish that the principal reason for the termination justifies it. The Industrial Tribunal decides whether the reason did in fact justify the termination (Crotty et al. 2000).

The ERA provides that reinstatement should be the primary remedy for an unfair dismissal. However, the Industrial Tribunal has broad discretion in determining whether this is a practical remedy in a particular case. It may render a special award not to exceed £27,500. The amount of the basic award is based upon age and years of service, with a maximum of £6,150. In addition, there may be a compensatory award that compensates the employee for loss of earnings, pension rights, injury to the employee's feelings, etc. This compensatory award is limited to £12,000, except in cases of race or sex discrimination, where there is no limit. If an employee is not granted reinstatement, he/she is entitled to an additional special training award, not to exceed £27,500. An employee may sue in civil court and recover damages for mental distress, anxiety, and illness (Crotty et al. 2000).

Practice in the Courts

Two Industrial Tribunal judges from the United Kingdom responded to our questionnaire, and both agreed that the burden was on the employer to prove cause for termination. One of them said that this needed to be by a preponderance of the evidence, and the other claimed that there had to be a "balance of probabilities" on the side of the employer. These opinions appear to be very similar.

The United Kingdom judges agreed that a case would usually be reviewed by several levels of management before making its way to court. One of them also mentioned ACAS conciliation as a regular occurrence.

As to the quality of the process, they agreed that the employer usually has competent representation. As to the competence of employee representatives, one of them said that employee representatives were usually competent, while the other responded that this was true only some of the time. One said that the court usually has sufficient information, while the other said that this was always the case. One responded that there was always pretrial discovery that was always worth the time and cost, while the other said that pretrial discovery only usually occurred, and that it was only usually worthwhile.

One of the judges strongly agreed that the system does a good job of protecting both employee and employer rights, while the other simply agreed with this. One agreed that the system is an efficient way of resolving workplace disputes, while the other was neutral on this. However, one agreed and the other strongly agreed that this system was preferable to that of the ordinary courts.

Advantages of the system include specialization and legitimacy (based upon tripartism), speed, and low cost. The disadvantages are the interface with nonemployment civil litigation, and the expense to employers in defending against "hopeless" employee claims. Even if the court awards the employer costs against the employee, this will rarely be enforceable as a practical matter.

Appendix B
The Research Sample
and Hypothetical Cases

THE SAMPLE

Our goal in constructing the sample for this research was to obtain responses from experienced labor arbitrators, employment arbitrators, peer review panelists, jurors with experience in employment discrimination cases, and human resources (HR) managers. In order to allow for a cross-cultural comparison, we also wanted to collect data from labor court judges in countries where for-cause standards are mandated by law. With regard to the labor arbitrators, we randomly sampled 200 labor arbitrators from the National Academy of Arbitrators Directory. Arbitrators were mailed the survey instrument and asked to mail the completed surveys to the researchers. Arbitrators were offered financial compensation for completing the survey, to ensure an adequate response rate. Eighty-two arbitrators provided responses, resulting in a response rate of 42 percent.

Employment arbitrators were identified from a list provided by the American Arbitration Association. In addition, we identified some 27 employment arbitrators who had published employment arbitration awards or otherwise identified themselves as employment arbitrators. Surveys were mailed to a random selection of 450 of these employment arbitrators (who were not already included in the survey of labor arbitrators). Half of the arbitrators were sent surveys that required the evaluation of cases from the standpoint of statutory claims. The other half were sent surveys that contained a for-cause standard in the instructions. Seventy-two surveys were received from employment arbitrators who received the survey with the statutory claim manipulation, resulting in a response rate of 32 percent. Sixty-eight surveys were received from employment arbitrators who received the survey with the for-cause manipulation, resulting in a 30 percent response rate. Again, financial compensation was offered to encourage responses to our survey.

With regard to peer review panelists, we identified two large manufacturing organizations that have active peer review systems at a number of their operations. Management officials cooperated with the research effort by sending the survey instrument to 141 employees who had served as peer review panelists in disciplinary cases. The peers were drawn from 11 different manufacturing facilities located in different parts of the country. All peers had been trained to evaluate disciplinary cases by their organizations, and had experience participating in peer review panels. We received surveys from 91 peers, resulting in a response rate of 64 percent.

With regard to jurors, with the cooperation of a federal district court judge, we obtained the names and addresses of jurors who had served in discrimination cases over the last several years within his district, which is located in the southeastern United States. Surveys were mailed to 112 jurors, and we received responses from 83, resulting in a response rate of 74 percent. As with most other parts of the sample, jurors were also offered a financial incentive to participate.

With regard to HR managers, we identified individuals with the titles of "HR Director" or "HR Manager" from a directory of manufacturing organizations located in the southeast. We also identified HR directors and HR managers based on job title listings in an alumni directory from a graduate program in human resources. From this listing of individuals, we randomly selected 200 individuals and mailed them the survey. We received 59 surveys, resulting in a response rate of 30 percent. A financial incentive was offered to encourage participation.

With regard to labor court judges, we relied on personal contacts to identify possible participants. Labor court judges were drawn from several countries (primarily in Europe) where judges were responsible for enforcing for-cause standards in termination cases. At their request, no financial compensation was offered to the labor court judges. In total, we received responses from 12 labor court judges from eight countries, giving us a response rate of 46 percent of the judges in 53 percent of the countries included in the survey.

THE TERMINATION CASES

Case 1 Summary

Case 1 does not involve allegations of illegal discrimination. Instead, it involves allegations of a violation of a contractual requirement that termination will be for-cause. Labor arbitrators were to evaluate the case from the standpoint of a labor contract, whereas jurors and employment arbitrators were to evaluate it from the standpoint of a provision in an employment agreement. Peer review panelists and HR managers were also told about the employment agreement requiring cause for termination. In this case, the alleged offense is severe (theft of valuable company property), and evidence against the employee is substantial. There are two witnesses to the offense, both of whom have long work histories with the employer. While the accused employee claims that the witnesses themselves are responsible for the theft, there is no evidence to support this. Further, evidence is presented that would suggest that it would have been difficult for the witnesses to have stolen the equipment. To the contrary, evidence is also presented to suggest that, given the nature of the accused employee's job, it would have been feasible for him to have stolen the property. Information presented about the employee indicates that he has a relatively short tenure with the firm. There is no evidence of any procedural problems with the dismissal or with the investigation.

In sum, evidence against the employee is strong, the alleged offense is severe, the employee's work history is relatively short, and there is no evidence of procedural problems with the termination or the investigation.

Case 2 Summary

Case 2 is similar to Case 1 on many dimensions. One key difference is that, except for decision makers who would normally have a for-cause standard (e.g., labor arbitrators and labor court judges), the case makes clear that this is an employment-at-will situation. The case contains an accusation of racial discrimination. As such, labor arbitrators and labor court judges would make a determination as to whether they were to find for the employee based on cause (influenced directly or indirectly by the alleged discrimination). Peer review panelists were to assess whether the termination was consistent with company policy and procedure (again, influenced directly or indirectly by the alleged discrimination). HR managers were to determine whether they supported termination in light of the alleged discrimination and other factors relevant to employee relations and organizational productivity. Finally, jurors and employment arbitrators were asked to determine whether they would find for the employee in light of the alleged discrimination. The facts remained constant across the different decision makers.

The employee is accused of theft by two long-term employees of good standing. The employee denies stealing the property and claims that the employees who accused him may have been responsible. Further, he claims he is being accused of theft because of racial discrimination. While the employee (a racial minority) states that he has heard racially oriented jokes, there is no other evidence available to support this claim—no corroboration regarding racial comments or jokes is provided. While the employee in question was in a position to steal the property, the two employees accusing him of theft were not well positioned to engage in theft.

In sum, the case involves a situation where racial discrimination is alleged but there is little evidence available to support the claim. The evidence against the employee is substantial, the employee has been with the firm a relatively short period, and there are no procedural problems with the termination or the investigation of the alleged offense.

Case 3 Summary

In Case 3, an employee is terminated for insubordination, but claims that the decision is due to discrimination on the basis of gender. For labor arbitrators and labor court judges, the case is one requiring cause. For other decision makers, it is an employment-at-will setting. Evidence with regard to discrimination is ambiguous. While the employee claims that she was treated with little respect by her supervisor, and that her male supervisor made inappropriate remarks about women, interviews with other employees fail to provide corroboration for this allegation. However, all other employees in the work unit are male.

Evidence of insubordination is limited to testimony provided by the supervisor. The alleged insubordination occurred during a private discussion regarding the need for the subordinate to assist another employee with his job responsibilities. The manager claims that the employee became abusive and insulting and refused to accept the order. The employee admits to challenging the need for obeying the supervisor's request, but denies becoming abusive or refusing the order. Instead, the employee claims that her challenge enraged her supervisor, resulting in the termination. The employee's work record is relatively short (four years). However, productivity data show that she is highly effective. Company policy states that termination for insubordination requires one written warning, and the supervisor claimed that he provided the employee with a verbal warning.

In sum, substantial ambiguity exists with regard to the evidence of discrimination and evidence of wrongdoing by the employee. Compliance by the employer with its own procedures is in question. Also, the employee is one with relatively short tenure with the organization.

Case 4 Summary

Case 4 does not involve allegations of illegal discrimination. Instead, it involves allegations of a violation of an employment agreement which stipulates that termination must be for-cause. Labor arbitrators were to evaluate the case from the standpoint of a labor contract, whereas jurors and employment arbitrators were to evaluate it from the standpoint of a for-cause provision in an employment agreement. Peers and HR managers were also informed of the for-cause provision in the employment agreement. In this case, the alleged offense is severe (theft of company property) and evidence against the employee is substantial. Indeed, the employee admits to the theft. Company policy states that theft of any company property, regardless of value, makes the employee subject to termination. However, the employee explains that he took property from the trash bin and assumed that doing so was acceptable behavior. The employee also points out that he has been with the firm for 20 years and has a good work record. No evidence is provided to show that there was inconsistency in how the firm has applied the rule. The focus, instead, is on the reasonableness of the rule, and what might be seen as disproportionate consequences for the employee, given the value of the property. There is no dispute about the facts of the case, and there are no concerns about the employer's compliance with contractually mandated procedures, or about the manner in which the firm investigated what happened.

Case 5 Summary

Case 5 does not involve allegations of illegal discrimination. Instead, it involves allegations of violation of an employment agreement.

Labor arbitrators were to evaluate the case from the standpoint of a labor contract, whereas jurors and employment arbitrators would evaluate the case from the standpoint of a for-cause provision in the employment agreement. Peer review panelists and HR managers were informed of the for-cause provision in the employment agreement. In this case, the rule is reasonable, in that it prohibits fighting within the workplace and makes fighting a basis for immediate employment termination.

An employee is accused by another employee of starting a fight, and there is only one witness (i.e., the employee making the accusation). The accused employee has a negative work history and a relatively short tenure with the firm. There are no obvious procedural problems with this case, no evidence of inconsistent treatment of employees, and no evidence that management failed to conduct a proper and appropriate investigation. The employee is challenging the termination by questioning the evidence against him. As stated above, there is only one other witness to the events: the other employee engaged in the altercation. While the employee being terminated contends that the other employee is only trying to get him in trouble, there is no evidence of any such motive.

In sum, the alleged offense is severe, there are no procedural problems with the case, and the employee has a negative work history. While there is evidence of employee wrongdoing, it is not conclusive.

Case 6 Summary

Case 6 does not involve allegations of illegal discrimination against the employee. Instead, it involves allegations that the employer violated an employment agreement that stipulates that termination must be for-cause. Labor arbitrators were to evaluate the case from the standpoint of a labor contract, whereas jurors, employment arbitrators, and others would evaluate the case from the standpoint of the for-cause provision in the employment agreement.

The employee was terminated for absenteeism problems that occurred over the prior year. The organization is in compliance with clearly stated policies regarding absenteeism. The employee received two written warnings during the last two months of employment and continued to have attendance problems after the final warning. No evidence exists to suggest that the firm was inconsistent in how the employee was treated, and there was no other indication of any procedural problems with manner of the termination. Mitigating circumstances are present, however: The employee is a long-term employee, and she had never received a disciplinary sanction prior to the last year. She also contends that the absenteeism was caused by family problems (illness of a parent, ending in death, combined with illnesses of her children).

In sum, termination is likely to be justified, in this case, unless mitigating circumstances are deemed to be relevant.

Case 7 Summary

Case 7 involves allegations of age discrimination. The employee in question was over 50 and was replaced by an employee below the age of 40. For labor arbitrators, labor court judges, and the appropriate subsample of employment arbitrators, there was a for-cause requirement for termination. Peer review panelists were instructed to ensure that the termination was consistent with company policy and procedures.

The employee, who was terminated for poor performance and insubordination, had received a below-average rating in the prior year and, according to his manager, had not improved his performance following this. Thorough documentation exists regarding the performance problem. Productivity statistics are provided and the performance evaluation form from the previous year contains a detailed explanation regarding the nature of the employee's deficiencies and the improvements needed. Company policy requires a written warning about performance problems before termination, and that written warning was provided. While the employee had not had performance problems prior to his last year employed, the job is one that changes over time and requires ongoing learning and development to perform effectively. Insubordination was alleged to have occurred in a meeting designed to discuss the performance problem. Two managers were present during the meeting, and both confirm that the employee became abusive and refused to follow suggestions made about how to improve performance. Nothing said or done by the managers in the meeting was deemed unprofessional. The employee had been with the firm for four years, and had received warnings for absenteeism. Evidence of discrimination is limited to a claim by the employee that the supervisor had made jokes about older workers, and no corroboration of this claim is provided.

In sum, the organization has strong evidence of wrongdoing in this case and has complied with its own procedures. Further, there is little basis for questioning the reasonableness of the rule, the employee's work history is not outstanding, and evidence of discrimination is limited.

Case 8 Summary

Similar to Case 7, Case 8 involves allegations of age discrimination. The employee in question was over 50 and was replaced by an employee below the age of 40. For labor arbitrators, labor court judges, and a subsample of employment arbitrators, there was—in addition to the claim of discrimination—a for-cause requirement for termination. And, as with all four cases, peer review panelists received instructions saying that the termination must be consistent with company policy and procedures.

The employee was terminated for poor performance and insubordination. He received a below-average rating in the prior year and, according to his manager, had not improved his performance following this. Other than the below-average rating, the performance evaluation form contains little specific information about actual productivity levels, or the nature of the employee's deficiencies. Testimony is provided by a coworker, indicating that the employee is good at solving technical problems and is frequently sought out by others for technical assistance. Company policy requires a written warning about performance problems before termination, and no warning was provided. While the employee had not had performance problems prior to the last year before termination, the job has changed over time and requires ongoing learning and development to perform effectively.

Insubordination is alleged to have occurred in a meeting to discuss the performance problem. Only the employee and his manager were present during the meeting. According to the manager (but denied by the employee), the employee became abusive during the meeting and refused to follow suggestions about how to improve performance. Nothing said or done by the managers in the meeting was deemed unprofessional. The employee had been with the firm for four years, and during that period, received warnings about absenteeism. Evidence of discrimination was limited to a claim by the employee that the supervisor had made jokes about older workers, but no corroboration of this claim was provided.

In sum, evidence of wrongdoing was modest in this case, and the organization failed to comply with its own procedures as they relate to termination for performance. However, there is little basis for questioning the reasonableness of the rule, the employee's work history is not outstanding, and evidence of discrimination is weak.

Case 9 Summary

Case 9 involves an allegation of age discrimination, although the issue of cause would also be relevant for some types of decision makers. The employee was terminated for poor performance and insubordination. He received a below average rating in the prior year and, according to his manager, had not improved his performance following this. Other than the below-average rating, the performance evaluation form contains little specific information about actual productivity levels or the reasons for the employee's deficiencies. Testimony provided by a coworker indicates that the employee is skilled at complex tasks and is frequently sought out by others for technical assistance. Company policy requires a written warning about performance problems before termination, and a written warning was provided one month prior to the termination. While the employee had not had performance problems prior to last year, the job is one that changes over time and requires on-going learning and development to perform effectively.

Insubordination is alleged to have occurred in a meeting to discuss the employee's performance problem. Only the employee and his manager were present during the meeting. According to the manager (but denied by the employee), the employee became abusive during the meeting and refused to follow suggestions made about how to improve his performance. Nothing said or done by the managers in the meeting was deemed unprofessional. The employee had been with the firm for four years, and had received warnings about absenteeism. The claim of discrimination is supported by two recently retired employees who confirm that they heard managers talk about the need to get rid of "old, deadwood employees." They also confirm that they heard the employee's supervisor make jokes about older employees.

In sum, evidence of employee wrongdoing was modest in this case, and there was some supporting evidence to justify the claim of discrimination. However, there is little basis for questioning the reasonableness of the rule, the employee's work history is not outstanding, and the organization is in compliance with its own policies and procedures.

Case 10 Summary

Case 10 involves an allegation of illegal age discrimination, although the issue of cause would also be relevant for some types of decision makers. The employee was terminated for poor performance and insubordination. He had received a below-average rating in the prior year and, according to his manager, had not improved his performance following this. Other than the below-average rating, the performance evaluation form contains little specific information about actual productivity levels or the nature of the employee's deficiencies. Testimony provided by a coworker indicates that the employee is skilled at complex tasks and is frequently sought out by others for technical assistance. Company policy requires a written warning about performance problems before termination, and a written warning was provided one month prior to the termination. While the employee had not had performance problems prior to the last year before termination, the job is one that changes over time, and thus requires ongoing learning and development to perform effectively.

Insubordination is alleged to have occurred in a meeting designed to discuss the performance problem. Only the employee and his manager were present during the meeting. According to the manager (but denied by the employee), the employee became abusive during the meeting and refused to follow suggestions made about how to improve his performance. The employee says that during the meeting, the supervisor became insulting toward him. The manager confirms this, but indicates that he did this in an effort to motivate the employee. The employee had been with the firm for four years, and during that period, he had received warnings about absenteeism. The employee claims that he had heard the supervisor make jokes about older employees. The supervisor denies this, and there is no evidence corroborating this claim by the employee.

In sum, evidence of wrongdoing is modest in this case. Furthermore, there is some indication that the supervisor's behavior might have provoked the behavior defined as insubordination. However, there is little basis for questioning the reasonableness of the rule, the employee's work history is not outstanding, the organization is in compliance with its own policies and procedures, and there is little evidence to support the claim of discrimination.

Case 11 Summary

Case 11 involves an allegation of illegal age discrimination, although the issue of cause would also be relevant for some types of decision makers. The employee, who was terminated for poor performance and insubordination, received a below-average rating in the prior year and, according to his manager, had not improved his performance following this. Other than the below-average rating, the performance evaluation form contains little specific information about actual productivity levels, or the reason for the ratings that were given. Testimony of a coworker indicates that the employee is skilled at complex tasks, and is frequently sought out by others for technical assistance. Company policy requires a written warning about performance problems before termination, and a written warning was provided one month prior to the termination. While the employee had not had performance problems prior to last year, the job is one that changes over time, and thus, requires ongoing learning and development to perform effectively.

Insubordination was alleged to have occurred in a meeting to discuss the performance problem, but only the employee and his manager were present during the meeting. According to the manager (but denied by the employee), the employee became abusive during the meeting and refused to follow suggestions about how to improve his performance. There was agreement that the supervisor behaved professionally during the meeting. The employee had been with the firm for 22 years and had never received a disciplinary warning prior to the termination year. Prior to the last year, the employee always received above-average performance evaluation ratings. The employee claims that he had heard the supervisor make jokes about older employees. However, the supervisor denies this, and there was no corroborating evidence.

In sum, evidence of wrongdoing is modest in this case. One possible mitigating factor is that the employee has a long and outstanding work history with the organization. However, there is little basis for questioning the reasonableness of the rule, the organization is in compliance with its own policies and procedures, and there is little evidence to support the claim of discrimination.

Case 12 Summary

Case 12 involves an allegation of illegal age discrimination, although the issue of just cause would also be relevant for some types of decision makers. The employee, who was terminated for poor performance and insubordination, received a below-average rating in the prior year and, according to his manager, had not improved his performance following this. Other than the below-average rating, the performance evaluation form contains little specific information about actual productivity levels or the reasons behind the rating that was given. Testimony provided by a coworker indicates that the employee is skilled at complex tasks and is frequently sought out by other employees for technical assistance. Company policy requires a written warning about performance problems before termination, and such warning was provided one month prior to the termination. While the employee had not had performance problems prior to last year, the job is one that changes frequently, and thus requires ongoing learning and development to perform effectively.

Insubordination was alleged to have occurred in a meeting designed to discuss the performance problem, but only the employee and his manager were present during the meeting. According to the manager (but denied by the employee), the employee became abusive during the meeting, and refused to follow suggestions about how to improve his performance. There is agreement that the supervisor behaved professionally during the meeting. The employee had been with the firm for four years, had received average performance ratings prior to the last year, and had received two warnings relating to absenteeism. The employee claims that he heard the supervisor make jokes about older employees, but the supervisor denies this, and there is no evidence corroborating this claim. The employee had some personal problems in the year prior to termination that might explain some of his recent performance problems. Nine months before his termination, the employee's wife developed a serious illness. She died prior to his termination.

In sum, evidence of wrongdoing is modest in this case. There is one possible extenuating circumstance relating to the recent illness and death of the employee's spouse. However, there is little basis for questioning the reasonableness of the rule, and the organization is in compliance with its own policies and procedures. Furthermore, the employee's tenure is relatively short, and his record was not outstanding during this time. Lastly, there is little evidence to support a claim of discrimination.

References

Abbott, Walter F. 1993. *Jury Research: A Review and Bibliography.* Washington, DC: American Law Institute.

Abraham, Steven E., and Paula B. Voos. 2000. "Empirical Data on Employer Gains From Compulsory Arbitration of Employment Disputes." *Employee Rights and Employment Policy Journal* 4(2): 341–363.

Advent, Inc. v. McCarthy, 914 F.2d 6 (1st Cir. 1990).

Air Line Pilots Association v. Northwest Airlines, Inc., 199 F.3d 477 (DC Cir. 1999), rehearing *en banc* 211 F.3d 1312 (DC Cir. 2000), *cert denied* 84 FEP Cases 544 (U.S. Sup. Ct. 2000).

Alexander v. Gardner-Denver, 415 U.S. 36 (1974).

Alternative Dispute Resolution Act. 28 U.S.C. §§657–658 (2000).

American Arbitration Association (AAA). 1999– 2001. *Employment Dispute Arbitration Reports.*

———. 2002. "ADR Legislation Moves Forward in California." *Dispute Resolution Times* (July–September): 3.

Appelbaum, Judith A. 1998. "Statement of Judith C. Appelbaum Senior Counsel and Director of Legal Programs National Women's Law Center." U.S. Congress. Senate. Mandatory Arbitration Agreements in Employment Contracts in the Securities Industry, 105th Cong., 2d sess., pp. 105–106.

Armendiaz v. Foundation Health Psychcare Services, 6 P.3d 669 (2000).

Bales, Richard A. 1997. *Compulsory Arbitration: The Grand Experiment in Employment.* Ithaca, NY: Cornell University Press.

Barnard, Chester. 1938. *The Functions of the Executive.* Cambridge: Harvard University Press.

Baugher v. Dekko Heating Technologies, 202 F.Supp.2d 847 (N.D. Ind. 2002).

Bell, James. 2002. Personal interview. Myrtle Beach, SC, September 28, 2002.

Bennett-Alexander, Dawn D., and Laura P. Hartman. 2001. *Employment Law for Business,* 3d Ed. Boston, MA: Irwin/McGraw Hill.

———. 2004. *Employment Law for Business,* 4th ed. Boston, MA: Irwin/McGraw-Hill.

Bentley's Luggage Corp. NLRB Case No. 12-CA-16658, *Daily Labor Report* (Bureau of National Affairs, September 25, 1995), p. D-4.

Bickner, Mei L., Christine Ver Ploeg, and Charles Feigenbaum. 1997. "Developments in Employment Arbitration." *Dispute Resolution Journal* (January): 8–15, 78–83.

Bingham, Lisa B. 1995. "Is There a Bias in Arbitration of Non-union Employment Disputes?" *International Journal of Conflict Management* (6): 369–397.

———. 1996. "Emerging Due Process Concerns in Employment Arbitration: A Look at Actual Cases." *Labor Law Journal* 47(2): 108–126.

———. 1997. "Employment Arbitration: The Repeat Player Effect." *Employee Rights and Employment Policy Journal* 1(1): 189–220.

———. 1998. "On Repeat Players, Adhesive Contracts, and the Use of Statistics in Judicial Review of Employment Arbitration Awards." *McGeorge Law Review* 29(2): 223–259.

Bingham, Lisa B., and Debra J. Mesch. 2000. "Decision Making in Employment and Labor Arbitration." *Industrial Relations* 39(4): 671–694.

Bingham, Lisa B., and Shimon Sarraf. 2004. "Employment Arbitration Before and After the Due Process Protocol for Mediation and Arbitration of Statutory Disputes Arising Out of Employment: Preliminary Evidence that Self-Regulation Makes a Difference." In *Alternative Dispute Resolution in the Employment Arena: Proceedings of the New York University 53rd Annual Conference on Labor.* Samuel Estreicher and David Sherwyn, eds. New York: Kluwer Legal International, pp. 303–329.

Block, Richard N., and Jack Stieber. 1987. "The Impact of Attorneys and Arbitrators on Arbitration Awards." *Industrial and Labor Relations Review* 40(4): 543–555.

Bompey, Stuart, and Michael Pappas. 1993–1994. "Is There a Better Way? Compulsory Arbitration of Employment Claims after Gilmer." *Employee Relations Law Journal* 19: 197–216.

Bompey, Stuart H., and Andrea H. Stempel. 1995. "Four Years Later: A Look at Compulsory Arbitration of Employment Discrimination Claims after *Gilmer v. Interstate Johnson Lane Corp.*" *Employee Relations Law Journal* 21(2): 21–49.

Brand, Norman, ed. 1998. *Discipline and Discharge in Arbitration.* Washington, DC: Bureau of National Affairs.

Bravin, Jess. 2001. "U.S. Courts Are Tough on Job-Bias Suits—Appeals Courts Overturned 44% of Plaintiffs' Wins Challenged by Employers." *Wall Street Journal*, Eastern ed. July 16: A2.

Brisentine v. Stone & Webster Engineering Corp. 117 F.3d 519 (11th Cir. 1997).

Brown v. ABF Freight Systems, Inc., 183 F.3d 319 (4th Cir. 1999).

Brown v. KFC National Management Co., 921 P.2d 146 (Hawaii Sup. Ct. 1996).

Bureau of National Affairs. 1994–2002. *Labor Arbitration Reports.*

———. 2001a. "House Democrats Introduce Legislation To Overturn High Courts *Circuit City* Ruling." *Human Resources Report* 19(25): 680–681.

————. 2001b. "Britain Proposes to Charge Workers To Take Cases to Employment Tribunals." *Human Resources Report* 19(30): 821–822.

Burstein, Paul, and Kathleen Monaghan. 1986. "Equal Employment Opportunity and the Mobilization of Law." *Law & Society Review* 20(3): 355–380.

Circuit City Stores, Inc. v. Adams, 532 U.S. 105 (2001a).

Circuit City Stores, Inc. v. Adams, 279 F.3d 889 (9th Cir. 2001b).

Circuit City Stores, Inc. v. Ingle, U.S. No. 03–604, cert. denied 1/21/04.

Circuit City Stores, Inc. v. Mantor, U.S. No. 03–605, cert. denied 1/26/04.

Clark, R. Theodore, Jr. 1997. "A Management View of Nonunion Employee Arbitration Procedures." In *Labor Arbitration Under Fire,* James L. Stern and Joyce M. Najita, eds. Ithaca, NY: Cornell University Press, pp. 162–181.

Cole v. Burns International Security Services, 105 F.3d 1465 (DC Cir. 1997).

Coleman, Charles J., and George M. Pangis. 2000–2001. "Mandatory Arbitration of Statutory Disputes: The View from the Fourth Circuit." *Journal of Individual Employment Rights* 9(4): 267–286.

Collins v. New York City Transit Authority, (2nd Cir. 2002).

Collyer Insulated Wire, 192 NLRB 837 (1971).

Colvin, Alexander J.S. 2001. "The Relationship Between Employment Arbitration and Workplace Dispute Procedures." *Ohio State Journal on Dispute Resolution* 16(3): 643–668.

————. 2003. "Institutional Pressures, Human Resource Strategies, and the Rise of Nonunion Dispute Resolution Procedures." *Industrial and Labor Relations Review* 56(3): 375–392.

Cooper, Laura J., Dennis R. Nolan, and Richard A. Bales. 2000. *ADR in the Workplace.* St. Paul, MN: West Group.

Crotty, M., G. Davenport, P. Torres, A. Trebilcock, and M.L. Ruiz Vega, eds. 2000. *Termination of Employment Digest.* Geneva: International Labor Organization.

D'Amato, Alfonse M. 1998. "The Chairman." U.S. Congress. Senate. Committee on Banking, Housing and Urban Affairs. Mandatory Arbitration Agreements in the Employment Contracts in the Securities Industry, 105th Cong., 2d sess., p. 24.

Dertouzos, James N., Elaine Holland, and Patricia Ebener. 1988. *The Legal and Economic Consequencesof Wrongful Termination.* Santa Monica, CA: Rand Corporation.

Dichter, Mark S., and Ian M. Ballard, Jr. 2001–2002. "Arbitration after Circuit City." *Journal of Individual Employment Rights* 9(4): 253–266.

Doctor's Associates, Inc. v. Casarotto, 517 U.S. 681 (1996).

Donohue, John J., III, and Peter Siegelman. 1991. "The Changing Nature of Employment Discrimination Litigation." *Stanford Law Review* 43: 983–1033.

Duffield v. Robertson Stephens Co, 144 F.3d 1182 (9th Cir. 1998)

Dumais v. American Golf Corp., 89 FEP Cases 1050 (10th Cir. 2002).

Eastman, Hope B., and David M. Rothstein. 1995. "The Fate of Mandatory Employment Arbitration amidst Growing Opposition: A Call for Common Ground." *Labor Law Journal* 20(4): 595–608.

Eaton, Adrienne E., and Jeffrey H. Keefe. 1999. "Introduction and Overview." In *Employment Dispute Resolution and Worker Rights in the Changing Workplace,* Adrienne E. Eaton and Jeffrey H. Keefe, eds. Champaign-Urbana, IL: Industrial Relations Research Association, pp. 1–26.

EEOC v. Circuit City Stores, Inc., 285 F.3d 404 (6th Cir. 2002).

EEOC v. Waffle House, Inc. 534 U.S. 754 (2002).

Eglit, Howard C. 1997. "The Age Discrimination in Employment Act at Thirty: Where It's Been, Where It Is Today, Where It's Going." *University of Richmond Law Review* 31(3): 579–756.

Equal Employment Opportunity Commission. 1997. "EEOC: Mandatory Arbitration of Employment Discrimination Disputes as a Condition of Employment." *Labor Relations Reports* (BNA) 8(405): 7511.

————. 2002. *A Study of the Litigation Program Fiscal Years 1997–2001.* http://www.eeoc.gov/litigation/study/study.html.

Estreicher, Samuel. 1997. "Predispute Agreements to Arbitrate Statutory Employment Claims." *New York University Law Review* 72(6): 1344–1375.

————. 2001. "Saturns for Rickshaws: The Stakes in the Debate over Predispute Employment Arbitration Agreements." *Ohio State Journal on Dispute Resolution* 16(3): 559–570.

Evju, Stein. Undated. "Norwegian Courts and Labour Jurisdiction." Unpublished Manuscript. Norwegian School of Management, Sandvika, Norway.

Ewing, David W. 1977. *Freedom Inside the Organization.* New York: McGraw-Hill.

————. 1989. *Justice on the Job.* Boston, MA: Harvard Business School Press.

Federal Arbitration Act, 9 U.S.C. §510 (2000).

Federal District-Court Civil Cases. 2001. http://teddy.law.cornell.edu:8090.

————. 2002. http://teddy.law.cornell.edu:8090.

Feingold, Russell D. 1998. "Opening Statement of Russell D. Feingold, U.S. Senator from the State of Wisconsin." U.S. Congress. Senate. Committee on Banking, Housing and Urban Affairs. Mandatory Arbitration Agreements in Employment Contracts in the Securities Industry, 105th Cong., 2d sess., pp. 2–5.

————. 2002. "Mandatory Arbitration: What Process is Due?" *Harvard Journal on Legislation* 39: 281–298.

Feldman, Daniel C. 1984. "The Development and Enforcement of Group Norms." *Academy of Management Review* 9: 47–53.

Ferguson v. Countrywide Credit Industries, Inc., 89 FEP Cases 706 (9th Cir. 2002).

Feuille, Peter. 1999. "Grievance Mediation." In *Employment Dispute Resolution and Worker Rights in the Changing Workplace,* Adrienne E. Eaton and Jeffrey H. Keefe, eds. Champaign, IL: Industrial Relations Research Association, pp. 187–217.

Flyer Printing Co. v. Hill, Fla. Dist. Ct. Appeals, No. 2D00–5008 (7/18/01).

Foulkes, Fred K. 1980. *Personnel Policies in Large Nonunion Companies.* Englewood Cliffs, NJ: Prentice-Hall, Inc.

Freeman, Richard B., and Joel Rogers. 1999. *What Workers Want.* Ithaca, NY: Cornell University Press.

Galle, William P., Jr., and Clifford M. Koen. 2000–2001. "Reducing Post-Termination Disputes: A National Survey of Contract Clauses Used in Employment Contracts." *Journal of Individual Employment Rights* 9(3): 227–241.

Gilmer v. Interstate/Johnson Lane, 500 U.S. 20 (1991).

Gould, William B., IV. 1987–1988. "Stemming the Wrongful Discharge Tide: A Case for Arbitration." *Employee Relations Law Journal* 13(3): 404–425.

Graham v. Scissor-Tail, Inc., 623 P.2d 165 (Cal. Sup. Ct. 1981).

Great Western Financial Corp. Case No. 12-CA-16886, *Daily Labor Report* (Bureau of National Affairs, September 25, 1995), p. D-4.

Green, Michael Z. 2000. "Debunking the Myth of Employer Advantage from Using Mandatory Arbitration for Discrimination Claims." *Rutgers Law Journal* 31: 399–471.

Green Tree Financial Corp. v. Bazzle, 2003 U.S. Lexis 4798 (June 23, 2003).

Grote, Dick, and Jim Wimberly. 1993. "Peer Review." *Training* (March): 51–55.

Guinther, John, and Bettyruth Walter. 1988. *Jury in America and the Civil Juror: A Research Project.* New York: Facts on File.

Hagedorn v. Veritas Software Corp. 250 F.Supp.2d 857 (S.D. Ohio 2002).

Halligan v. Piper Jaffray, Inc., 148 F.3d 197 (2nd Cir. 1998).

Harkavy, Jonathan R. 1999. "Privatizing Workplace Justice: The Advent of Mediation in Resolving Sexual Harassment Disputes." *Wake Forest Law Review* 34: 135–163.

Hayford, Stephen L. 1995. "Agreements to Arbitrate Statutory Fair Employment Practices Claims: Unforeseen Consequences for the At-Will Employer." *Labor Law Journal* 46(9): 543–569.

Hodges, Ann C. 2001. "Arbitration of Statutory Claims in the Unionized Workplace: Is Bargaining with the Union Required?" *Ohio State Journal on Dispute Resolution* 16(3): 513–558.

Hollander, Edwin P. 1958. "Conformity, Status, and Idiosyncrasy Credits." *Psychological Review* 65: 117–127.

Hooters of America, Inc. v. Phillips, 173 F.3d 933 (4th Cir. 1999).

Howard, William M. 1995. "Arbitrating Claims of Employment Discrimination." *Dispute Resolution Journal* 50(Oct.–Dec.): 40–50.

Ingle v. Circuit City Stores, Inc. 328 F.3d 1165 (9th Cir. 2003).

International Labor Organization (ILO). 1948. Declaration of Philadelphia. Geneva, Switzerland. http://www.ilo.org.

———. 1982. *Convention on Termination of Employment*. Geneva, Switzerland. http:// ilolex.ilo.ch:1567.

Jung, David J., and Richard Harkness. 1988. "The Facts of Wrongful Discharge." *The Labor Lawyer* 4(2): 257–269.

Jury Verdict Research. 2001. *Employment Practice Liability: Jury Award Trends and Statistics*. Horsham, PA: LRP Publications.

———. 2002a. "Median Awards for Discrimination Show Increase of 177% from 1994 to 2000." *Employment Practice Liability Verdicts and Settlements* 4(8): 1–2.

———. 2002b. "Juries Render Plaintiff Verdicts in 67 Percent of Employment Practice Liability Trials During 2000." *Employment Practice Liability Verdicts and Settlements* 4(6):1–2.

Kandel, William L., and Sheri L. Frumer. 1994. "The Corporate Ombudsman and Employment Law: Maintaining the Confidentiality of Communications." *Employee Relations Law Journal* 19(4): 587–602.

Kaswell, Stuart J. 1998. "Prepared Statement of Stuart J. Kaswell, Senior Vice President and General Counsel, Securities Association." U.S. Congress. Senate. Committee on Banking, Housing and Urban Affairs. Mandatory Arbitration Agreements in Employment Contracts in the Securities Industry, 105th Cong., 2d sess., pp. 88–92.

Keeler Brass Automotive Group, 317 NLRB 1110 (1995).

Keller, William L., and Timothy L. Darby. 2002. *International Labor and Employment Laws, 2002 Supplement to Vol. 2*. Washington, DC: Bureau of National Affairs.

Kennedy v. Superior Painting Co., 215 F.3d 650 (6th Cir. 2000).

Kittner, Michael, and Thomas C. Kohler. 2000. "Conditioning Expectations: The Protection of the Employment Bond in German and American Law." *Comparative Labor Law and Policy Journal* 21: 263–330.

Klaas, Brian S., and Daniel C. Feldman. 1993. "The Evaluation of Disciplinary Appeals." *Human Resource Management Review* 3: 49–81.

———. 1994. "The Impact of Appeal System Structure on Disciplinary Appeals." *Personnel Psychology* 47: 91–108.

Kuruvilla, Sarosh. 1995. "Industrialization Strategy and Industrial Relations Policy in Malaysia." In *Industrialization and Labor Relations*, Stephen Frenkel and Jeffrey Harrod, eds. Ithaca, NY: Cornell University Press, pp. 37–63.

LeRoy, Michael H., and Peter Feuille. 2001. "Final and Binding . . . But Appealable to Courts: Empirical Evidence of Judicial Review of Labor and Employment Arbitration Awards." *Program Materials, 54th Annual Meeting, National Academy of Arbitrators* Sec. 2-A: 1–47.

——. 2002. "When Is Cost an Unlawful Barrier to Alternative Dispute Resolution? The Ever Green Tree of Mandatory Employment Arbitration." *UCLA Law Review* 50: 143–203.

Lewin, David. 1990. "Grievance Procedures in Nonunion Workplaces: Empirical Analysis of Usage, Dynamics, and Outcomes." *Chicago-Kent Law Review* 66(3): 823–844.

Lipsky, David B., and Ronald L. Seeber. 1999. "Top General Counsels Support ADR: Fortune 1000 Lawyers Comment on its Status and Future." *Business Law Today* 8: 20–30.

Little v. Auto Stiegler, 29 Cal. 4th 1064, 63 P.3d 979 (2003).

Litras, Marika F.X. 2000. "Bureau of Justice Statistics Report on Civil Rights Complaints Filed in U.S. District Courts." *Daily Labor Report,* January 10: E-5–E-17.

Locke, Edwin A. 1986. "Generalizing from Laboratory to Field: Ecological Validity or Abstraction of Essential Elements?" In *Generalizing from Laboratory to Field Settings*, Edwin A. Locke, ed. Lexington, MA: Lexington Books, pp. 1–20.

MacCoun, Robert. 1989. *Experimental Research on Jury Decision Making.* Santa Monica: Rand Corporation.

Malin, Martin H. 2001. "Privatizing Justice—But By How Much? Questions that *Gilmer* Did Not Answer." *Ohio State Journal on Dispute Resolution* 16(3): 589–631.

Maltby, Lewis L. 1998. "Private Justice: Employment Arbitration and Civil Rights." *Columbia Human Rights Law Review* 30(29): 29–64.

Markey, Edward J. 1998. "Opening Statement of Edward J. Markey, U.S. Representative in Congress from the State of Massachusetts." U.S. Congress. Senate. Committee on Banking, Housing and Urban Affairs. Mandatory Arbitration Agreements in Employment Contracts in the Securities Industry, 105th Cong., 2d sess., pp. 5–10.

Martin v. Dana Corp. 135 F.3d 765 (3rd Cir. 1997).

McCabe, Douglas M. 2002. "Administering the Employment Relationship: The Ethics of Conflict Resolution." *Journal of Business Ethics* 36(1): 33–48.

McDermott, E. Frank. 1995. "Survey of 92 Key Companies: Using ADR to Settle Employment Disputes." *Dispute Resolution Journal* 50: 8–29.

McDermott, E. Patrick, and Arthur Eliot Berkeley. 1996. *Alternative Dispute Resolution in the Workplace.* Westport, CT: Quorum Books.

Meeker, James W., and John Dombrink. 1993. "Access to the Civil Courts for those of Low and Moderate Means." *Southern California Law Review* 66(5): 2217–2231.

Midworm v. Ashcroft, 200 F.Supp.2d 171 (E.D.N.Y. 2002)

Morrison v. Circuit City Stores, 317 F.3d 646 (6th Cir. 2003).

National Arbitration Center. 2002a. AAA Amends Arbitration Rules. www.lawmemo.com/arb/res/aaa-employment.htm.

———. 2002b. California Statutes Regulating Arbitration Enacted in 2002. www.lawmemo.com/emp/docs/ca/arbitration.htm.

National Employment Lawyers Association. 2002. Mandatory Arbitration Subverts Civil Rights Laws. www.nela.org.

Neal, Alan C. 2001. "Recent Developments In Unfair Dismissal." *NJL Employment Law Supplement.* December 7, 2001, pp. 1801–1802.

Nelson v. Cyprus Bagdad Copper Corp., 199 F.3d 756 (9th Cir. 1997).

Organisation for Economic Co-operation and Development (OECD). 1999. *Employment Outlook, June, 1999.* Paris: Organisation for Economic Co-operation and Development.

Palefsky, Cliff. 1998. "Opening Statement of Cliff Palefsky, Chairman Securities Industry Arbitration Committee on Behalf of the National Employment Lawyers' Association." U.S. Congress. Senate. Committee on Banking, Housing and Urban Affairs. Mandatory Arbitration Agreements in Employment Contracts in the Securities Industry, 105th Cong., 2d sess., pp. 17–19.

Paladino v. Avnet Computer Technologies, Inc., 134 F.3d 1054 (11th Cir. 1998).

Parry, John. 1998. "American Bar Association Survey on Court Rulings Under Title I of Americans With Disabilities Act." *Daily Labor Report* June 22: E-1–E-3.

Patterson v. Tenet Healthcare, 113 F.3d 832 (8th Cir. 1997).

Plaskett v. Bechtel International Inc. 243 F.Supp.2d 334 (D.V.I. 2003).

Pryner v. Tractor Supply Co. 109 F.3d 354 (7th Cir. 1997), *cert denied* 74 FEP Cases 1792 (U.S. Sup. Ct. 1997).

Public Citizen. 2002. *Cost of Arbitration: Executive Summary.* www.lawmemo.com/arb/res/cost.htm.

Quint v. A.E. Staley Manufacturing Co., 172 F.3d 1 (1st Cir. 1999).

Ragsdale v. Wolverine World Wide, Inc. 535 U.S. 81 (2002).

Rogers v. New York University, 220 F.3d 73 (2nd Cir. 2000).

Schjoldager, Harald. 1976. "Norway." In *International Handbook on Contracts of Employment,* Claude Serge Aronstein, ed. Deventer, Netherlands: Kluwer, pp. 191–196.

Scott, William G. 1988. "The Management Governance Theories of Justice and Liberty." *Journal of Management* 14(2): 277–298.

Shankle v. B-G Maintenance Management of Colorado, Inc., 163 F. 3d 1230 (10th Cir. 1999).

Sherwyn, David J., Bruce Tracey, and Zev J. Eigen. 1999. "In Defense of Mandatory Arbitration: Saving the Baby, Tossing out the Bath Water, and Constructing a New Sink in the Process." *University of Pennsylvania Journal of Labor and Employment Law* 2(1): 73–150.

Silverstein, Eileen. 2001. "From Statute to Contract: The Law of the Employment Relationship Reconsidered." *Hofstra Labor and Employment Law Journal* 18: 479–527.

Singletary v. Enersys Inc. unpublished (4th Cir. 2003), *Labor Relations Week* 17(8): 233–234.

Southland Corp. v. Keating, 465 U.S. 1 (1984).

Sparks Nugget, Inc., 230 NLRB 275 (1977).

Spielberg Manufacturing Co., 112 NLRB 1080 (1955).

St. Antoine, Theodore J. 2001. "*Gilmer* in the Collective Bargaining Context." *Ohio State Journal on Dispute Resolution* 16(3): 491–512.

Sternlight, Jean R. 2001. "Mandatory Binding Arbitration and the Demise of the Seventh Amendment Right to a Jury Trial." *Ohio State Journal on Dispute Resolution* 16(3): 669–733.

Stirlen v. Supercuts, 60 Cal. Rptr. 2d 138 (Cal. Ct. App. 1997).

Stone, Katherine Van Wezel. 1999. "Rustic Juctice: Community and Coercion under the Federal Arbitration Act." *North Carolina Review* 77(3): 931–1036.

Summers, Clyde. 1992. "Effective Remedies for Employment Rights: Preliminary Guidelines and Proposals." *University of Pennsylvania Law Review* 141: 457–546.

Suviranta, A.J. 1999. "Finland." In *International Encyclopedia for Labour Law and Industrial Relations*, Vol. 6. Roger Blanpain, ed. Deventer, Netherlands: Kluwer, pp. 1–200.

Tajfel, Henri. 1979. "Individuals and Groups in Social Psychology." *British Journal of Social and Clinical Psychology* 18: 183–190.

———. 1981. *Human Groups and Social Categories*. Cambridge: Cambridge University Press.

United Nations. 1948. Universal Declaration of Human Rights. New York.

U.S. Departments of Commerce and Labor. Commission on the Future of Labor-Management Relations. 1994. *Report and Recommendations—Final Report.*

U.S. General Accounting Office (USGAO). 1994. *Employment Discrimination: How Registered Representatives Fare in Discrimination Disputes.* GAO/HEHS-94-17.

————. 1995. *Employment Discrimination: Most Private-Sector Employers Use Alternative Dispute Resolution.* Letter Report, 07/05/95, GAO/HEHS-95-150.

————. 1997. *Alternative Dispute Resolution: Employers' Experiences With ADR in the Workplace.* Letter Report, 1997, GAO/GGD-97-157.

United Steelworkers v. American Mfg. Co., 363 U.S. 564 (1960).

United Steelworkers v. Enterprise Wheel & Car Corp., 363 U.S. 593 (1960).

United Steelworkers v. Warrior & Gulf Navigation Co., 363 U.S. 574 (1960).

United Technologies Corp., 268 NLRB 557 (1984).

Vargyas, Ellen J. 1998. "Letter to Mary L. Schapiro, President, National Association Of Securities Dealers Regulation, Inc." U.S. Congress. Senate. Committee on Banking, Housing and Urban Affairs. Mandatory Arbitration Agreements in Employment Contracts in the Securities Industry, 105th Cong., 2d sess., pp. 118–120.

Volz, Marlin M., and Edward P. Goggin, eds. 1997. *Elkouri and Elkouri, How Arbitration Works,* 5th Ed. Washington, DC: Bureau of National Affairs.

Ware, Stephen J. 2001. "The Effects of *Gilmer*: Empirical and Other Approaches to the Study of Employment Arbitration." *Ohio State Journal on Dispute Resolution* 16(3): 735–758.

Werhane, Patricia H. 1985. *Persons, Rights and Corporations.* Englewood Cliffs, NJ: Prentice-Hall, Inc.

Wheeler, Hoyt N. 1997. "Evolutionary Employment Relations: An Introduction and an Approach." In *Proceedings of the Forty-Ninth Annual Meeting, Industrial Relations Research Association.* Madison, WI: Industrial Relations Research Association, pp. 1–6.

Wheeler, Hoyt N., Brian S. Klaas, and Jacques Rojot. 1994. "Substantive Principles of Justice at Work: An International Comparison." *Annals of the American Academy of Political and Social Science* 536: 31–42.

Wilensky, Ron, and Karen M. Jones. 1994. "Quick Response Key to Resolving Complaints." *HR Magazine* 39(3): 42–47.

Wilko v. Swan, 346 U.S. 427 (1953).

Willborn, Stephen L., Stewart J. Schwab, and John F. Burton, Jr. 1993. *Employment Law.* Charlottesville, VA: The Michie Company.

Wolterstorff, Nicholas. 2001. "Ivory Tower or Holy Mountain? Faith and Academic Freedom." *Academe* (January–February): 17–22.

Worker Protection and Working Environment Act (WEA). 2001. Norway. www.loc.gov/law/guide/norway.html.

Wright v. Universal Maritime Service Corp., 525 U.S. 70 (1998).

Zack, Arnold M. 1999. "Agreements to Arbitrate and the Waiver of Rights under Employment Law." In *Employment Dispute Resolution and Worker Rights In the Changing Workplace,* Adrienne E. Eaton and Jeffrey H.

Keefe, eds. Champaign-Urbana, IL: Industrial Relations Research Association, pp. 67–94.

Zalusky, John. 2002. "Circuit City is to Workplace Justice as Voting in Florida is to Democracy." Paper presented to 54th Annual Meeting of Industrial Relations Research Association, Atlanta, Georgia, January 6.

Zimmerman, Philip. 1997. "First Alternative Dispute Resolution Conference." *The CPA Journal* 67(7): 10–11.

The Authors

Hoyt N. Wheeler is Professor of Management and Business Partnership Foundation Fellow at the Moore School of Business, University of South Carolina. He holds a Ph.D. in Industrial Relations from the University of Wisconsin and a J.D. from the University of Virginia. His publications include *The Future of the American Labor Movement* (Cambridge University Press 2002), *Industrial Conflict: An Integrative Theory* (University of South Carolina Press 1985), *Workplace Justice: Employment Obligations in International Perspective* (coeditor, University of South Carolina Press 1992), and articles in such journals as *Industrial Relations, Industrial and Labor Relations Review, Labor Studies Journal, Personnel Psychology, Bulletin of Comparative Labour Relations, British Journal of Industrial Relations,* and *Annals of the American Academy of Political and Social Science.* He is a former national president of the Industrial Relations Research Association, a member of the National Academy of Arbitrators, and was a founder and co-chair of the Study Group on Employee Rights and Industrial Justice of the International Industrial Relations Association.

Brian S. Klaas is a Professor of Management and Chair of the Management Department at the Moore School of Business, University of South Carolina. His research interests include workplace dispute resolution, employee relations, compensation, and human resource outsourcing. He received his Ph.D. from the Industrial Relations Research Institute, at University of Wisconsin–Madison. He has published in such journals as *Personnel Psychology, Industrial Relations, Academy of Management Journal, Academy of Management Review, Industrial and Labor Relations Review, Journal of Management, Journal of Labor Research, Journal of Applied Psychology,* and *Human Resource Management.*

Douglas M. Mahony is an Assistant Professor of Management at the Moore School of Business, University of South Carolina. He holds an M.A. and a Ph.D. in Industrial Relations and Human Resource Management from Rutgers University. His research interests include alternative dispute resolution systems and the effects of participatory work practices on unions, organizations, and employees.

Index

Page numbers followed by a *t* refer to a table.

About the Institute

The W.E. Upjohn Institute for Employment Research is a nonprofit research organization devoted to finding and promoting solutions to employment-related problems at the national, state, and local levels. It is an activity of the W.E. Upjohn Unemployment Trustee Corporation, which was established in 1932 to administer a fund set aside by the late Dr. W.E. Upjohn, founder of The Upjohn Company, to seek ways to counteract the loss of employment income during economic downturns.

The Institute is funded largely by income from the W.E. Upjohn Unemployment Trust, supplemented by outside grants, contracts, and sales of publications. Activities of the Institute comprise the following elements: 1) a research program conducted by a resident staff of professional social scientists; 2) a competitive grant program, which expands and complements the internal research program by providing financial support to researchers outside the Institute; 3) a publications program, which provides the major vehicle for disseminating the research of staff and grantees, as well as other selected works in the field; and 4) an Employment Management Services division, which manages most of the publicly funded employment and training programs in the local area.

The broad objectives of the Institute's research, grant, and publication programs are to 1) promote scholarship and experimentation on issues of public and private employment and unemployment policy, and 2) make knowledge and scholarship relevant and useful to policymakers in their pursuit of solutions to employment and unemployment problems.

Current areas of concentration for these programs include causes, consequences, and measures to alleviate unemployment; social insurance and income maintenance programs; compensation; workforce quality; work arrangements; family labor issues; labor-management relations; and regional economic development and local labor markets.